Oink!

Only in Korea!

Based on true events that happened in and around the

Demilitarized Zone, Republic of Korea

circa 1980

David H. Osterhout

The O•Zone Press
El Paso, Texas

Oink!
Only in Korea!

The O•Zone Press, 2015
© By David H. Osterhout

ISBN-13-978-1508472605
ISBN-10-1508472602

David Osterhout is a former Army Intelligence Officer who was stationed on the DMZ during 1980. He received a severe injury while patrolling inside the DMZ but didn't realize the effects until nearly a year later. Spending eight months in Brooke Army Medical Center in San Antonio, Texas he penned the manuscript while it was fresh in his memory. Thirty-five years later, not much has changed in Korea. There is a republic in the south and a maniacal dictator in the north. His DMZ story is as valid today as it was then.

Dedication

To my brother John who challenged me by writing his own book, to Barbara Villemez, an old pro who told me I could do it, to my editor George Verongos for his fine work but mostly to my wife for everything good that ever happened to me.

Table of Contents

CHAPTER 1

Turtle

The occasional moan from the other men on the ward and the relentless scurrying of the orderlies in their military whites; looking like giant lab rats in a maze of hospital beds, exacerbated my inability to sleep. However, the singular prevailing factor causing my insomnia was the pain. Pain, is current, and can be tolerated and even endured if it is persistent, but the memory of the pain and all of the choices that led up to its manifestation is haunting and sometimes never lets a man find his peace. With spiral notebook, ballpoint pen, and plenty of time on my hands, every night when sleep was nowhere to be found, I began to write in a desperate attempt to exorcise the memory of the pain and put it on paper.

After Vietnam and well before Desert Storm, America was experiencing a period of peace. Feeling guilty over completely missing out on Vietnam— neither fighting for it nor protesting against it—I joined the Army in the spirit of '76, the nation's bicentennial. Trying to make up for my past apathy, I volunteered to go to Korea, the only official peacetime "conflict" left in the world. I got there eventually, but I had to spend two years training and another two years in Alaska. So, as a first lieutenant, I finally got my wish, I was headed to Korea, but as they say, "Be careful what you wish for." How would I have ever guessed, that I, the Oscar Deuce, would be sent home eleven months later in a C-9 Nightingale medevac airplane.

North Korea: the Peoples Democratic Republic of Korea, and South Korea: the Republic of Korea (ROK), are adversaries separated by a four kilometer wide strip of land called the DMZ (Demilitarized Zone): a divided land and a divided people. There was officially no end to the war, but a tenuous truce was declared. In 1980, twenty-seven years after the end of the Korean conflict, isolated hostilities sometimes broke out in spite of the truce. Two American officers were killed at Panmunjom, the negotiation village in the DMZ, the same year I joined the Army. They were beaten to death with axe handles.

At 1535 (3:35 PM), our van pulled into the 2nd Infantry Division Replacement Company parking area at Camp Casey, which seemed to have all of the amenities that one would find on a stateside fort. I was looking for adventure when I volunteered for this "hardship" tour, but now I was afraid that it was just going to be another Headquarters Company assignment on a large Americanized post.

We un-assed the van, stacking our bags in a painted square on the pavement. We entered the Quonset hut that had In Processing printed over the door. The adjacent Quonset hut was labeled Out Processing. The female clerk handed us some papers and told us to fill them out and bring them back at 0900 tomorrow. Then she suggested that we go to Finance if we needed money, it would be closed in thirty minutes. The five of us in processing needed some cash to help us get settled in so we damn near trampled each other trying to get out the door. We hailed one of the light blue PX taxis. I was the first man in and four others piled in behind me. The Korean taxi driver was shouting something about regulations allowing him to only carry four passengers, not five.

I tried bribing him, but he just said, "No can do."

Then a private sitting next me said something to the driver about bitch slapping him into next Tuesday. Being the officer, I felt I was obligated to do something about the private's less than professional attitude, so I just said, "Hey!" Not exactly a strong display of command presence on my part. We all then fell silent as the driver slammed the taxi into gear and squealed the tires. Well, the sound may have actually been the screeching transmission of the miniature 1972 Hyundai trying to peel rubber with six people in the car.

We received our pay even though it was "too late in the day." The next taxi took us straight back to the "turtle farm," as the driver called it. Once inside, I asked the clerk why the Korean driver called this place "the turtle farm."

She told me that although the in-processing and out-processing doors were only twenty feet apart, it took a year to get from one door to the other. "Slow as a turtle. New troops are referred to as turtles and all new troops are grown right here, the Turtle Farm," she said proudly.

I grabbed my bags and flagged another PX taxi. I was going to visit my friend Mike at Camp Hovey, the adjacent compound. I was let out near the 23rd Infantry's area when I saw Mike surrounded by ten other officers. It looked like a fight was about to break out. As I got closer, I saw Mike standing on a rock about three feet long, two feet wide, and a foot tall.

He spread his arms out as if to take flight, raised one leg behind him and started singing, "All the way to ROK land just like this. All the way to ROK land just like this."

All 23rd Infantry turtle officers had to sing that tune while standing on a rock as an initiation. I got that part but why they had to spread their arms and raise their leg like a bird, I'll never understand, nor could I imagine what sort of stupid initiation was in store for me.

We walked up to the small Brigade Officer's Club and had a pizza. Without actually discussing it, we decided to go "down range," into the local village. After supper we went to Mike's room to change into civilian clothes. Mike had only been "in-country" five days, and I was half way through my second day. The locals called us "cherry boys" which is a "turtle" who hasn't popped his Korean cherry yet.

After changing clothes, we hit a double time into the Korean night. We had about a half-mile to run before we got to the back gate of Camp Hovey. I suppose it was a habit from OCS but Mike and I jogged everywhere. A little village called Tokko-ri lay just outside the gate. Mike and his buddies had been down there once on a 'thunder-run,' which is code for a drunken binge, so he knew where most of the clubs were located. The gate guard checked our IDs. Officers didn't need passes to go down range, but most enlisted personnel did. We stepped through the gate and officially declared ourselves "down range."

We walked about a quarter of a mile along the main drag and then it forked. We went left into an alley. With the sun just below the horizon, the alley was dark and ominous. There were only half a dozen streetlights in the whole village and, of course, none were allocated to this particular alley. I could see well enough to recognize that the building on our left was a church; knowing that the Koreans weren't heathens made me feel a little better.

After a short block, we came to the street that had most of the bars on it. The first bar was two blocks down on the right: The Peace Club, good a place as any to start. The Peace Club was pretty much a building all to itself because there were small alleys down each side. I glanced down the nearest alley as we approached the front door. We stopped and stared, as any cherry boys would. There was an old Papa-san squatting down with his bicycle, using his bike and his body to make a strange kind of yoga looking tripod. His pants were down around his knees and he was defecating through the bicycle frame.

"Mike," I said. "That guy's taking a shit in the street."

"I guess they do that here," he said. "C'mon, let's go in."

Immediately, I thought, I hope I don't have to take a shit before we get back.

We went into the club. There were five "mature" women and no customers. Two women were huddled by the stove, one sat at the bar and two worked behind it. All five fixed their eyes on us.

"Let's get out of here, the women are all pushing thirty," Mike said as we turned to leave.

"So are we," I said as I trailed Mike out the door.

Then I heard one of the women ask, "Where you go?"

I probably would have told her if I'd known.

The next club was down the street on the left, the Sunshine Club. Half a block away we could hear the rock music reverberating from the club walls. Once inside, the music was so loud that we couldn't talk. We couldn't even yell and understand each other, so we left. I did notice that the women were younger and dressed more western than those of the Peace Club. We went out the door, down one block and turned left into an alley. There was a porcelain urinal attached to the wall of the building in the alley.

"Hey Mike, when you're in Korea and you want to take a piss, where do you do it?"

"Well, if you piss on the wall in the alley," he said, "you're probably pissing in the right spot."

We turned down another alley that was even smaller than the one we were in. I was thoroughly lost and stumbling around like a "one legged man in an ass kicking contest," as Mike so deftly put it. Mike stands 6'4" and always moves with a purpose. At 5'9", I had to hustle to keep up with him. I fell over—or at least stumbled over—every trash pile in the alley.

We made one more turn down a sidewalk-size alley and found what we were looking for, Rosa's Cantina. All the bars and clubs had a sign on the outside that said "On Limits to U. N. Personnel." It was kind of like the Good Housekeeping Seal of Approval. Mike walked into Rosa's like he owned the place. It took a few seconds, but we stared everybody down and took a table against the wall. This club was a little larger than the others. In it were nine soldiers and an even dozen women. Within seconds there was a woman on each side of us. The waitress was soon to follow:

"What you want drinky?"

"What do you have?" asked Mike.

"All kinds," said the waitress.

"Okay," he said. "We'll take one."

The waitress was confused, but she brought four beers anyway. I don't drink, so I gave mine to Mike. The two main beers brewed in Korea are O. B. and Crown. Mike drank a glass of each. When I ordered the second round, I ordered a Coke for me. Korean Cokes tasted flatter than American Cokes. I guess the secret recipe lost something in translation but Korea was known as the "Land of the Not Quite Right."

The girls asked questions while we played octopus with them. All Korean businesswomen invariably ask the same questions: "What company, what rank, what name, and overnight pass?"

Mike explained to me that we should lie about everything except our names and then we should only tell them our first names. Sometimes the girls grabbed your dog tags to see if you were lying. That's the only thing that they could easily check. Mike felt safer not telling anybody that we were intelligence officers. The reasons he gave were twofold: the command didn't like officers in the village chasing the same women that the enlisted men chased and there were spies and North Korean sympathizers around that would love to catch them a U. S. Intelligence Officer. I thought that reason number two was slightly ludicrous but I was a cherry boy and had a lot to learn.

Deciding to move on, I gave the waitress a twenty-dollar bill and she brought back a handful of Korean change. For some reason, it was a habit when I was with Mike to catch the check. He was the finest of men and the best of friends and I could always expect some huge gift in the near future to make up for all the little things for which I paid.

The New Seoul Club was directly across the road. A young lady came out of it wearing short-shorts, halter-top with sequins and a flower in her hair. She waved us over. It looked ridiculous to see a woman wearing so little clothing on such a cold evening. The three of us walked into the club arm in arm. What a zoo! There were fifteen, maybe twenty women dressed in spangles, sequins, and glitter. One girl was wearing a traditional Korean dress and another a black silk dress slit up the side to the hip. One had on a football jersey, one a strapless something or other with a cowboy hat and one had on a leopard leotard and a black patch over her left eye. If there was ever a male sexual fantasy, it could be found here.

We sat down and the women came. I talked with three and Mike four but we didn't see any "trinkets" that we liked. Trinket is a colloquialism name for a young businesswoman (prostitute). Mike stood, prying a woman off his arm and bounded for the door. I was left to pay for eleven drinks, 6500 won. A hair over ten bucks.

I got out on the street just in time to see Mike go into the next club. It was called the Airiang. It was a zoo, too. The women in the Airiang were more up front about their business. I wasn't in the joint two minutes before one of them asked me if I wanted a "short time" which meant straight intercourse for about thirty or forty-five minutes. Price: ten dollars give or take. It was a little too coldhearted for me so I told them "no." I learned quickly that it was cheaper to say "no" right off the bat because I didn't have to spring for drinks. We stayed long enough to get a good look at every woman there. None really interested us. I paid the bill, 4000 won, cheapest club yet. Learning to say "no" was really paying off.

There was only one more club that we could readily see. It was about two blocks down on the right, the Papa-san Club. When we were about halfway to it, a woman came out of a store and crossed the street right in front of me. I said, "Hello."

She was the most natural looking woman I'd seen all night. Her hair was cut in bangs and it was long, halfway down her back. She had on no makeup. She stopped in front of me and asked, "How are you?"

I told her the truth and it came out of my mouth before I could stop it. She smiled and said that she could help me with that. She pointed to a door saying that she lived right there and I could come up and have a cup of coffee if I wanted. I yelled at Mike and told him to go on and grab a beer and I'd catch up with him later.

This woman took me to a door locked with a U. S. government series 200 lock, which cost Uncle Sam about five bucks. A soldier could get a "short time" for one because Korean locks weren't worth a damn. There was a courtyard inside where there were seven hooches in a semi-circle around a water faucet. Five of the hooches had two pair of shoes lined up out front, one large pair and one small pair. The soldiers were home with their women.

My new friend opened another series 200 lock and slid her door to the side. She automatically kicked off her shoes and told me to come in. She put a paper sack on the floor for me to stand on while I untied my shoes. When I stepped out of them, she aligned them perfectly just like the other shoes on the front porch. She hung her coat in one of two large black wooden armoires covered with mother of pearl dragons, swans and pheasants.

The room was furnished meagerly but had a full size mattress on the floor. There was a small ondol stove in the center of the room. A brass teapot sat upon the stove. She pointed to a quilt on the floor and said, "Sit down." She folded the quilt back and put her hand on the yellow linoleum floor. "It's hot," she said explaining that charcoal briquettes are rotated through the stove and placed under the floor keeping it hot for several hours. There was a line from a GI poem I'd heard my entire career that said, "…heated floors and slant-eyed whores." I'd found the heated floor and I was pretty sure I was conversing with the other party in the poem.

As I sat on the floor, she turned the radio to AFKN, (Armed Forces Korean Network) the only English speaking station in the Republic. She moved to the stove and warmed her hands a minute, then she asked me if I wanted some tea or coffee. I opted for tea. She poured two steaming China cups full of water from the brass pot. She went to one of the small cabinets to get the tea. I'll be damned if half the PX wasn't in there. She had coffee, Vaseline, shampoo, cocoa, dairy creamer, and Tang. All of which were U. S. Post Exchange controlled items. A soldier can only buy a limited quantity of these things each month for personal use. Korean Nationals were not allowed to have them because it was against regulations. I never could figure out why the U. S. Army couldn't let a Korean have a freaking glass of Tang but it didn't matter, that regulation obviously went to hell in a duffel bag.

She brought a cup of tea to me and then sat beside me on the floor. She was a little woman. She smiled often and could speak English with relative ease. A Korean businesswoman who spoke English well had been around the block several thousand times. Her name was Miss Yi, a very polished twenty-six year old. She had a Yobo who recently went stateside.

A Yobo is a "spouse." A soldier finds a businesswoman who wants to make a more permanent arrangement than short times and overnights. The soldier will pay the woman a monthly salary to service him only. Sometimes cooking, cleaning and sharing a hooch goes along with the fee. The prices range from fifty to five-hundred dollars a month depending on the quality of the relationship, the attractiveness of the woman, the rank of the soldier and the fidelity level expected of the businesswoman. Obviously, the more you pay the woman, the more faithful she is. More often than one would expect, soldiers marry their Yobos and take them back to the States.

We finished our tea and I asked her, "Where's the latrine?" She looked at me a little funny, as I asked her again, "Where's the restroom?"

She said, "You need a pee?"

Yes, I certainly did. I'd been drinking Cokes all evening with a cup of tea to top it off. She got up and went to the corner and brought back a little silver pot with a top on it. She put it down beside me and said, "Pee Pot." My mind immediately reeled, *Am I supposed to take a piss in this?* I couldn't tell if I only thought that or actually asked that out loud. She nodded her head and said, "I won't look, Cherry Boy."

I must have acted like I'd just flown over on the turnip plane. She went to the clothes closet and pretended to be straightening things. I took the pot to the far corner. We looked like fighters ready to square off. She in her corner, me in mine.

I placed the pot down on the floor and looked back over my shoulder. She was still straightening clothes. I knew it would be impossible for me to hit the little sugar bowl size pot from a standing position so I knelt down and unzipped my pants. Peeing from the kneeling position was very awkward. Trying to hit the three-inch opening of a pot in the corner of a room with someone watching was even more uncomfortable. I aimed the best I could at the small hole in the top of the pot. My urine tinkled into the silver pot with an alarming sound. I finished and replaced the top.

"Where do you want me to put it?" I asked.

"Leave there," she said, and I did.

I went to the stove and warmed myself. She met me there and stood very close. I could feel her long silky hair brush against me. I could smell her perfume and I knew right then that I would succumb and she knew it too.

She hugged me, her chin against my chest, her arms wrapped around me, and asked, "Do you want to makey love?"

For some reason, still unbeknownst to me, I actually had to think about that for about two point two seconds. Then, "Yes," I said.

She laughed, more like a giggle, "Cherry Boy," she whispered.

I stretched out on a mink blanket on top of the king size mattress. The mink wasn't really made of mink, that's just what they called it, but it was fuzzy, double thick and plush. I watched Miss Yi move gracefully around the room.

"Go on, take off clothes," she said. I sat up on the edge of the mattress. She laughed again.

"What are you laughing at?" I asked.

"Cherry Boy," was all she said.

She moved over to me, stood for a moment then knelt down and methodically removed my socks. She started to unbutton my shirt. I stopped her and said that I would do it. She laughed again and went back to the cabinet. I removed my clothes and crawled under the mink blanket. I propped up on an elbow and watched her flit around the room. She pulled the light cord hanging in the middle of the ceiling and the white neon light went out and a dim blue bulb came on. She checked the charcoal in the stove and locked the door.

Finally, she began to undress. First her blouse and then her bra. She had tiny breasts with exceedingly long and apparently hard nipples. She pulled her jeans off and folded them on the couch. She poured some water from the brass teapot into a bowl and carried it to the corner with the "bathroom" in it. She squatted over the little silver "pee pot." She told me not to look and I halfway turned my head. I heard her urinate in the silver pot and then wash herself in the warm water.

She slipped into bed beside me before I got a chance to look at her crotch. For an instant I really thought that there might be a difference between Caucasian and Oriental women.

She snuggled close to me; her hair fell across my chest, tickling my senses. We kissed deeply and she threw a leg over mine. I couldn't wait any longer and had to reach down between her legs to see if Asian women really were different down there. How stupid did I feel?

I rolled over on top of her, bracing on my elbows so I could look at her beneath me in the blue light, and I was lost...at least for the next glorious six and a half minutes. It probably would have been less if not for the condom I'd slipped on.

I was just about to get the last lace on my shoes tied when she said, "Don't forget why I do this." I assumed that she was referring to money. I wasn't too sure how much to pay so I asked her, but she wouldn't quote a price. I gave her a ten and she seemed happy. We chatted a minute and I told her that I was going into the Papa-san Club to find Mike. She said she worked there part time. It seemed that all businesswomen are affiliated with one club or another and must pay a tax to the Madame who owns the establishment.

As I walked to the club, "heated floors and slant eyed whores" kept running through my mind.

Mike was at the bar with a beer in his hand. There were three women around him. When they saw me, they gave me that "I know what you've been up to" look.

"How was it?" asked Mike.

I sort of shrugged my shoulders.

"How much?"

"Ten," I said

"Number hana (one) short time, huh?" asked the bargirl.

"What?" I retorted.

"Short time, number one, okay?" she said.

"Sure, real fine," I said.

For the next few minutes the women asked many questions and we effectively lied to them. Miss Yi walked in and everyone laughed while she pretended to be embarrassed. She stood by my side and held my arm. I bought beers for everyone and asked Mike how he did. He shook his head 'no.' I inconspicuously slipped Miss Yi another ten and pointed to Mike.

"Tell him, meet me outside," she said as she left.

"You wanna get laid?" I asked Mike. He alerted like a bird dog.

I waited a few seconds and said, "That girl told me she likes tall men.

She's waiting for you outside." Mike spilled his beer on two of us and knocked his bar stool over getting out the door. Those left behind were wide eyed in amazement at how fast, but ungraceful, the big man could move.

I continued to practice lying to the businesswomen while waiting for Mike to return. Thirty-five minutes later, Mike stuck his head in the door, grinning from ear to ear. Deep down, Mike was an honorable man and may not have done anything, but he sure seemed happy. I bought another round for everyone.

At 2330 (11:30 PM), a local military patrol chases all the soldiers out of the bars to make sure they get back to compound by the midnight curfew. The senior C. P. (Courtesy Patrol) came into the club and told us to go home or find a hooch to hole up in for the night. I paid the bar bill and bid the girls 'adieu' and we began jogging back to the compound. We were joined by scores of other soldiers and made it back to the gate at 2352 (11:52 PM). Serving in the Army in Korea was considered to be a hardship tour. Surely partying and chasing women wasn't the reason why.

CHAPTER 2

Hello DMZ

I showed up at the Turtle Farm at 0830, speculating that I would be assigned to the ASIC, All Source Intelligence Center. A staff sergeant walked in and mechanically read the roster. Only half the people that were supposed to be there showed up, after all, it was Sunday morning.

At exactly 0900, a female lieutenant came in and collected our paperwork from the previous day. She read off a list of assignments. When she got to my name she could have said that I was assigned to Bumfuk Egypt because I didn't recognize a thing that came out of her mouth. She said the name of a Korean town, a Camp name, some other numerical designation, and then the Western Corridor. I didn't recognize any of that crap.

I found myself at the back of the room, searching a large map for the Western Corridor. I looked at every mark, pin, and label on the map, but couldn't find where I was going. I asked a soldier, who had been in-country for four months, but he didn't know, nor did he care, where it was. The second soldier I asked said that the Western Corridor was the 3rd Brigade Area at Camp Howze.

Camp Howze was located west of Camp Casey. It had a small village outside the main gate. In light of the new assignment, I now assumed that I would be a Brigade Intelligence Officer. I'd just finished two years with the 172nd Light Infantry Brigade in Alaska. I reckoned I could be a Brigade Intelligence Officer again for another year.

At 1300 (1 PM), I got into a van at the Turtle Farm. It was just the driver and me. I riddled him with questions that he couldn't answer. He didn't know anything about Camp Howze. He was stationed at Camp Casey and only made the drive back and forth. It didn't really matter what the place was like, I'd be stuck with it.

Some time later, we turned off the main road into a small village. We drove a block and came to the main gate of Camp Howze. The van pulled into a parking space beside the ceremonial cannon beneath the flagpoles. After I told the driver to watch my gear and wait for me, I went into the Headquarters building and found the S-1 office. (S-1 was the Adjutant who dealt with personnel, S-2 was intelligence, S-3 was operations, and S-4 was logistics and supply.)

I found the Adjutant (S-1). He was a major, a little man, almost comical looking. He sat behind a large desk that made him look even smaller.

"Sir, I'm Lieutenant Osterhout."

"Goddamn, Son, where have you been? The colonel's been waiting for you for two days." I didn't know if he wanted an answer to that or if it was just a rhetorical statement. I chose to respond.

"I got in-country Friday, spent one night at Camp Coiner another at division Headquarters—"

"Never mind that," he cut me off in midsentence. "Get in there and report."

I said, "Yes Sir" and went to the brigade commander's office. I knocked on the door once, twice; then I walked back to the Adjutant's office.

"He's not in," I said.

"Aw shit, where's Colonel McLain?" bellowed the Adjutant.

A Korean secretary came scampering around the corner with a surprised look on her face. She was a gorgeous woman with big boobs, which is very unusual for a Korean woman. I assumed that it was a special qualification for working at brigade Headquarters.

"Him go D. M. Gee" she said, nodded, smiled and left.

The Adjutant put his face in his hands as if he had a headache and leaned against the top of his oversized desk.

"Aw shit, that's right. Just take a seat in the hall and wait for him to get back!"

"Yes Sir."

I sat in the hall near the secretary pool. There were two women working. Both of them were very attractive. The one with the biggest boobs was nearly intimidating. Fifteen minutes later a private came running through the foyer yelling that the colonel's chopper had just landed. The Adjutant made a mad dash through the Headquarters screaming for all the clerks to get things squared away. The colonel walked in wearing full combat dress.

"Tench Hut!" and the Headquarters snapped to attention in unison.

"Carry on," and we all relaxed. The colonel secured himself in his office. I went to the Adjutant's office and asked if I was supposed to go in.

"Goddamn, are you still here? Get your ass in there; he's been waiting for two days I told you."

I nearly laughed at the major's question, "Are you still here?" I started to say, "Who are you talking to if I'm not here?" but decided I'd better not. I went to the door and knocked.

"Come in."

I marched to within three feet of the colonel's desk, saluted as smartly as possible, and said, "Sir, Lieutenant Osterhout reports to the brigade commander."

I held my salute until he returned it. He was in the process of taking off his gear.

"Relax," he said.

I snapped to the position of parade rest.

"Sit down, sit down," he said nonchalantly and pointed to a chair. I sat.

He took off his forty-five-caliber pistol and stuffed it in his desk drawer. He sat behind his desk and smoothed back his graying hair.

"Lieutenant Osterhout, we've been waiting for you for two days. You've been handpicked."

Oh God, for what, I thought.

"You'll be going to the 1st of the 9th at Camp Greaves, it's an infantry battalion. They're on the mission at this time. I want you to report today.

"Yes, Sir." I was dismissed, snapped a salute, did an about face and exited out the door. The first interview was certainly brief and to the point. I now knew my unit but I still didn't know where it was and I didn't have the faintest idea what mission they were on.

I passed the Adjutant's office. "You better get your ass in gear, he wants you up there today," the last words I ever heard from the brigade adjutant.

I got back in the van and told the driver to go to 1st Battalion, 9th Infantry at Camp Greaves.

"Oh shit, you going there?"

"Yeah," I said. "What's wrong with that?"

"Hell, I won't even spend the night there."

"Why," I asked.

"I don't like it."

I was hoping for a little more definitive answer than that. I'd just have to wait. I'd be there in thirty minutes.

The road was comparable to most state highways, paved with drainage ditches on both sides. We passed a couple of American compounds on the way: Camp Pelham and Camp Edwards. After Camp Edwards, we started passing dragon's teeth and tank walls. Then we drove through a village called Uchon-ni.

The driver said, "That's it."

"What do you mean?" I asked.

"That's the last village. There aren't any more."

I watched the village pass before my eyes. The rooftops and storefronts were brightly colored in an attempt to make everything seem more pleasant and happy. Beyond the tank wall at the end of the village was a pretty bleak looking scenario: a muddy river, rice paddies, lots of barbed wire, and a big-ass bridge. There were several buildings and statues near the bridge. The largest building was the Imjin-Gak, a restaurant that was the heart of the national monument. The bridge used to be part of the Trans-Siberian railway that ran from Paris to Pusan. The DMZ cut the line and killed it.

We stopped in front of a guard shack at the beginning of the bridge. An armed guard came over to check our orders and IDs. The bridge was only a single lane, so traffic had to be stopped at either end to let the others pass. There were two guards on the bridge and a spotlight on either side. The first 100 meters of the bridge was a flat deck with a wooden guardrail for aesthetic purposes. The next couple of hundred meters had a huge through-truss system of girders. A couple of guards at the far end of the bridge stood by their shack and nonchalantly saluted and waved us through.

There was a metal building off to the right: Freedom Bridge Security Platoon. The road turned sharply up a hill. A ROK (Republic of Korea— Korean soldiers were called ROKs) compound was embedded at the elbow in the road. We topped the hill and the two story white Korean CIA building masquerading as a hospital came in to view. It displayed a large white flag with a red cross on it.

An American compound, Camp Greaves, was on the right. There were Quonset huts and temporary buildings helter-skelter across the compound. I noticed a couple of American guards at what appeared to be an ammo dump. Korean guards were at each of the two entrance gates to the compound. A double barbed wire fence, seven feet high, with concrete posts, surrounded the compound. I could see a church steeple deep in the valley. There were colored rooftops near the church steeple. Was there a village up here after all?

We turned right, into the Camp Greaves compound. The Korean guard at the gate gave us the once over as we came through. We parked in front of the Headquarters building and I got out of the van and stretched. The driver threw my bags on the ground and drove away without as much as a "By your leave, Sir." The only people I could see on the grounds were the perimeter guards.

I hoisted up my bags and headed for the door. There was a long row of jeeps parked in front of the building. They had white wooden signs with black lettering that said: DMZ POLICE. *That's a lot of MPs*, I thought

Carrying my bags, I walked in the foyer where there were twenty soldiers anxiously milling around. There wasn't even room to walk in with my gear. I left my bags outside and waded in, pushing through the sea of soldiers. The soldiers were all dressed in field uniforms, helmets, flak jackets, pistol belts and all had weapons. I shouted that I was looking for the battalion commander. A guy turned around and shouted back, "Hey, here's a new lieutenant!" They all started shouting, "Get him! Take him!" I thought I might have to fight somebody.

A distinguished looking major stuck his head around the corner and hollered, "Fresh meat? George, take him. Nelson, fix it!" He ducked his head back around the corner. A stocky redheaded captain pushed his way over to me and asked me my name.

"Osterhout," I said in a loud military voice.

"No shit, I'll never remember that. Goddamnit, Nelson, let's get this show on the road."

A red haired lieutenant came over to me and asked, "What do you have?" I didn't know if he was talking about a sexually transmitted disease or what.

I looked at him dumb founded and said, "Huh?"

"Do you have a DMZ pass, flak jacket, helmet and arm band?"

"No, nothing's ready, everything I have is in a bag outside the door," I said and the lieutenant disappeared back into an office.

"The cherry lieutenant's on his ass," said the captain. "He's been here two minutes and he ain't good to go." I thought that the captain may have been kidding, but I wasn't sure.

"What's going on?" I asked.

"We're going to Panmunjom," said someone.

"Nelson, Goddamn! Let's go, we're fifteen minutes late already," roared the captain.

"Comin' over!" The red haired lieutenant, who must have been Nelson, slung a flak jacket over everybody's head. It bounced off two enlisted men and the wall before it came to rest at my feet. The crowd responded with obscenities.

"Heads up!" a helmet came winging over. I caught it and placed it on my head. Amazingly, it fit fairly well. Someone handed me a pistol belt and harness. I grabbed it and put it on. There was a yellow smoke grenade taped to the suspender. The ammo pouches had two empty forty-five magazines in them. There was a holster on the belt, but it was empty also.

"Does he have a DMZ pass?" an anonymous voice asked.

"No," I said.

Magically, a little blue card appeared from an outstretched hand. It was a pass that gave me free reign inside the Southern Boundary of the DMZ.

"Ya got your dog tags?" a southern voice asked.

"Yes."

"ID card?"

"Yes."

I had a funny feeling that he might ask me if I had a rubber and a ten-dollar bill, like all the ladies did last night. Last night already seemed like a light year away.

"Are we ready, Nelson?" asked the captain.

"I think so, Sir," said Nelson.

"Well, load up, Goddamnit. Don't stand around here!" said the captain in perfect command pitch.

We started filing out the door. A deuce-and-a-half (two and a half ton truck) driver caught the high sign from the captain and brought his open bed truck around. I was hoping that it wasn't going to be a long ride. It was seventeen degrees and I didn't relish the thought of riding in the back of an open vehicle for very far. The guys began to load on to the truck bed, handing their M-16's up to the men ahead of them and then climbing on.

Nelson came out the door, "Hey Turtle!" I didn't have to go through thirty-four weeks of intelligence training to figure out that he was calling me. He threw an M-16 my direction. I caught it, pulled the charging handle to the rear; the chamber was empty. Nelson then threw a magazine at me. I caught it against my chest. I depressed the cartridges with my thumb to find that there were eighteen rounds in it. Nelson also gave me a black armband with MP in white letters on it. The rest of the soldiers were also putting on their MP armbands. I'd just figured out who the DMZ police were.

The truck eased its way on to the M.S.R. (main supply route—the road to Panmunjom). As we crested the hill, the church steeple and village came into view again. It was a quarter of a mile off the M.S.R. It was called Unification Village.

"What's that place like?" I asked.

"It's off limits, that's what it's like. It's just for show—propaganda. If you go over there to get a piece of ass or something, you'll be in Kansas before you can say 'on your horse in the motor pool!'" said the sergeant next to me.

"On your horse in the motor pool?" I said.

"Yes, sir, it's a Korean word, means 'hello' or something like that."

"You mean it sounds like 'on your horse in the motor pool', right?" I asked.

19

"Yes, sir, that's what I said, and the ville's off limits too."

"Check," I said.

I hadn't had time to unpack my parka and I was beginning to freeze my gonads off. The sandbags we were sitting on were like blocks of ice. The sandbags lined the bed of the truck to minimize injury to the personnel in the back if the vehicle were to detonate a mine. Basically, they were there to keep our frozen gonads from being blown off. We passed an artillery firing battery on the left called 4PI (four papa one) and a ROK check point about a mile on down the road.

A quarter mile farther down were a couple more military complexes located on either side of the road. Camp Kitty Hawk, the one on the left, was a large, well-constructed compound. It was a United Nations command outfit with Korean and U.S. soldiers. Their task was guarding the Joint Security Area (JSA) at Panmunjom. Two officers from Camp Kitty Hawk were axed to death in the JSA back in '76.

Camp Liberty Bell was a poorly built compound situated on the right side of the road. It was the home of 1st Battalion 9th Infantry's Alpha Company. Camp Liberty Bell was nestled at the foot of some hills that marked the actual Southern Boundary of the DMZ. Ten years ago, a North Korean raiding party swooped down out of those hills like a band of marauding Indians and machine-gunned three Alpha Company soldiers to death while they were eating chow. The mess hall burned during the attack and the concrete slab was the only thing remaining.

The road adjacent to Camp Kitty Hawk was blocked by a small barricade labeled UNC Check Point Number 1. The guard came out to verify our I.D.'s. and a column of UNC jeeps pulled up in front of our truck. A captain got out, "Get in our jeeps. Hurry, let's move, it'll get dark on us if we don't watch out. We're twenty minutes late already."

We got into the caravan of UNC jeeps and rushed through Check Point Number 1. The American UNC captain, with the little blue diamond patch on his tanker's jacket, led the way. The blue diamond indicates a soldier who patrols the Joint Security Area. It's a very small plot of ground, several acres at the most. The focal point of the JSA is Panmunjom.

Passing several more checkpoints, we came upon a blue sign that arched across the roadway denoting the "Southern Boundary of the Demilitarized

Zone."

The first day in my unit, hell, my first ten minutes, and I was inside the DMZ. It didn't look anything like I thought it would, besides the armed guards at every checkpoint and the minefields on either side of the road. It had rice paddies, haystacks, and even some Korean farmers milling around in the fields. The only village inside the DMZ, Tae Song Dong, was located in the American sector. It was a propaganda village.

A large hill came into view on the left. It was laced with trenches, bunkers, sandbags, and barbed wire. A great black cloud of smoke was billowing off its crest.

"What the hell's that?" I asked.

"That's Guard Post Collier," said the sergeant sitting beside me.

"What's the smoke?" I asked.

"They're burning shit, no commodes. You know what I mean, Sir?"

"Is that part of our unit?"

"Yes."

I was afraid of that. I wasn't worried about the guard post's combat responsibilities; however, I could envision one of my extra duties being the shit-burning officer.

Off to the right I saw another bunker system with smoke pouring off it too.

"How many guard posts are there?" I asked.

"For us, just two, Guard Post Collier and Guard Post Ouellette."

A sign appeared on the right side of the road just past the Guard Post Ouellette cutoff that said: ONLY JSA VEHICLES BEYOND THIS POINT. I knew we were getting close to Panmunjom. We pulled into a parking lot near a small metal building. The convoy halted and we all piled out. The UNC captain said, "This is the Quick Reaction Force (QRF) staging point." That's all he said. It wasn't worth getting out of the jeep. I was still freezing my ass off.

A little further down the road we ran into UNC Check Point Number 5. The guard waved us through. Another quarter of a mile brought us to the front of Freedom House where we parked the vehicles. It was a beautiful white building with a pagoda. The pagoda was intricately painted with many bright colors and had a sunken garden in front of it.

The UNC captain began to give an orientation, "This is Panmunjom. The line running down the middle of that building is the Military Demarcation Line (MDL). It separates North and South Korea. There is a conference table in the building and the North Korean contingent sits on the North end of the table and the Admiral and the UNC contingent sits on the South end. Needless to say the MDL divides the table down the middle also."

He continued his spiel, pointing out the Pan Mun Gak, which was the North Korean equivalent of Freedom House. The Pan Mun Gak was only a facade. It was taller and larger than Freedom House, or at least it appeared that way. The North Korean building was only four feet thick. It was constructed for show in the game of "one-upsmanship" between the two countries.

The captain pointed out some North Korean guard towers and other strategic points in the terrain. Then we moved across the yard, parallel to the Military Demarcation Line. We came upon a concrete marker embedded in the side of the hill. The UNC captain looked me straight in the eye and said, "Lieutenant, when you get the call, I want you to take your men, lead them around this ridge, seal off that avenue of approach and kill everybody in the valley."

I started to say, 'Hell, Sir, the only man I have to lead is a clerk typist,' but I decided that I better not, instead, in spit-shined military fashion, I said, "Yes Sir."

The captain highlighted several points of interest, including the Bridge of No Return and 72 Hour Bridge. The Bridge of No Return got its name at the end of the Korean conflict in '53. When prisoners were exchanged at Panmunjom, they were given a choice of staying with their captors or returning to their homeland. If they decided to go back and cross the bridge, they would never be allowed to return, thus the name. The 72 Hour Bridge was constructed and named in '76. Prior to '76, all nationalities, North Korean, South Korean, American, Czech, Polish, Swiss, and Swede could move about freely in the Joint Security Area. After the North Koreans attacked the American officers and killed them with axe handles and clubs, they fled across the Bridge of No Return. The United Nations then enforced the rule about crossing the MDL that ran through the middle of the bridge, which was the only North Korean egress into the Joint Security Area. Since the North

Koreans couldn't get into the area anymore they had to construct a new bridge and did so in three days, thus its name, 72 Hour Bridge.

I was standing with my boot touching the concrete MDL dividing marker. I leaned over a little to get a better look down the road to the bridge. I thought my head might have been hanging into the North Korean air space. Then I felt it. Some people say that they can tell when they're being watched. They can feel the back of their neck begin to tingle. Not me, but I felt it just the same. My nipples got hard, or maybe it was just the cold seeping into the flak jacket.

"Don't make any quick movements!" ordered the UNC captain. "They may fire on us." Two North Korean soldiers stood beside the guard tower across the small valley. One held binoculars to his eyes while the other aimed his AK-47 automatic rifle at my face. I heard someone in our group behind me say, "Exit, stage fuckin' left."

Our little mob slowly turned and ran away in such an exaggerated, cartoon like slow motion that it would have been funny if I hadn't been half way expecting to get a new orifice ripped in my ass by a 7.62 millimeter chunk of lead.

We moved on to an observation post. It was a small concrete tower/bunker that was designed to hold about seven troops. As any cold infantrymen would do, we squeezed eighteen people into the space for seven. It was warmer, but someone farted one of those long, three tone farts. I mentally clocked it and it lasted approximately six seconds. During the first two seconds the conversation completely lagged and during the next four seconds there was only silence … except for the last two tones of fart.

The UNC captain could barely keep a straight face, but he concluded his speech with a history lesson. He told us that the Armistice Agreement was signed on 27 July '53, "in that building." He pointed to a small museum on the North Korean side, the Peace Museum, with a descending dove above the front door. It was really a propaganda building, filled with atrocities from the war, all slanted against the Americans.

He told us about the Neutral National Supervisory Council (NNSC). These were the Czech/Poles who lived on the North Korean side and the Swiss/Swedes who lived on our side. They had small compounds close to the JSA and were tasked with investigating any allegations of Armistice Agreement violations.

The signing of the Armistice Agreement was only a truce. It's the longest running truce in the world. The Koreas are officially at war. The cease-fire is broken from time to time, actually quite often, as I would find out later. The captain finished and we rode in the jeeps back to Camp Kitty Hawk. Then we froze our asses off again in the back of the trucks.

The sun was just about to set on the North Korean horizon when we got back to Camp Greaves. I went to the arms room to turn in my weapon. It was a dumpy looking building that could be broken into with a can opener. Of course one of my responsibilities was weapons security. The armorer and I got to talking about one thing or another when an awful racket broke loose outside.

"What on earth is that?" I asked.

"You ain't never seen the DMZ Disco?" he asked.

"No, I ain't," I smiled.

"You a turtle, huh, Sir?" and he smiled.

"Yeah, I'm a turtle, just what is going on out there?"

Three trucks pulled up in front of the arms room. Fifteen or twenty soldiers dressed in combat uniforms were in the back of each truck. Each man was banging an axe handle against the metal side of the truck. A whistle blew and everyone bailed out of the trucks and formed a wedge in front of the vehicles. A couple of men remained in the bed of the truck with weapons pointed over the cab. Another whistle sounded and the wedge of men began moving forward. They'd take a half step with their lead foot and drag the other one up even. Done in unison, it gave a sense of rhythm to the wave of soldiers.

"That, Sir," said the armorer, "is the Quick Reaction Force (QRF) doing the DMZ disco, the stomp and drag."

The series of whistles continued and the soldiers went through an assortment of gyrations. They individually ran back to the trucks and traded the axe handles for M-16s, they fixed bayonets with a simultaneous battle cry, donned protective mask and changed formations. All in all it was very impressive.

This act was designed to control riot situations in the JSA, but everyone pretty much suspected that such a highly structured routine would fall flat on its ass if a riot was in full swing, especially a riot with armed North Korean soldiers. I hoped that we wouldn't try to bust up North Korean extracurricular machine gun play with axe handles, but I'd never know until it happened.

I went back to the Headquarters building to find the battalion commander so I could report in. However, I didn't really think that he would be available Sunday evening. Lieutenant Nelson was waiting for me at the Headquarters.

"Colonel St. John wants to see you," and Nelson pointed to a door.

I reported. Lieutenant Colonel St. John was an impressive man, tall, distinguished, smoked a large cigar, wore glasses, and was red headed.

He explained the mission of the battalion to me and wanted a written transition schedule between me and my predecessor. The transition plan would delineate responsibilities during the period that there were two intelligence officers for the one office. He puffed twice on his cigar and dismissed me. I went out to find Nelson waiting for me in the hall.

Nelson greeted me with, "Captain Starns wants to see you in the bunker."

"Where's that?"

"Follow me."

We went behind the Headquarters building to an underground structure. It was an operations center and S-2 office for the battalion. Nelson gave the high sign to the face looking through the peephole on the iron security door and we entered. A red haired captain met me just inside the door. He was extremely happy to see me, to say the least. If he'd been a dog, he'd probably have wagged his tail and dribbled pee on the floor. We sat and talked about patrols, guard posts, and the QRF. He was surprised about how knowledgeable I was, after all, I'd already been inside the DMZ, toured Panmunjom, seen my first North Korean soldier, saw the troops burn shit on the guard post and watched the QRF do the stomp and drag.

Captain Starns and I talked for an hour. He told me to go ahead and sleep-in tomorrow because of jet lag and all. "Come in at eight," he said.

Nelson waited for me outside the bunker, "Let's go eat some steaks at the Officer's Club." He and I packed my bags in the duty vehicle and we rode a quarter of a mile to the Officer's Club on the cliff overlooking the Imjin River and Freedom Bridge. The river was frozen and reflected the security lights from the bridge. It appeared very peaceful

Nelson told the duty driver to wait for him. We went into the club and took a seat near the door. Little did I know that this club was going to be the only sanctuary I had. There was a bar in the back that ran the length of the room. There was a Ping-Pong table, a pool table, and a TV. That was the extent of the recreational facilities in the club. In addition, there were two "silver bullet" diesel-burning stoves that provided the heat.

A waitress came over to the table and took our order, steaks, potatoes, and tea. The waitress was middle aged and walked with a distinctive limp from a stiff leg.

Nelson challenged me to a game of Scrabble. Scrabble? Something didn't seem right about this place. It was truly the Land of the Not Quite Right. The mere mention of the game brought another officer over to the table. Lieutenant Nelson introduced me to a warrant officer, Chief Kiel, a physician's assistant, our battalion "doc." The first thing that I noticed about this pleasant looking man was his head of red hair. I began to feel out of place, all five officers I'd met so far had red hair.

"May I join you for a game?" asked the doc.

The Scrabble board was brought out and the game began. Nelson was the undefeated battalion champion. We played until our food was served. The steaks were tender and juicy and relatively inexpensive, five bucks. The steaks were on special that night. They weren't any cheaper, there was just an abundance of them, and you could get them served a little quicker. After getting warmed up by the silver bullet and getting a steak and spud in me, I was content and needed sleep. I asked Nelson where my quarters were.

"It's not far, c'mon, let's finish the game," he suggested.

Of all things, I didn't feel like playing Scrabble, but more than that, I didn't want to alienate anyone on my first day. We continued to play. At 2240 (10:40 PM), the management threw us out of the club so they could close. I emerged the new Battalion Scrabble Champion.

The duty driver was still waiting for us. Nelson shouted to him something about the Turkey Farm. The vehicle followed as we walked down a hill toward the river. We came to a Quonset hut near the edge of the cliffs. There was a perfect view of the bridge from the door. Home, Sweet Home; a room in a tin Quonset hut. There was one shower, one commode, one urinal, and seven other men to share them with… the Turkey Farm.

I quickly threw some sheets and a blanket over the mattress on the metal bunk and plugged in my two electric alarm clocks, one across the room, and set them for 0630. I left the rest of my junk in the middle of the floor, Nelson said good night and I died in bed.

I woke up a couple of hours later with goose bumps. I covered up the best I could and doubled up in a knot. A couple of minutes after that, I woke up to an explosion that rattled my windows. My first thought was the bridge blew up, our only escape route. I ran out the front door to see if the bridge was still there. It was. No one was running around screaming frantically like in all the war movies I'd ever seen, so I assumed the explosion was part of the status quo.

The sound was actually a sonic boom from a SR-71 reconnaissance plane flying overhead. The officers got to a point where they couldn't go to sleep until they heard the boom. Then they could sleep peacefully knowing that the enemy was being watched. I glanced at my clock, 0200.

"Lord, let me sleep," and I did.

CHAPTER 3

1st Patrol

Through the haze of my awakening brain I could make out movement in the hall of the Quonset hut. I glanced out the window, the sun was up, but a ground fog obscured everything from view. "What the hell time is it?" I looked at my clocks ... both of them read 0430. *Holy Shit, what the hell time is it?*

A Korean man opened the door, "Helro, you new S-2." I don't think it was a question.

"Yes," I said.

"I'm Mr. Yi, houseman, you worky today?"

"Yes, what time is it?"

"Seben forry fife."

"Seven Forty Five!" I echoed in the King's English.

I sprang out of the bunk, madly threw on my fatigues, and ran to the latrine. Mr. Yi was making my bed when I left the building ten minutes later.

The ground fog was dense and I couldn't see fifty feet in front of me. I didn't remember how to get to the Headquarters but I knew it was a quarter of a mile away on a road. I was on a road so I ran down it making a couple turns that I wasn't sure I was supposed to make. I was right. I wasn't supposed to make them because I came to a locked gate. The ammo dump I'd seen earlier was on my left and Charlie Company Headquarters was on my right.

Damn, I'm lost. I went into the Charlie Company Headquarters and found the company commander who pointed me in the right direction. When you know where you are going and the fog as lifted a little, getting to the battalion Headquarters is a piece of cake. I rang the buzzer on the bunker and a pair of eyes peered out at me from the peephole in the iron door.

"I'm Lieutenant Osterhout, the new S-2, intelligence officer."

The little window shut. I stood there for a few minutes waiting on the guy to get back with confirmation of my name. The door swung open and I went into the bunker. I slithered around the radio operators, the assistants posting the map and the Fire Support Team. Captain Starns was buried in a mass of papers in the far corner of the room. The first thing I asked him was: "Did the power go out last night?"

"It always does," he replied.

"It does?"

"Yeah, sometimes four or five times a day. You obviously have an electric alarm clock?"

"Yes, Sir, two of them, and neither one's worth a shit."

Captain Starns told me that every time it rained, the electricity failed. The record was eight power failures in one twenty-four hour period, which occurred during the monsoon season.

Captain Starns forgave me for being late because nothing of importance happened during the night. However, a patrol would be leaving soon that needed to be briefed and I was supposed to sit in on the briefing. While I was waiting, I met the rest of the crew: Sergeant First Class Haifley, Staff Sergeant Pettit and Private First Class Hancock (Stan the Man). All of these men, like everybody else, would rotate out of country before I would.

I spent most of my first day getting to know the operations. I read all our contingency plans, walked the compound perimeter and checked all the guards. I walked a mile down to the bridge and checked the security operations there. I sat in on patrol briefings and debriefings. I monitored the radio traffic coming in from the guard posts and watched the radio operators pass the information up to brigade. The mission was just about all the battalion was doing. The mission consisted of several moving parts:

Manning two large platoon size guard posts inside the DMZ,

Maintaining the platoon size Quick Reaction Force,

Sending a minimum of five different 6 to 10 man patrols a day into the DMZ,

Providing soldiers for many smaller two man check points and essential guard posts,

Supplying two platoons to guard Freedom Bridge.

That was 200 men a day carrying a loaded weapon. It was a total commitment and it took every man we had to conduct the mission properly.

It was 2030 (8:30 PM) when I finally finished my "transition plan" for the battalion commander. I took it into his office and was going to leave it in his "in" box. To my surprise the battalion commander was still working. I realized that working from 0530 to 2030 (5:30 AM to 8:30 PM) was just a normal day.

The battalion commander and I talked a little while. From his conversation I gathered that he, the Executive Officer (XO) and the Operations Officer (S-3), the three highest ranking officers in the battalion, were all from the Pentagon and had taken this assignment to "groom" themselves for better things. When we finished talking, he looked up at me from behind his desk, puffed on his big cigar and said, "Well Dave, take the rest of the day off," and he was serious.

I had managed to either work through lunch and supper or I was somewhere on the far side of the perimeter and missed the hours that the Headquarters' mess hall was open. I was starving and I went directly to the Officer's Club craving another steak and potato. When I got to the club it was closed for cockroach fumigating. I went hungry. Heading to my room, I dreaded the chore of putting all my things away.

Before I entered my Quonset hut, I stood on the patio overlooking the river. The village across the river to the south was lit up and the bridge looked almost majestic. It was a pretty sight. Peaceful. Peaceful? Shit, what did I know at that time?

I went into my room and was surprised to see everything in its place. The dresser drawers were filled with my socks and underwear and the closet had all my uniforms dress-right-dressed, boots, and shoes all in a line and spit shined. It was amazing. I walked over to the bed and looked at my clocks. They were four hours behind. I set the time and the alarms for 0500 and hoped that I could wake myself up, because I sure didn't trust the electricity. I went to bed.

I no sooner closed my eyes when an explosion rattled the windows again. I fought the urge to check the bridge so I listened carefully for the sounds of men running and shouting in panic. There were no sounds. I slept.

I was very restless. I could usually wake myself up at the proper times if I never fell into a sound sleep. I woke up three times during the night, the clock read 12:30 AM the first time, 0230 the next, and about an hour later it showed 0238. It was obvious that the electricity had gone off. I laid awake waiting for noises from the hall. It was still dark outside so I wasn't extremely late, at least not yet. After several millenniums of keeping my eyes open, I heard the hall phone ring. There was only one phone in the building. A door immediately banged open and I could hear bare feet pad down the hall at a double time.

"Captain Starns.... Have you reported it to brigade? ...Don't report it yet. .... Right, I'll be down in a minute."

I thought 'Well, what the hell, it's my job too!'

My fatigues were laid out for emergencies so I wouldn't have to go digging around in the dark for them if the electricity was off, which it was. I met Captain Starns in the hall. We looked at each other inquisitively, the "What the hell are we doing up at this hour" look, although I didn't know what time it really was.

We went toward the bunker. Halfway to the Headquarters we were halted by one of the Korean guards. Every time they challenge someone they jack a round into the chamber of their M-16s. I was a little afraid of Koreans to begin with, since I was so new to the country, however, I was deathly afraid of Koreans with automatic rifles. I remained afraid of that kind of Korean my entire tour.

We entered the bunker and the Officer in Charge immediately began to brief Captain Starns. I already felt a little out of place. I didn't fit in, not yet anyway. No one would come to me or call me as long as the guy I was replacing was still here. He had seen them through most of the mission and they trusted him, even though they thought of him as a "flaming asshole."

Captain Starns finally got a handle on the situation. I just listened. Evidently an enemy patrol was reported approaching the DMZ. Captain Starns got some of the radars that report to us to swing around and try to locate the enemy personnel. He got the scouts in the towers on the DMZ guard posts to go outside and use their starlight scopes. He called the ambush patrol to alert them. He contacted the South Barrier Fence Guards and briefed them. He called the adjacent ROK units and got their report. Then he called the United Nations Command Operations Center and asked them if their patrols or guards at the Joint Security Area knew anything. He compiled his information on an extended message form and gave it to the operations center officer and told him to send it up to brigade. It took fifteen minutes to get the paragraph size message reported.

"Now we sit and wait."

"What for?" I asked.

"Nuclear Detonation."

Captain Starns got a cup of coffee and sat at his desk. I sat at the little field desk set up beside his. I felt like I was relegated to the kids' table at Thanksgiving. Ten minutes later the brigade operations center called back and answered our message with a dozen questions that we'd already answered.

Finally they asked, "What was the battalion commander doing about it?"

We could have answered this a million ways but we decided to tell the truth—the battalion commander was doing nothing. We told higher Headquarters that the guard posts and patrols were aware of the suspected infiltration and we would advise the brigade operations center of any new information. For the time being, it satisfied them.

We'd been at it for an hour and forty-five minutes—it was 0500. The phone must have awakened us at 0315. Captain Starns and I sat around and wrote a three-page summary of all the events that just took place starting from the initial report from the guard post to the time that the brigade signed off the air. When we got through writing it up, it was time for breakfast.

The next couple of days dragged on just like the first. We got calls in the middle of the night regularly. Guards were checked and rechecked. Patrols were briefed and debriefed. My transition plan with Captain Starns was going as scheduled. It had been four days and I already thought nothing could surprise me. But something new always came up. I didn't know it at the time, but tomorrow would be the turning point of my Army career and my life. I was going on my first patrol inside the DMZ.

Most of the night before was spent learning the rules of engagement (when to shoot and when not to shoot) and the patrolling SOP's (standard operating procedures). When I thought I had them all memorized I turned out the light and set the alarms on my two new wind-up clocks, purchased at our tiny PX.

I woke up at 0530, a good night, no phone calls. I dressed and took the proper clothing to the bunker with me. The patrol was scheduled to leave friendly front lines at 1100. I briefed the battalion commander at 0730 and told him that I was going to "check out of the net" for the afternoon because I would be on patrol.

The battalion commander seemed pleased, he said, "Well, it's about time." I think he was serious; after all I'd been there five days and 1st Battalion, 9th

Infantry Manchu Warriors are supposed to be leaning forward in the saddle.

Most patrols have rehearsals, but this one didn't. I pulled out my map and checked the route one more time. It was a rather long route that had a start point, five check points, and a pick up point. I put the map away and began checking myself from the bottom up: wool socks, leather boots, overshoes, long-john bottoms, fatigue pants, field pants, T-shirt, long-john shirt, O.G. wool shirt, parka, pile cap, helmet, black gloves with inserts, trigger finger mittens with inserts, flak jacket, harness, pistol belt, compass, map, binoculars, two smoke grenades, a flare, a bayonet, 196 rounds of ammunition (seven magazines), protective mask and chemical detection paper and decontamination kit. I had my DMZ pass, ID card, dog tags, and MP armband. My M-16 was cleaned and oiled and my face was blackened with camouflage face paint. I probably weighed 300 pounds with all the gear on. How did the Army expect me to be hostile, agile, and mobile when I could barely put one foot in front of the other?

My job title for the duration of the patrol was assistant patrol leader. I was a first lieutenant and the patrol leader was only an E-5 sergeant. We had two radio operators, an aid man, a point man, a 203 (grenade launcher/M-16) gunner and a rear security man. The 203 gunner was also our KATUSA soldier. A KATUSA is a Korean Attached to the U.S. Army. All patrols needed a KATUSA. Their job was to interpret for the patrol leader if we found any Korean Nationals inside the DMZ. This happened quite frequently since there was a propaganda village consisting of some 130 residents located within the southern boundary of the DMZ. If we ran across any of these residents, we were to challenge them for their credentials. If everything was in order, we'd carry on. If not, we would arrest them and take them in for questioning.

I'd only heard of a few incidents when the residents of Tae Song Dong, the propaganda village, didn't have the proper identification. Most of the time they came along willingly and when questioned, were found to have only forgotten their papers. One time a sixty-year old woman was discovered without her papers. The patrol did their duty and began to haul her in. A young Korean man, probably a relative, started to give the patrol a hard time, calling them "stupid GIs" and "motherfuckers." The patrol leader had his hands full trying to watch his prisoner and keep the patrol members from butt-stroking the Korean man in the face with their rifles. Finally the patrol leader had taken enough bullshit and asked the young Korean man for his papers. The Korean man backed off immediately. The patrol surrounded the young man and asked him again for his papers. He tried to run, but the soldiers kept shoving him back into the center of the circle. To the glee of the patrol it became evident that this man had no papers either. It was with much pleasure that the patrol bound his hands firmly behind his back and led him off with the old woman. Later, the two were confirmed to be official residents of Tae Song Dong and fined severely for not having the proper credentials.

Our patrol made the necessary radio checks and loaded in the back of the sandbagged deuce-and-a-half truck. It was very solemn as the soldiers passing around the last cigarette. The truck bed was covered with a canvas so no one could see that a patrol was going out. I sat next to the tailgate and could see out a crack in the back flap. The propaganda village passed by. There was a bus stop near the road and several Korean villagers loitered nearby. They waved at us as we passed. I had this terrible feeling that they knew we were in the back of the truck, knew exactly where we were going and knew what we were going to do. My hands were already getting cold. These Army gloves aren't worth a damn. Firebase Four Papa One passed by and my toes started getting cold, Army boots aren't worth a damn. We passed a fifty-caliber machine gun at the ROK checkpoint as the last cigarette butt was extinguished on the sandbags.

We stopped at the last barricade before entering the DMZ. The truck flap flew open and a Spec/4 asked, "Is ya'll the patrol for eleven hundred?"

"Yes."

"Let me see ya'll's ID cards and DMZ passes. Ya'll lock and load one magazine but do not chamber a round unless you're fired upon or the patrol leader tells you to. Ya'll have a good'un now, y'hear," and the corporal with the southern accent disappeared from view.

Click—click—click, and the magazines all snapped into place. The proper radio transmissions were made and the patrol leader barked out the last minute instructions: "First man out, head up the bank and check the woods. Second man out—stand by the truck and help the radiomen out of the back. When the radiomen are out, everyone heads for the wood line. Make a three sixty perimeter and we'll make the next radio check before we move out."

The truck came to a stop and the first man bailed out of the back. He took one step sliding three feet on the ice, then a hop, two skips, and a nosedive into the ditch beside the road.

Well, I thought, *we have a good start.*

35

The first guy bounced up and disappeared into the woods. The radiomen jumped out and the rest of us followed as the truck was taking off. We got into the woods and after a little shuffling around, managed to make a circle and face out. The radio checks were made and I pulled out my map to make a quick azimuth check. The patrol leader did the same and the point man was up and ready to take off. The patrol leader pointed in a direction and off we went. The first leg of the route wasn't very hard at all. It was about 500 meters long and took us around the base of Guard Post Collier. As long as we kept the guard post hill on our right we couldn't be too far off course.

The first segment went quickly and we set up a small perimeter on the west side of Guard Post Collier. I pulled out my map and made another azimuth check. The patrol leader was doing the same while the primary radio operator called in 'check point one'. My hands were getting really cold. When I put my map back in my field pants I didn't close the pocket properly because my hands were too cold to feel the small metal snap. I was afraid that my confidential map might fall out and of course it did, somewhere between Check Point 1 and Check Point 2. At Check Point two, the rear security man gave it back to me. I was very thankful. It could have been one of those "Oh shits" that ruined my career.

Check Point 2 was about twenty meters short of the hard surface road to Panmunjom. I assumed a position thirty meters to the right of the main body of the patrol and the rear security man, called Showboat, was going to the left. The purpose of the flanking movement was to warn the others if the enemy was anywhere close or if a vehicle was coming down the road so we could get out of sight. We weren't supposed to be seen by any Neutral Nations Supervisory Council personnel, who might be in any vehicle. The Armistice Agreement stated that automatic weapons were not allowed inside the DMZ. American soldiers are issued M-16s, which have the capability of firing fully automatic, as are the North Korean's AK-47s. In order to disguise the fact that we break the Armistice Agreement, we hide from everybody so no one will know. Everybody knows anyway. It's one of those stupid games we play. The troops don't understand why we do it, the command doesn't understand, nobody does, but we do it. It's the Army way.

I got into position and looked down at Showboat—he was also in position, sixty meters on my left. I glanced down the road to the right and stared into the wood line. Nothing. I waved the first man across. He moved up to the road, looked both ways, and sprinted across. He searched the far side of the road for a few minutes and then gave a signal for the next man to cross. Showboat and I gave signals and the next man sprinted across. Within minutes everyone but Showboat and me was on the far side. I was going to be the last man across. Showboat stood up to cross the road, but I waved him back down. A deuce-and-a-half was headed this way from friendly front lines. It was probably a guard post's chow truck, but we had to follow the rules and hide. We hunkered down by the side of the road with our M-16s underneath us. This way, if we were spotted, whoever saw us wouldn't be able to see our illegal weapons, they would just see a soldier lying on the side of the road for no apparent reason. How stupid did I feel?

The truck passed us and when it was out of sight, Showboat sprinted across the road. Then I gave a look both ways and began running to the other side. Snow had fallen the last few nights and it was a smooth virgin white. My footprints would be the first mark on it. I couldn't see anything at all on the ground just the snow. Every step I took was based on faith. A young lady once told me that faith was like jumping from a tree to the green grass and knowing that the ground was underneath to hold you up, even though you couldn't see it. I had faith, how could the ground not be under the snow?

I must have been a backsliding, heathen, son-of-a-bitch, because on the third step on the far side of the road, the ground disappeared. In a small hollow spot, my boot became wedged in a maze of hidden barbed wire called tangle-foot. It was designed to make men fall and it worked wonderfully. I fell uncontrollably down a small hill into a sharpened stake. I landed squarely on my left knee, bounced a little, and then came to rest with my knees buried in the snow at the bottom of a pit.

The impact startled me and I didn't realize I was hurt until the snow showed some red bloody spots. I tried to stand up and a damned stick was hanging out of my leg. "Oh God." I could feel it up underneath my kneecap somewhere. No wait, I think it passed right through. I don't know. "Shit," I breathed deeply. I took two more deep breaths, reached down, and pulled the stake out. The cold air seared my lungs as I sucked in a silent scream.

I picked up my M-16 and nodded to the patrol leader. He nodded back. When we regrouped Showboat asked me if I was okay. I told him that I'd make it. I thought maybe I lied, but I was going to try. We were just on the third segment—less than halfway. Check Point 3 was still 700 meters away. Thank God it was fairly easy-going terrain. We had left the hills and were on frozen rice paddies. I was going to try to be a functional member of the patrol, but I was mostly concentrating on just walking. My knee felt fairly well intact, it just hurt like hell. We were moving across the open ground quickly because we didn't want to be exposed to the enemy view for too long. The quickened pace made it even more difficult for me to keep up. I prayed and swore alternately, but I wasn't going to quit. I thought that I might pass out but I wasn't going to quit.

Check Point 3 was at the bottom of the Guard Post Ouellette hill. It was heavily vegetated, but again all we had to do was keep the hill to our right and we wouldn't be too far off. Check Point 4 lay directly beneath the outdoor shit-house of Guard Post Ouellette. The game plan was to hike around the slope of the hill until we could see the shit-house directly up the hill from us and then we'd take another azimuth reading and head for check point five. So, there I was, in some state of being wounded, scanning the rim of the hill, hoping to see the shit house.

The vegetation became extremely thick. It was surprising to see the leaves still on the trees in the dead of winter. The patrol began to angle down the hill because gravity naturally pulled our 300-pound bodies downward. Besides, soldiers generally always followed the easiest route. In combat situations, that's what got people killed—laziness. We were even lazier on this patrol. It was daylight and our patrol leader said that he had been on this route several times before.

We were just about at the bottom of the hill and the terrain had really flattened out. I felt sure that we were semi-lost. That meant we didn't know exactly where we were, but we weren't in North Korea getting our asses shot off. Even through the pain, I felt a mild case of panic. The patrol leader halted the patrol and radioed in Check Point 4. I was only a fair map reader, but I could tell that this wasn't Check Point 4 because when I looked up, I saw sky and not a shit house. I glanced at my watch—it was time to be at Check Point 4. I guess the patrol leader just called it in anyway. The folks back in the rear would never know.

The patrol leader gathered us into a tight perimeter and told us that he wanted to go on a short leader's recon. That meant he was going to walk around a little and try to figure out where he was. As soon as he got back he signaled for everyone to get up and resume the patrol. I knew immediately that we were going in the wrong direction. I glanced back at Showboat.

"This isn't the right way," I whispered.

"Tell him," he said, pointing to the patrol leader

I passed it up to the next man, "We're going the wrong way."

After fifteen minutes, which seemed like forever, the patrol suddenly stopped and to my disbelief we had come upon a tennis court. It had a green playing surface with a dark maroon out-of-bounds area. The snow had been cleared off and it was ready for play. The net was a brand new shiny white and there was a seven-foot chain link fence around the court. Nothing else was in sight, just the woods, and the tennis court. I hoped everyone else's first instinct was to run because that was mine. We stared for a minute from the concealment of the wood line. The patrol leader walked toward the tennis court. Everyone jacked rounds into their weapons and I could hear the distinctive click of the M-16s being taken off safe. I thought, *what the hell is he doing?*

The patrol leader moved to the fence and touched it, as if it may not be real. He moved across the open area and out of sight into the woods on the far side of the tennis court. We remained in our over-watch position.

He came back and gave us the high sign to move out. We did and right smartly, too. We ended up going back the way we came for a hundred meters and then turned nearly straight south. We were supposed to be going southwest but halfway in the right direction beat being in North Korea getting our asses shot off. That became my litmus test for how bad conditions were, "Are you in North Korea getting your ass shot off?" If the answer was "no," then things couldn't be too bad. I was just happy that we were moving again. The faster we got this thing over with the better. I had a noticeable limp now.

After humping through some brushy terrain, we set up a perimeter and the radioman was instructed to call in Check Point 5 even though we were about 250 meters short. I thought, *No wonder we get people killed, this patrol leader sucks.* I made a time check and we were twenty minutes behind schedule, which meant a sprint for the pickup point. We got a "roger" on Check Point 5 and we were off to the races. All patrol tactics were thrown out the window and it became a fast hump through the bush. I could barely keep up. I was falling behind and separating from the patrol. I fought hard to keep the separation to a minimum. When the front half of the patrol reached the pickup point I was sixty meters behind. The forward radioman called for the pick up vehicle and was just finishing his transmission when I collapsed in the perimeter. My knee was a raw nerve. No matter what position I held it in, it still hurt badly.

The chill began to creep in after only a few minutes. The race against the clock wasn't a very good idea. We were sweaty now, but in minutes we'd be on the verge of hypothermia. Maybe the truck wouldn't take too long to arrive. The cold seemed to soak into my knee and stiffen it. Within five minutes the whole patrol was experiencing the first stages of hypothermia and we were essentially defenseless. All of us were curled into little balls trying to keep in some of the heat.

The sound of a truck coming brought the patrol to life. The patrol leader went to the road to signal the vehicle but it was the Guard Post Ouellette re-supply vehicle and just passed him by. The patrol leader came back and looked into all the anxious faces. "Wrong truck. Radio in that we're still waiting at the pickup point,"

The reply was that the truck had been dispatched twenty-five minutes ago. "We're at the wrong place," I said, and pulled out my map and surveyed the situation. Sure enough, we looked to be 400 meters from the proper location.

"Let's move out," the patrol leader barked.

We rucked up and started a fast, non-tactical walk to the truck with everyone cursing under their breath. My knee was hurting so badly that I had to use my M-16 as a crutch to support my weight. My feet were numb, my hands were numb, and my cheeks and nose were raw from the cold. And worst of all, I feared that my knee might be permanently damaged. The truck was waiting for us by the side of the road. The driver was nervously smoking a cigarette when we linked up with him.

"Where the hell you been?" the driver asked.

"You're in the wrong place," said our patrol leader.

"You must'a been lost and now you're gonna blame it on me." With that, the driver got back into the cab and started the engine. The tailgate was down and the radiomen were assisted in. I was the last man to mount and I had to have someone pull me up. We closed the truck flap and sat back on the frozen sandbags trying to keep warm.

After clearing our weapons, we settled into the debriefing room. The debriefing was very simple. The patrol leader said he had negative results, he didn't see anything, he didn't hear anything and all routes were clear. Sergeant

Pettit took copious notes of the "nothing" the patrol reported. There was no mention of my swollen, bloody knee; there was no mention of the tennis courts, no mention of being lost and no mention of the tangle-foot wire booby trap. Sergeant Pettit, the debriefer, dismissed the patrol and they filed out heading for chow. I reported the real story to the sergeant and mentally began to plan some intense remedial patrol tactics training, beginning with that patrol leader. Also, the next patrol that I dispatched went out with wire cutters and picks to clear the booby trap I'd fallen into.

I limped into the operations center portion of the bunker and found Captain Starns running through the daily intelligence reports.

"Sir, are there any tennis courts in the DMZ?"

Captain Starns just laughed.

"I saw one," I said.

He laughed again, "There's an aerial photograph of this area in the cabinet. Take a look for yourself." I limped to the cabinet and searched for the photographs. Captain Starns asked me if I was hurt and I told him the story of falling down.

"Go to the Aid Station and get it taken care of. That's an order," he said and continued his work.

"Yes, Sir, in just a minute."

I unraveled a mosaic photograph that must have been ten years old. It was dark and very poor quality. I couldn't find a tennis court on it anywhere. There weren't very many aerial photographs of this area because aircraft were not allowed to fly into the Buffer Zone around the DMZ. My compound was on the edge of the Buffer Zone. Special permission had to be granted at God-level to allow airplanes and helicopters to fly into the Buffer Zone. The exception was the SR 71 spy plane and I wasn't at a pay grade that had permission to discuss it, let alone get to see any resulting imagery.

The mystery of the tennis courts baffled me. I knew that the patrol had been outside the U.S. Sector. Could we have been in North Korea? I shuddered to think of it. After further research in the coming weeks, I found out that the tennis courts belonged to the Neutral Nations Supervisor Council Swiss/Swedish delegation. However, all I needed to worry about right then was getting to the dispensary.

I tried to find a jeep around Headquarters to take me to my Quonset hut so I could store my gear. I couldn't find a driver, but there were several jeeps out front. I thought about stealing one, but started walking instead. I turned in my M-16 at the arms room along the way and continued my walk. When I was halfway to the dispensary, I was wondering why I was stupid enough to wear my flak jacket and helmet. I could have left them in the bunker. Every ounce felt like a ton on my knee. The doc was at the dispensary treating VD cases. He treated some 1200 cases per year. There were only 800 men in my unit, which was an annual average of one and a half cases per soldier.

I told the doc's assistant what happened and I got moved to the head of the line. Doc Keil punched and pulled on my leg a little, but couldn't tell anything conclusive. He cleaned off the blood and medicated the punctures. The stake went in the front, bounced off my tibia, and poked out the side. He wrote out an X-ray request and summoned his ambulance driver to take me eighteen miles to the rear to Camp Edwards. It was about 1700 (5 PM) when I got to Camp Edwards and all the rear echelon pukes were off work already. I had to wait for an hour and a half while the clinic clerk called the X-ray technician back from the local bar.

When the rear echelon puke finally showed up, the X-ray process only took ten minutes. After he took the pictures, I sat and waited for another hour until a duty NCO (Spec/5) came out and said nothing was broken. He held the X-ray in front of the light and pointed to a pinhead size blemish on the bone just below my kneecap.

"There's a funny spot here, but it's not broken. You can go back to your unit now." The Spec/5 disappeared down the hall. I woke up the ambulance driver and we headed back to the DMZ. It was 2030 (8:30 PM) when I arrived. I went to the bunker first and checked in. There wasn't much happening so I went up to the Officer's Club. There wasn't much happening there either. However, there was a startling new member of the Officer's Club staff. Her name was Miss Yi. She was small, slender, had dark hair, dark eyes and perfect olive colored skin. She looked wonderful. She moved gracefully and had a genuine smile. She was quiet and shy and I loved her immediately, as did every other soldier. Of course she'd been an employee for three years, therefore, she'd seen over 2400 soldiers come and go. It would be a tough chore getting to know her. I asked one of the officers what the story was on Miss Yi. He told me that he thought she was married. Miss Yi brought me my large plate of fried rice (flied lice). As I ate it, Doc Keil came over to me with a cane in his hand.

"Here, you may need this," he tossed it to me. "What did the X-rays show?"

I told the doc that the Spec/5 at the medical facility just said that nothing was broken, and I should go back to duty. I finished my rice, paid Miss Yi and said good night to her. I limped down the hill to my Quonset hut and collapsed on my bunk. The phone rang. I sprang up in time to hear Captain Starns answer it. I fell back into a daze.

"I think they gave him a very poor once over—I'm not sure if he's all right—Keil said nothing's broken, okay—good night, Sir."

It was Lieutenant Colonel St. John, the battalion commander calling to see if I was all right. I was functional but I wasn't all right.

CHAPTER 4

Guard Post

A couple of weeks went by and I still limped a little but the cane was no longer necessary. I was getting well just in time for the Lunar New Year. It's a festive occasion, very similar to our New Year however, I decided to see in the Lunar New Year at Guard Post Ouellette, spitting distance from North Korea.

I arrived on the guard post at 1100 riding the chow truck. I met the guard post commander who was a very likeable black lieutenant named Bill Ross. Then I wound my way through the bunker system and emerged in front of the scout tower. There had been very few spot reports throughout the day because it was a Korean holiday.

The main event for the afternoon was the three enemy soldiers hanging around North Korean Guard Post 222. Besides the three soldiers, there was a dog, a goat, and two chickens in the vicinity. The scouts ask me if they were supposed to report the animals to higher Headquarters. I thought, *why not, this ought to be amusing.*

They started with the dog. After the scouts reported everything but the name, rank and serial number of the dog, the brigade operations center asked the sixty-four thousand dollar question, "Was it a trained dog?"

After a short, dramatic pause, our radio operator provided the perfect response, "I don't see him jumpin' through no hoops."

We resumed radio traffic with the goat report: "One goat—tied to small bush—near North Korean Guard Post two, two, two—undetermined if goat is North Korean—time is twelve fifteen—with leash and harness." And the added insult to higher Headquarters, "And the goat ain't jumpin' through no hoops either."

The radio operator at higher Headquarters must have been satisfied because no comment other than "Roger" came back. We all looked at each other not really believing what we were doing. Then our radio operator asked me if he was supposed to send anything about the chickens. I nodded my head, affirmative. No one gave a rat's ass about two chickens but I just wanted to mess with brigade.

"X-ray seven-five, this is X-ray two-three, do you want the rest of the report? We have two probable communist chickens, over." I'd never seen grown men with M-16s giggle like schoolgirls before.

"Wait, over," came the reply.

Obviously the radio operator had run off to ask someone in authority if he was supposed to take the report on the chickens. Two minutes went by and the squelch broke as the radio crackled: "This is seven-five. Negative, do not report chickens. Over."

The corporal operating our radio just said, "Wow, that was fun."

The reverie of the moment was snapped quite abruptly when gunshots rang out from the east. They were barely audible from inside the closed scout tower. I reported it to the guard post operations center and stepped outside, standing behind a waist high wall of sandbags. I surveyed the area with my binoculars. The guard post commander reached the tower within forty-five seconds. He asked, "What is it?"

"Shots fired, at least three, approximately four-hundred meters away, down by the stream," I pointed to a frozen rice paddy area. He and I stood watching the area closely with our binoculars.

"Go ahead and report shots fired to battalion," I said over my shoulder to the scouts. "Do you see anything, Bill?" I asked.

"Not yet," said Lieutenant Ross. "Do you think we ought to 'stand to' the guard post?"

"Let's hold off a few more minutes. Where's the recon patrol right now?"

The scouts in the tower started earning their $450 a month. One was contacting battalion to find the exact location of the recon patrol. One was formulating the spot report for transmission to higher Headquarters and the other high-tailed it through the trenches to the far bunker to get a better look. It wasn't long before the far bunker reported that two North Koreans with AK-47s were spotted near a small clump of trees 200 meters north of the MDL. They were carrying a pole ten feet long and several inches in diameter.

One of the scouts looked at me questioningly and I nodded again. The scout efficiently began writing a spot report about the two soldiers and the pole. The radio became a constant burst of static from higher Headquarters inquiring about the shots fired. Our answer was "No further details at this time." We kept putting the battalion and brigade off until the S-3 himself came on the horn and demanded a situation report immediately.

Lieutenant Ross and I looked at each other hoping the other one would volunteer to take the call. Eventually I said that I would do it and reached for the microphone. I delayed until one of the scouts copied the message from the far bunker. Meanwhile the S-3 came back on and asked if the guard post was under attack and wanted to know if we needed the Quick Reaction Force. The scout called back a "negative on the Quebec Romeo Foxtrot."

The message from the bunker said that the two North Koreans emerged with what appeared to be a dead water deer hung from the pole between them. We suspected it was New Year's dinner. We called in our report—shots fired at the game animal, not at friendly forces. Finally, after thirty minutes, we got it all straightened out and settled back to enjoy the rest of the afternoon.

I spent most of my time in the scout tower, but I did move around a little. I passed through the operations center and barracks rooms, the small mess hall and made a necessary stop at one of the dozen "tubes" on the guard post. On our compounds, pipes four inches in diameter are driven into the ground for our urinals. They're called "piss tubes." Most of the buildings didn't have latrines, but there was always a "piss tube" stuck into the ground somewhere close.

Evening chow was prepared and the soldiers coming on duty for the night shift got a pep talk from the guard post commander in the mess hall. Lieutenant Ross tried to emphasize that tonight might be a little different since it was the Lunar New Year. "You should be prepared for anything." Equipment was checked and they were sent through the trenches to the bunkers.

It was getting late and the sun was setting over the North Korean hills. I went back to the tower to watch the scouts prepare for the night. Ships binoculars were put away and night observation devices were brought out. Each scout grabbed his M-16 and locked a magazine into it.

"Are you supposed to have these weapons loaded?" I asked.

"No, Sir, but have you been up here at night?"

"No," I said.

"You'll see then, Sir. No disrespect intended."

"I'll just wait and see for myself."

I didn't have long to wait. As soon as the sun's tip disappeared behind the mountains, propaganda music started playing from "speaker hill." On North Korean Guard Post 214 there were a dozen speakers piled as high as a house. They played music, sang songs, recited speeches and poems, but with no doubt everything was done to praise Kim il Sung, the North Korean dictator.

Kim il Sung has been the North Korean dictator since 1972. He's nearly a god in their eyes. North Korea has such a closed society that the people really don't know anything about world politics. Radios in their country can only be tuned to one station, the national station. One time the South Koreans sent a batch of propaganda leaflets over to North Korea with instructions on how to change the radios to pick up more than one station.

The sun was down and the woods were black, but the sky still glowed a little orange. I hated this time of the day. You just could not see anything. The music from speaker hill stopped and a scratching noise could be heard, like the end of the record. Then silence.

A bugle blasted from the speakers and sent showers of sound across the frozen DMZ. Bugles were used in the war to signal attacks. Now they were used to scare hell out of American soldiers and it worked very well. All the scouts reached for their M-16s and cradled them in their laps. I slowly slid a magazine into my M-16. The one scout, whom I'd asked earlier about loading his weapon, looked over at me and then slowly turned his head back to stare out of the Plexiglas. The bugle ceased and a man's screams filled the air. At first it sounded like someone being tortured. The KATUSA in the tower said the voice was just screaming and didn't mean anything intelligible. The longer we listened, the more it just sounded like a drunken idiot.

We listened. We waited. We thought that maybe the screams were designed to cover up some other kind of activity. We called all the bunkers and reinforced that they should be prepared for anything. We reported the screams to higher Headquarters and we waited some more. An hour passed and the screaming man let out one final cry. Then there was silence. Everyone leaned forward anticipating another scream. We nearly fell out of our seats when it didn't come which made us all very antsy. We reported to the higher Headquarters that the screaming had stopped. Another conference call was made to the bunkers just to make us feel better. No one had sighted anything unusual. Good!

Five minutes went by and there was complete silence. The far bunker called in for permission to "lock and cock" their weapons. The operations center denied permission. It didn't matter, they did it anyway. Ten minutes of silence had passed when we heard a scratchy noise again. Instead of a record, a woman's voice came over the air. The voice sounded like the Korean equivalent of Marilyn Monroe. Her voice was deep and rich, full of cream and honey. I thought about the legendary Tokyo Rose.

Our KATUSA began to translate as she talked. Each one of us in the tower took turns copying the translated sentences for our G-2. She spoke of a wonderful life in North Korea, where everyone had plenty of food, where the jobs were high paying and the standard of living was excellent. She credited it all to the masterful leadership of Kim il Sung. She ended her speech with the most effective propaganda of all. She said she was lonely, just like thousands of young single women in North Korea. If we would come across the MDL (Military Demarcation Line), she and her sisters would meet us and comfort us.

I was experiencing a strange feeling. I think she was somehow getting to me. Not that I wanted to cross the MDL, but I could sure use some of that "comfort" she was talking about. The peaceful after thought of Korean Rose's speech was broken by a shouted American voice—

"Bring your North Korean cunt sisters over here and suck my cock!" A pause—and then, "Bitch!"

"Great," I said sarcastically under my breath. I didn't want to get a shouting war started. We weren't supposed to yell at them because it could be considered a provocative act according to the Armistice Agreement. The troops could give a shit about that, what the officers on the guard post didn't like was that if you ever yelled back, the North Koreans felt like something they were doing was affecting us, so they'd yell all damn night long. Another conference call went out to the bunkers, but no one would fess up to who yelled back. Lieutenant Ross put out the word that the next guy who hollered back would get an Article Fifteen.

The North Koreans really started yelling after the American reply. They didn't know what we had yelled and we didn't know what they were yelling, but we were getting it from all sides. At least three North Korean guard posts were yelling at us. Our KATUSAs tried to translate as much as they could but it was coming too quickly. Most of it was garbage about the greatness of North Korea. One sentence did catch our attention. It was spoken in English, a rarity for North Koreans assigned to the DMZ. It was spoken in a distinct fashion and was amplified by the mountain of speakers on North Korean Guard Post 214.

"Did you hear that?" I asked the scout beside me.

"Yes, Sir."

"Send it up immediately."

The scout pulled out a message form and wrote: Spoken in English, "WE WILL DESTROY SEOUL SOON."

I turned to Ross, "Do you think they'll start now?"

"Start what? Destroying Seoul? Hell, they can destroy Seoul all they want. We never get down there anyway. As long as they bypass this piss-ant little guard post, it's fine with me."

"They'll attack us just to get warmed up." I added.

"Maybe they won't kill any Americans because they'll be afraid that we'll enter the war in strength," Ross said with eyebrows raised.

"I haven't been here long but you can bet, they'll figure out a way to attack and kill all 800 of us and make it look like we started it."

"You're making me feel secure. Isn't that your job, security?"

"You got twenty armed men in a circle around you. What more do you want?" I asked jokingly.

He turned serious, looked me straight in the eye and said, "I just want to go home."

Several hours wore on and Lieutenant Ross went to check the bunkers. He'd been gone thirty minutes when he called the tower and said he'd remain at the helm in the operations center for the duration. I informed him that I would be in the tower or on the bunker line.

At 2300 (11 PM) the yelling from North Korea finally stopped. The last one to quit sounded like that original drunken soldier yelling in a megaphone. We didn't think he was ever going to stop. He yelled for three hours about wanting to meet us on the Military Demarcation Line. He wanted to get to know us better and give us a present. According to our KATUSA's translation, he either wanted to stick something up our asses, shoot us in our asses or fuck us in our asses.

When it was over, we realized the silence was boring. Everyone grew edgy waiting for their next antics. Lieutenant Ross sent out another conference call. "Increase readiness from now until I send out word after midnight," was the order. The far bunker called back with a statement: "Increase readiness? Our assholes are already so puckered shut that you couldn't drive a nail up 'em."

We sat and waited for the approach of midnight. At five minutes until midnight, Lieutenant Ross came into the tower. He startled one of the scouts by his unannounced entry. The scout snapped his M-16 to his shoulder with the muzzle pointed at the center of Ross's flak jacket.

"Goddamn it, Sir, I asked you to knock or sound off before you barge in here."

"Sorry," and the soldier leaned his M-16 against the wall.

"I couldn't sit in the Ops Center at midnight. I'm too fidgety," said Ross.

"Well, as you can see we're just a calm, cool, collected bunch of tower rats," said the scout. Ross smiled. "Yeah, I can tell."

We sat quietly in our watchtower. The minutes dragged on. Finally, "Midnight, Sir," said one scout.

"And there it goes!" said another.

We wheeled around to the Northwest. "It" was illumination flares; red, green and white star clusters, ten or twelve of them, three parachute flares, two red and one white. "What in the world is goin' on over there?"

"I don't know."

Another conference call went out. All bunkers saw no movement and heard nothing except the 'pop' of the illumination. Everyone in the bunkers was wide-awake, fully alert, locked and loaded and on rock and roll (automatic fire).

I was too. I was afraid to move around on the guard post because one of our own men might shoot me.

"Report the flares," I said. "You know what?"

"What?"

"I think that's the North Korean version of fireworks. Do they have fireworks in North Korea?"

"Hell, I don't know. You're the intelligence officer."

"I'll be damned if I know," I said. "What's the location of the origin of the pyrotechnics?"

"Huh?" said the scout.

"Did you see where the flares came from?"

"Oh, yes, Sir—New Propaganda Village." North Korea's version of Tae Song Dong and Unification Village.

"Yeah. They cropped up right underneath the flagpole. It's got to be military fireworks. Report our theory," I said.

"Huh?" said the scout again.

"Tell 'em we think it's fireworks."

"Oh, yes Sir."

Twenty minutes passed and no movement was observed by any of the bunkers or the tower. However, the radio crackled and a message from brigade filled the air.

"Higher wants to know why you think the illumination wasn't a signal of some kind," said the radio operator.

"Tell them." I paused. "Give me the handset." The scout passed it over to me. "X-ray seven-five this is.... Who the hell are we?" I asked the scout.

"Two-three, Sir."

"X-ray seven-five, this is X-ray two-three. I think it was a display of fireworks because I've never seen a signal that had fourteen flares in it—four red star clusters, two green star clusters, five white star clusters, two red parachute flares and one white parachute flare. Out."

"I guarantee you the G-2 thinks they're attacking and the fireworks are the signal." I threw the handset down on the counter.

"Do you want us to 'stand-to' the guard post?" asked Ross.

"Shit, let's just keep checking the bunkers and make sure everyone is alert. I'll settle for at least awake."

"I'll go," said Ross.

"I'll tag along," I said.

We grabbed our weapons and walked out of the tower and into the trenches. We wound our way through the line from bunker to bunker. Everything was quiet. At the far bunker, the guards challenged us with the sign and we had to give the countersign. We talked with them a while and then we moved back to the tower. Another couple of hours wore on and Ross headed to the Ops Center to rest on his cot, boots on, of course. I stayed in the tower. At 0215 we spotted a single individual at the perimeter fence. He crept up on his hands and knees right before our eyes. We couldn't believe it.

"Did you see...?"

"Yes, call battalion, alert Ops, get in the bunker, and man the claymores (mines)." There was a sandbagged bunker right below the tower. There was a trap door in the floor of the tower through which soldiers could drop into the bunker. The bunker was there in case explosions started going off near the tower.

One scout got on the horn to battalion, one was on the field phone to the Guard Post Ops Center and the other was crawling through the trap door into the bunker below. I saw the North Korean move again and I jumped out of the tower with my M-16 at my shoulder. I had a set of night observation goggles hanging around my neck. I put the goggles on my face and crouched behind the sandbag wall just outside the tower. My M-16 was at the ready and aimed down towards the small defilade position where the North Korean was last seen. We had a five-meter blind spot at the edge of our perimeter fence and that's where he was. He couldn't move without exposing himself. It was a standoff ... I waited ... he waited.

We had him cold. All he had to do was show himself for an instant and I'd ... I balked. I'd what? I'd kill him. *Why?* I thought. *Don't think about it now,* I told myself, *worry about that later...just pull the trigger when the time comes. Stay calm ... be steady ... just squeeze the trigger.*

"Sir—he's gone."

"What?" I think I said that like I might have been disappointed.

"When you were going out the door he ran back."

"You're shittin' me? It only took a second and a half for me to get out here."

"Yes, Sir, I know, but he's gone. It's happened before."

"You mean they've come to the perimeter before?"

"Yes, Sir. Sometimes we don't even bother to report it."

"Why not?"

"We end up doin' six hours work and waking everybody up to 'stand to' the guard post—all for a five second incident."

Ross came running up in his undershirt, flak jacket, and helmet with a forty-five in one hand and night vision goggles in the other. "What's going on?" He crouched behind the wall with me.

"A North Korean ran across the MDL and camped out in the dead space at the edge of the perimeter for about two seconds and then he took off. The scout says he's already gone home. I never saw the bastard go back, to be honest."

"Did you report it?"

"Yes."

"Aw shit—Barbed Wire Bob (the 2nd Infantry Division commanding general's nickname) will have this place on alert all night long."

"Maybe not. Bring the scout out of the bunker. Report to battalion that he's already gone back and be sure and put that 'clacker' (claymore mine detonator) in your pocket," I told the scouts. "Maybe battalion won't report it to brigade."

"What do you think the chances are of that?"

"I'm afraid it's one of those 'does a bear shit in the woods?' situations." I said.

The guard post was alerted, as always, about thirty minutes after the fact. The troops hated it because it took them from a semi-warm sleeping bag into a frozen dark bunker, from the land of slumber into another type of dreamland—that of the nightmare.

We remained at "stand to" for thirty minutes. When higher Headquarters felt like it, they let us "stand down" and assume our normal nighttime posture.

Thirty minutes after the "stand down," a rock-throwing contest started between us and the North Koreans. It seems that they started bombing our far bunker with stones. It didn't take a major political decision for the American soldiers to know what to do. They threw rocks back.

Lieutenant Ross and I decided not to report this to battalion. We didn't know where to start the explanation and worse, it would be embarrassing to admit that we were losing. We had policed up all the rocks on the guard post years ago. So we had very little ammunition. We basically had to throw back the rocks they threw at us.

I went to the far bunker just to see the show. When I arrived on the scene, the soldiers manning the far bunker slowed up just enough to tell me that it wasn't their fault. The North Koreans attacked without reason. The guards said they had not provoked the North Koreans and they must be just plain mean bastards to perform such a hostile act as rock throwing. The most articulate of the soldiers in the far bunker described it as "the most blatant fucking act" he'd ever seen.

I agreed with him. As I crouched behind a sandbagged wall, a hailstorm of rocks was landing on the far edge of the bunker. A small piece of gravel *pinged* off of my helmet. The soldiers around me waited to see what I would do.

"Hot damn," I said, "give me a rock!"

A young private snapped one into my outstretched hand. I got up on my good knee and threw the rock doing my best imitation of John Wayne throwing a grenade. I couldn't see the rock fly through the darkness, but I heard it crash in the bushes. I put my night vision goggles on and scanned the wood line. It looked clear.

I asked, "Where are they? I was just throwing blind."

"They're over to the right a little, by that big tree."

Five North Koreans ran out of the tree line and hurled a volley of rocks. We ducked behind the sandbags as the stones landed all about us. One somehow hit the bottom of my boot. Lieutenant Ross came scrambling up right in the middle of the barrage and dove in on top of us.

"What the fuck? Over," he asked.

"We're throwin' rocks. What's it look like?" I returned.

"It looks like you're trying to get queer for Private Baker." There were four of us huddled behind a three-foot high, four-foot wide wall.

"If you don't want to huddle up with us, then you stand up and see what you get. Take a look at the wood line by the large tree," I instructed. Ross put his goggles on and watched the five North Koreans throw a double volley. Again we all piled on top of each other behind the wall.

"Damn, Ross, now what are you, queer for me all of a sudden?" I accused.

"Screw you. Somebody's gotta find another place to hide, Baker, you and Matson..."

"Watson, Sir," corrected the sentry.

"Yeah, Baker, you and Watson get back in the bunker and knock off this foolishness. Ya'll don't throw any more rocks, understand?"

"Yes, Sir."

"Come on, Dave, let's go back to the tower." Ross turned to go back and exposed himself to the enemy.

CLANK! A rather large rock bounced off Ross's helmet. 'Oh fuck' I thought as I nearly strangled myself choking back laughter.

"Goddamn it, give me a brick. Baker, Watson, get out here."

"Yes, Sir", they hollered as they stumbled all over themselves getting out of the bunker.

"Get me a BFR (in GI terms, a Big Fuckin' Rock). I'm gonna cold cock me a chink."

I was still incapacitated with laughter. "Aren't you glad you had your helmet on?" I barely choked out the question.

"Shut up," Ross grinned. All I could see were his teeth. "Now, we've got to do this in a military manner."

"What! Throw rocks at the enemy?" I'm still choking down a giggle.

"Yeah, Watson, Baker, get behind your bunker and throw three rocks apiece as fast as you can when I give you the signal."

"What's the signal, Sir?"

"I'll say, 'Throw the rocks.'"

I'm dying laughing now.

"Can you throw very good?" Ross asked me.

"I was an all-district baseball player in high school, but that was ten years ago," I said.

"That's good enough. As soon as we hear Baker and Watson's rocks hit the bushes, we'll throw our rocks and catch them when they step out of the woods to throw theirs. They'll think we've thrown our volley, ya see?"

"Yeah, I guess." Made as much sense as throwing rocks at men with machine guns.

Whack! A North Korean rock bounced off the Plexiglas of the bunker's window.

"Okay, everybody ready?"

"Yes, Sir."

"Well then, throw the rocks."

"What?" said Baker.

I started to laugh again.

"Throw the fuckin' rocks."

Within two seconds, Baker and Watson launched six rocks into the air. The first one hadn't touched down when the last one was thrown into the blackness. It was left up to fate where they would fall.

When we heard the rocks start to crash through the brush, Ross and I stood up and threw like center fielders going for the out at home plate. We threw two good size rocks apiece, after which we crouched back down and held our night vision goggles to our eyes.

The North Koreans stepped out like a chorus line and let go a salvo.

Schlock! A sound similar to a golf ball being driven into a pine tree trunk emanated from the woods.

"I don't believe it," I gasped.

"That's what I'm talkin' about!" said Ross.

To this day I'm not sure which one of us did it, but we hit the second North Korean from the left, right between the eyes with a rock the size of a chicken egg. He grabbed his face, fell on both knees and then passed out backwards with his legs underneath him. The North Koreans acted out their version of a Chinese fire drill. They ran around him in a circle twice, then ran into the woods. Their comrade still lay on the ground.

"Get your weapons," Lieutenant Ross said. I had the feeling that this all of a sudden became a very grave matter.

"Maybe we killed the son-of-a-bitch," I said.

"That's what I'm afraid of."

"Don't anybody fire no matter what happens," I yelled to the other guys. "They can't go back to their superiors and tell them that we killed him with a rock, can they?" Ross shook his head. "I think they're going to try to cause a serious incident. You get my drift. They're going to come out shooting and get us to fire back. Then they can fix it so it looks like we gunned him down. What do you think?"

"It's kinda farfetched, isn't it?

"I don't know. Killing the asshole with a rock seemed kinda far fetched thirty seconds ago."

We sat, crouched in a fighting position, ready for anything. I felt the late hour's effect on my body. I think I heard Baker start snoring off to the right. How could you sleep with an enemy soldier laying dead forty meters to our front? I guess he was dead. If he wasn't, he sure lay there in the freezing weather longer than I would have. My first body count and I killed him with a rock. We waited longer. I spent half my military career waiting for something— medical shots, chow, pay—always waiting. Then there was movement in the bushes.

"I hear it. Can you see anything?"

"Not yet," I said.

Pucker factor was high.

"You want to provoke it?" I said. "I'll throw a rock down there."

"Don't raise up for shit. Throw it from behind the wall," suggested Ross.

"Damn right I won't raise up," I readied myself. "Be frosty over there."

"Roger." I heard Baker and Watson shuffling around a little.

I was almost afraid to throw the rock. "Don't shoot unless you see one in the perimeter wire."

"Roger."

I let go with the rock. It crashed through the woods and thudded on the frozen ground. I pressed my helmet down on a sandbag.

Shots rang out. "Six—seven—eight. Eight shots, two weapons. "Report it on the field phone, Baker, and don't say anything about the rock throwing. Bill, I hate to suggest this but we have to 'stand to' the guard post again."

"Shit." The guard post commander's whistle sounded. It took three minutes to fill every bunker. I looked up over the sandbags. The body was gone. They must have laid covering fire to drag the body back.

"We're going to have to spread the word through the bunkers not to fire back unless they are shooting directly at us."

"Okay, I'll go do it personally." Ross ran off.

"Don't get shot by one of our own guys," I warned as he disappeared in the darkness.

During the night two more shooting incidents occurred, but nothing major. They were just firing over our heads trying to get us to fire back. We didn't though. Our soldiers showed great discipline. We spent a tense, sleepless night, but we had the last laugh. In some bunker system somewhere in North Korea four North Korean privates were standing in front of a high ranking North Korean officer trying to explain how the American Capitalist Pigs used their great technology and killed their comrade with a rock.

In the morning, I went back to battalion Headquarters the same way I came out, riding the chow truck. I felt a little badly about leaving everyone up there, but I had my job to do and they had theirs.

CHAPTER 5

Ambush

Another few days passed quickly. I couldn't remember when one started and another ended. I was getting burned out and I hadn't even been in the country a month. I needed a break and the Good Lord provided. The Division was going to start outfitting the line battalions with a small tactical radar, the AN PPS-15. The intelligence sections were assigned the task of teaching the rest of the battalion the usage of the radar. My whole shop got a three-day reprieve to Camp Casey for radar school. We couldn't all go at once, so Stan the Man went first, Sergeant Pettit next, and I went last.

I called my friend Mike and told him that I would be down for a couple of days and he said he'd be waiting. I arrived at Camp Casey on a late bus. When I got to Mike's hooch, he and seven other officer buddies were well on their way to being intoxicated. I only had time to throw my gear down before all nine of us headed for a thunder run. This time we went to Tongduchon, commonly called TDC.

We ventured down a street that had row after row of clubs. Each one had more going on than a three-ring circus. Mike pointed out several women who were famous in their own right: one dressed like an Indian, "Pocahontas," and another blonde haired oriental woman who always dressed in black, the "Dragon Lady."

We lost at least one of our group in every club. At the fourth club, the Las Vegas Club, the thunder run officially ended because Mike and I were the only ones left. Then Mike found a legitimate female friend he met in the laundry and left with her. After an eternity, thirty seconds, of sitting by myself, a cute, young woman came up to me and sat in my lap.

"You short time me?"

"What's your name?"

"Helenth."

"Nice Korean name," I said.

"Yesth." The girl talked with a lisp.

"No, I don't think I want a short time."

"No? Youth cherry boy?"

"No, I don't want to short time any Korean woman with a name like Helen."

"What name you want me to be?"

"No, I'm not going to play that game."

"What game you wanna play?"

"I don't want to buy a businesswoman. I want to sit and talk like friends."

"No friend hereth, soldier boy. You want friends you go home, you want fuck, you pay me ten dollar."

This was quickly becoming an embarrassing situation. I got up to walk out and the girl and one of her friends followed me to the door screaming obscenities at me. It was all I could do to hold my hostility back. I wanted to turn around and knock the bitch out but I held it in. They were still calling me names as I walked down the street. They were making me feel guilty and I hadn't done anything wrong. I needed to hit something.

Maybe I better go back to the compound, I thought. I started walking in that direction, heading down a dark stretch of road called blowjob alley, where all the Mama-sans come out and try to get you to meet their daughters, sisters, and other businesswomen. They promise a good show, women on women, two women on one man, anything a heart desired. More appropriately, anything a "hard" desired.

An old woman with a few teeth still intact stepped out of the dark.

"Go away, Mama-san. I don't want any of it tonight."

"You want oral sexy?"

"Go away," I said.

Koreans make a weird noise when they're excited or mad. It's the same kind of noise Americans make right before they spit up a wad of phlegm. I walked away leaving the old Mama-san spitting a blue streak. I crossed some railroad tracks where the taxis were lined up on the main drag. I thought I'd take a taxi to Tokko-ri and find the girl I was with before, but a man stepped out of a corner in the alley. "Hey," he said and motioned for me to step closer to him. I did. He whispered in my ear.

"You want cocaine?"

"Not tonight, Brother," I said as I tried to keep walking but he grabbed me by the arm, "I give you good deal you cragee to pass up."

"Let go of my arm." I stared him down and he let go.

"You too good to buy from me, too good to help out me."

"Help you out? You asshole, get a job?" I started walking off again.

"This my job, good job."

This time I called him over to me. "How much cocaine do you have?"

"How muchi you want buy?" he asked as he walked over to me.

"All of it," I said.

The Korean got excited and pulled out a heavy sandwich bag full of cocaine. He ran his fingers across the seal and it popped open. He pinched some between his fingers and held it up front of my face. He smiled and so did I. We stood for a second longer, each of us with a big shit eating grin.

"How much?" I asked.

"Thousand dollar ounce," he said.

"How many ounces do you have there?"

"Ten," he said as I started digging in my pocket as if I were magically going to come up with 10,000 dollars. Instead, I slapped the bag out of his hand. He made a one syllable guttural sound similar to what I make when I get a digital prostate exam. His face also looked like he just had something shoved up his ass.

It snowed cocaine all over the alley and a cloud of white smoke floated off in the wind. The Korean truly looked as if I'd killed his mother. He probably preferred that I had killed his mother. He made that irritating spitting sound and came toward me. I left hooked him, right crossed him and kicked him in the balls. He clutched his nuts with both hands and fell over in slow motion like a tree going "timber." I walked off and thought, *why the hell did I do that?* I consoled myself with knowing that I saved some soldiers 10,000 dollars. I'd never done anything like that before.

I went through the compound gate at 2300 (11 PM). The last buses on the compound quit running at 2230 (10:30 PM). I didn't feel like riding in a taxi anymore, so I walked. As I passed the PX, I noticed a light on in the steam-bath massage parlor. I thought a "steam and cream," as the soldiers called it, would be nice. The door was locked but I knocked and peered into the small porthole style window. I saw movement inside.

"Sorry, we closed," sang out a woman's voice.

"It's cold outside. Could I come in and warm up?"

She came to the porthole, "We closed."

"I know, but could I come in for a minute?"

"What you want?" she asked with her head cocked slyly to one side.

"Just to warm up."

"You miss bus?"

"As a matter of fact, I did."

"You leave when I say you leave?"

"You're the boss." I was blowing on my hands while rubbing them together, stomping my feet and generally pretending like I was freezing to death.

The door opened. "Me get trouble if Mama-san know you here."

"I won't tell anybody," I lied.

She motioned for me to come in and pulled the curtain across the little window.

"What name you?" she asked in standard Korean English.

"David."

"What compound?"

"I'm not from here. I'm from the DMZ."

"D-M-Gee Huh? Not good place?"

"It's a number ten. Are you a massage girl?"

"Neh, (yes) my name Miss Kim."

"Can I get a steam bath so I can warm up?"

She blushed, "Steam bath closed."

"I know that, but it's just you and me here. How 'bout I give you a steam bath and massage?" I asked. She really blushed then. "C'mon, I'll give you a good massage," I said as I took her hand and led her off down the hall.

"Wait, wait," and she pulled free to lock the front door. She giggled as she walked back to me.

"How muchi is massagee?" she asked.

"Twenty dollars," I said.

"I no have that muchi," she said, as we played a role-reversal game.

"How muchi do you have?" I asked.

"Fifteen dollar only."

"No can do," I said and we both laughed. We walked back to room number three. In the room, there was a large tile bathtub, a small steam bath that closed around you when you sat in it that looked like an old washing machine, a massage table and a large oil-burning stove.

"Have you givie a massagee before?" she asked.

"No."

"Let me show you first."

"Gladly," I said.

"You make yourself com-fort-a-ble," she had a little trouble saying that word. She turned on the water in the large tile bath and left. I took my clothes off and stood by the stove. She returned after turning off all the lights in the building except the one in room number three.

"You cold?" she asked.

"Yes."

"You hairy too," she said and touched my chest.

She mechanically picked up a stool and placed it in front of the tub. Then she scooped a big bowl of water out of the tub and poured it on the stool.

"Stool warm now. Sit."

When I sat down, she dumped a very hot bowl of water over my shoulders.

"Too hot?"

"No." I lied a little then too.

She dumped three more bowls of water over the rest of my body. Then she soaped up a rather rough sponge and scrubbed the living hell out of my back. She held up each of my arms and washed under them. Then she scrubbed my chest, legs, and feet. She handed the sponge to me and indicated that I should wash my own genitals. Then she rinsed me off with several more bowls scooped up from the steaming tub.

"You want steam bath or tub bath?"

"Can I have both?"

"Neh."

She went to the washing machine looking steam bath and turned on a faucet that started small puffs of steam shooting out from the floor.

"Get in," she said.

I sat on the wooden bench seat inside and she closed the contraption around me.

"Ten minutes okay?"

"Okay," I agreed.

She shut and locked the steam machine door and placed a towel around my neck to keep the heat from escaping from the head hole. "Call me if you too hot, my name Miss Kim, remember?" And she left the room.

I felt a little guilty about taking a steam bath when all the other guys were back up on the line bustin' their asses. About thirty seconds of remorse was all I allowed myself. However, after five minutes I was ready to get out. I started looking for a way to release the latch; *surely they wouldn't make one of these things that you couldn't get out of from the inside.* Then the terrible realization hit, 'This is Korea, the Land of the Not Quite Right.'

"Kim!" I called out. No answer, I thought maybe that the bitch had taken off.

"Kim!" I screamed a little louder. I heard her scurrying back to the room from the lobby.

"You too hot?" she asked.

"Gettin' there." She came over and flipped the latch and the door popped open. I felt five pounds lighter.

"Sit," and she pointed to the stool.

She threw a few more bowls of water over me.

"You do okay?" she asked.

"Yeah, I'm fine."

"Sit tub now."

I got in the tub and it was damn near as hot as the steam bath. After a few minutes in the hot water I noticed that my wounded leg began to feel better. *I should do this more often.* Nearly every compound had a steam bath on it but of course ours, up on the Z, didn't.

Just before becoming prune-like, I got out of the tub. Miss Kim dried me off and told me to lie down on the table, face down. She covered my buttocks with a towel, and the massage began. She slapped, beat, and gouged every inch of my body. She even pounded the soles of my feet. She cracked my fingers and my toes, popped my elbows, shoulders and vertebrae. When she snapped my wounded knee, my scream almost made her cry. I explained that I was wounded.

"Ah-po," she said. It meant hurt or pain, a word that became an integral part of my vocabulary. She resumed the massage and I floated again.

"Now what you want, Dabid?" Koreans had a hard time enunciating the letter V.

"What do you mean?"

She giggled, "Don't be shy."

"What's next?" I asked, playing dumb.

"I sometimes massagee man where he likes."

"Where?" and she went for it.

Afterwards, when I became conscious of my surroundings, the time was 0100. It was after curfew and she was trapped in the steam bath for the rest of the night. I was free to move around inside the compound but she couldn't go home.

I massaged her next. It took hours and she really enjoyed it because Korean women don't get much attention. In her society, the woman's function is to please the man. Miss Kim was very good at it too. We took turns massaging each other until we couldn't tell who was doing what to whom. When the sun came up, we found ourselves on the couch in the lobby. The stoves had long since burned out of fuel and it was cold enough to see your breath. Our bodies were still entwined, for warmth, not affection, and we had a dozen layers of towels wrapped around us. My head pounded when I opened my eyes.

"It's cold," I said as I shivered. She just buried her face in the towels, still half asleep. I got up to find my clothes, shaking and shivering as my bare feet tread on the icy floor. When I got back to room number three, I found all my things as I left them. I turned the tub water on thinking that I might as well take a bath. It will be the last one for a long while. It felt good and made my stiff knee loosen up. After soaking, I dried off, dressed, and walked back to the front lobby. Miss Kim was still asleep among the towels. I took a twenty-dollar bill out of my wallet and left it on the coffee table, thinking that it was well worth it, especially since she didn't ask for any money at all.

I could barely stay awake during radar class. It was a typical Army class, dull and by the numbers.

"Gentleman," the instructor said, "this toggle switch turns the machine on and, as you can see, it also turns it off." It must have taken a genius to figure that out and so went the first day of the course. We broke down into groups to practice putting the radar together and breaking it down.

The only question I asked all day was, "Is it GI proof?"

The instructor said, "I assure you, Sir, these radars are virtually indestructible and soldiers can not possibly damage them. They can only be put together one way and that's the Army way, Sir." Now, I knew better than that. GIs can break anything. As a matter of fact, as I was talking to the instructor, I glanced over his shoulder and one of the soldiers in our group was putting the radar dish on the tripod upside down. It wasn't a perfect fit so he was bending the dish to make it fit the way he wanted. Without saying a word, I pointed behind the instructor. He spun on his heels to see the soldier mangling the radar dish.

He ran over to the soldier and screamed at the top of his lungs, "What flavor of dog shit do you have for brains, private?" I wondered how anybody could possibly answer that question. None of the parts of that soldier's radar fit together properly after that and I feel sure that he had just ruined Uncle Sam's $15,000 toy.

The sergeant in charge of the class came up to me afterwards and told me that I didn't have to attend class since I was an officer. "Just take these brochures and read them."

"Roger, out," and that's the last the radar instructor saw of me.

I spent the rest of the morning shopping but buying little. I ate several varieties of Korean food, all of which tasted hot, bitter or rotten. At some point I ended up in a meat market. Meat wasn't on my shopping list but curiosity overcame me. In the back of the shop, behind the counter, I found a rack of skinned and gutted small dogs hung up by their hind legs.

By noon, I called Captain Starns to tell him I was coming back early, said goodbye to Mike and departed on the bus. I had a dozen manuals on the operation and maintenance of the radar, but all were unread. As the bus started to pull away, a soldier came running out of the PX Arcade and flagged us down. The driver opened the door and the soldier started to get on. Then he hesitated, "Where does this bus go?"

He looked at the front plate on the bus, "Oh shit, I don't want to go there ... ever." Then he ran in another direction. The sign on front of the bus read, DMZ EXPRESS.

The ride from Camp Casey to Camp Greaves took an hour and a half. We travelled through a village called Yon Gu Gol. It was considered by most connoisseurs of the fairer sex to be the VD Capital of the World. There must have been 100 whores in town on any given day and twice that on pay days. Most of them looked like whores too. They lined the road to wave at the bus and we all waved back.

I put my head against the window and tried to sleep, attempting to dream myself away from all this. After three major bumps that banged my head against the glass so hard that I thought it might break (the glass that is, not my head), I gave up on trying to rest. I just waited for the miserably cold ride to end. At last, the bus passed under the tank drop and entered the no man's land of the frozen rice paddies and thousands of strands of concertina barbed wire.

I could see the bridge and my Quonset hut on the far bank of the river. It felt like coming home.

The guards from the bridge searched the bus and checked ID's. The guards had finally gotten so they could recognize me, after all, I'd been down to the bridge raising hell with the operation on a daily basis. I was, on paper, the advisor to the Freedom Bridge Security Platoon. However, I got a lot of help from the battalion sergeant major. Between his guidance and mine, we managed to keep the Freedom Bridge Security Platoon marginally squared away.

The bus pulled up in front of the main gate and several of us got off. The Korean gate guard saluted me as I walked through the fence. I went directly to the bunker to report in.

"You better get some sleep," the first words out of Captain Starn's mouth.

"Damn, do I look that bad? Here's some manuals for our radar instruction," and I plopped them down on the desk.

"Go to the hooch and get some sleep."

"Why? It's only 1530 (3:30 PM), the recon doesn't come in for an hour, and I want to sit in on the debriefing. I'm not that worn out."

"You will be when you get in from the ambush patrol tonight," and Captain Starns smiled.

"Ambush!" I said loudly enough to turn everybody's head in the bunker. Then I lowered my voice to a loud whisper, "Damn it Sir, I don't believe you scheduled me for an ambush patrol with only a few hours notice."

"What would you have done differently if I gave you a day's notice?"

"I could have brushed up on the patrolling procedures."

"You won't need it, it'll be alright. You're on the early ambush."

"Thanks a lot, Sir," I said as I stormed out of the bunker. I had four hours until departure of friendly front lines.

I went to my Quonset hut and pretended like I was going to sleep. I turned the blankets back and then jerked them off the mattress and threw them across the room. I went to my desk and pulled out two camouflage sticks. I didn't even know the route, call signs, insertion point or anything else. Most of my gear was already stored in the bunker so I only needed a few things from my room. I grabbed a Gerber stiletto, a small pair of binoculars, and a miniature Bible that my best friend, Jim Locke, sent me from Texas. I stopped by the arms room and checked out my M-16, a compass, a starlight scope that weighed twenty-five pounds and a pair of night vision goggles. I entered the bunker, banging around and making as big a spectacle as possible because I was pissed-off and wanted everyone to know it.

"What's the route?" I yelled to Captain Starns.

He handed an overlay to one of the "bunker Rats" who brought it over to my desk. I began plotting the azimuths and marking the paces for each leg. It took a good twenty minutes to figure it out and re-check it. I wrote down all the call signs and frequencies for the time period of the ambush and the subsequent time period, just in case we got lost, heaven forbid. I checked the rosters and found out that the patrol leader was another E-5, Sergeant Turner. I called the patrolling Company and asked where I could find Sergeant Turner. They told me that he was a member of the 2nd Platoon. I went to find their billets and get face to face with him. When I tracked him down, he told me we'd meet in his room two hours prior to departure time for the briefing.

"When is the rehearsal?" I asked.

"What?" Sergeant Turner looked dumbfounded.

"Forget it," I walked off. *This place is driving me crazy.* I went back to the bunker and gathered all my gear together, strapped it all on and went to my hooch to get the proper clothing. Temperatures were supposed to drop to fourteen degrees above zero. Our ambush was to last five hours and it's hard to dress for fourteen-degree weather when you have to be totally immobile. I put every piece of clothing on that I could find. My face was camouflaged and my gear was strapped down and taped so it wouldn't rattle or shine. I was heavier by ten pounds than I was on the first patrol and I hadn't even picked up my ammunition or pyrotechnics. I took my M-16 and locked the door behind me. I beat feet to the 2nd Platoon's area. Hell, I was worn out by the time I walked the quarter mile and I had a good mile and a half to walk on the ambush patrol.

I found Sergeant Turner in his room. He was alone and had a thousand rounds of ammunition piled up in front of him. He handed me seven magazines and three flares: a white, a red, and a green.

"Where is everybody?" I asked.

"Sir, you're early. They still have thirty minutes before it's time."

"I'm going to hit the latrine."

"Yes, Sir." I couldn't imagine him saying "No, Sir" to a statement like that.

I clambered down the hill to the latrine. It was the only shower facility to service both the 2nd and 3rd Platoons. I walked up to the urinal and was faced with a near panic situation. I was about to pee myself from nervousness and I had to unzip my field pants, fight through the liner, unzip my fatigue pants, dig through my long johns and then somehow pull down my jockey shorts and hold all five layers open while I pulled it out and peed. It was very cold which shortened the barrel so to speak; so aiming at the commode was done by trial and error. When I started the flow it went sideways so I had to turn sideways to hit dead center. If my bladder hadn't been about to burst, it would have been funny.

I re-straightened, re-zipped and re-buttoned and went to the mirror to check my camouflage. Of course it was all screwed up. I pulled out one of the few sticks of dark green face paint left on the compound and filled in the light spots. It was my personal camouflage stick; after all, I did personally steal it from supply.

I felt some things in my field trouser pocket that I couldn't immediately identify. I pulled them out. They were a bent up stick of gum, a condom, and a business card that had an advertisement written on the front that entitled me to one free sex act with the person of my choosing. *Where in the hell did these come from?* They were all tossed in the trash and forgotten as I headed back to the 2nd Platoon area.

Only one other patrol member was there when I got back. The longer we waited, the more I began to sweat making it necessary to open some of my clothing. At T minus one hour, we were still missing one of the patrol members. I was just about to get pissed off when he walked in the door. The patrol leader didn't say a word, he just started his patrol order briefing, but it didn't tell me anything I didn't already know.

We divided the remainder of the ammo, made a radio check with the battalion operations center, and loaded on the truck. We stopped at battalion HQ for a final brief to see if the situation had changed. I was praying that they would call off this patrol or at least postpone it for a year or two. No dice, the truck started rolling and we were on our way. I asked the patrol leader if he knew the azimuths and the pace counts. He said he did. He also said he had been on this route before.

The night was black and cold. There was no moon with sub-freezing temperatures. I was hoping that the Americans were the only ones dumb enough to be out in weather like this. Our instructions for this patrol were so sketchy that if we got hit, there would be no way we could remain a unit and fight through it. I prayed that nothing would go wrong.

"Sergeant Turner, which stop do we get out on?" I asked. I could see all the faces of the patrol members in the glow of a final cigarette. They were all staring at Sergeant Turner.

"Stop number two, Sir," he said, in as confident a tone as possible.

We quietly sat in the back of the enclosed truck. Sergeant Turner and I frequently exchanged glances in the dark. I had a very bad feeling about this patrol. We were systematically checked through the two barricades leading into the DMZ and the truck made its first false insertion, a fake stop to fool the enemy about the location of the patrol's start point.

"Are you going to give us some last minute instructions? After all your patrol briefing was rather sparse," I inquired.

"No," said Sergeant Turner. "We've all been together on patrol before. We know how each other operates."

"That's curious," I said. "I don't remember going on ambush patrol with any of you before."

A light bulb finally popped on in Sergeant Turner's wee little brain—"Oh, that's right."

"Well, it's too late now," I said as the truck ground to the second halt.

"This is it," said Turner.

We all prepared to bail out of the back. As soon as the truck was dead in the road the first two men jumped out. One went to the near side of the road and one went to the far side. That wasn't the way things were supposed to be done. Turner knew it was wrong and gave me a 'go to hell' look. Another man jumped out and ran to the wrong side of the road. It became obvious to me that his men didn't know where in the hell they were supposed to be going.

"Damn it," swore Turner.

I eased out of the truck and lay down in the ditch beside the road. The truck started to pull away after being stopped for a few seconds. The last man was sitting on the truck bed, half in and half out. Inertia caused him to stay in place when the truck accelerated and the vehicle literally drove out from underneath him. He dropped down and his canteen got hung up on the bumper. The truck started dragging him down the asphalt road. The only thing touching the asphalt were the heels of his boots. His arms were flailing about as if he were weightless in outer space. His helmet snapped off his head and rolled around in a circle and his M-16 cart wheeled to the pavement and clattered with the awful sound of metal and plastic.

Sergeant Turner ran after the truck screaming, "Stop, stop, stop!" The truck driver stuck his head out on the third shout to see what was behind him. He saw Turner running after him and came to a halt beside the road. The driver immediately got out of the truck and ran back a few steps to meet Sergeant Turner. "Holy shit, sarge, did you fall out of the back of the truck?"

"Fall out! Look at that." and he pointed to our man hanging by his canteen from the bumper.

"What happened?" asked the truck driver innocently.

Turner's face swelled up like a bullfrog, made even more grotesque with the camouflage paint.

"You asshole!" yelled Turner, "You drove off before we got unloaded. I'll deal with you when we get back," Turner screamed at the driver.

"But," the driver retorted.

"But nothing, asshole! You fuckin' motherfucker! You fucked up my whole patrol!" swore Turner.

Meanwhile, I got what was left of the patrol together near the back of the truck. We policed up the helmet and M-16. Turner was still "cussing out" the driver. I pointed to the guy hung up on the bumper, "Help him off that thing," and the two radio operators began assisting the soldier who, for all intents and purposes, looked like he had a trailer hitch stuck up his ass.

"Sergeant Turner, get the patrol squared away. We'll figure out what happened later," I ordered. Turner walked to the side of the road and began checking the map illuminated with his red filtered flashlight.

The young truck driver came over to me. "Sir," he said, "I was instructed to let you off at the third stop, not the second."

"I don't doubt that a bit, continue the mission."

"Yes, Sir."

We all regrouped around Turner who was still hyperventilating.

Without me saying a word, Turner looked at me and said, "I've got it now, Sir."

"Did you allow for being in the wrong place?"

"What do you mean, 'wrong place?'"

"We got off the truck at the wrong stop. We were scheduled to get off at stop number three."

"How do you know that?" blurted out Turner.

"The driver told me."

"You believe that private over me?"

"That's right," I pulled out my map and we both crawled underneath a poncho and turned on our red filtered flashlights. After a ten-minute conference, we decided that we were at least eight hundred meters from our drop point. We were also fifteen minutes late.

In order for us to get back on schedule, Sergeant Turner ordered the patrol to double time to the proper start point. We began at a nine-minute mile pace but soon wore down to a fifteen-minute mile walk. Sweat was pouring off all of us. It was a devastating pace with all our gear on. As we made our way to the planned start point, Guard Post Collier was making a spot report to battalion about hearing someone screaming the word 'stop' three times and hearing some other loud, but unintelligible conversation. We would definitely have to explain that when we got back.

We were thirty minutes late when we reached our planned start point and we were already exhausted. We had just run a half-mile with seventy pounds of gear strapped on our bodies. We had another three-fourths of a mile to hump before we reached our ambush site. The patrol leader gathered us together and gave us a little speech. "I know where we are now, so we won't stop any more for pace count or azimuth checks. I've been to the exact ambush site before."

I pulled Sergeant Turner over to the side, "Listen, I'm about ready to call this thing off. We're thirty minutes behind schedule, we're all exhausted and you don't know what the hell you're doing."

"Sir, give me the benefit of the doubt. I know where I am now and what I'm doing. I can handle it."

"I don't like the idea of foregoing the pace count. That's how people get lost or dead."

"Sir, this is my patrol and we're going to move on."

"It's all yours," I said.

Sergeant Turner began to speak to the whole group. "We're thirty minutes late so we'll have to double time again." Groans of disgust were heard from the blackness the patrol occupied.

"Saddle up," said Turner.

Turner led the way. Again it started out at a very quick pace but fizzled to a fast walk. I unzipped my flak jacket to prevent overheating. I had on four layers of clothing wrapped in a vinyl covered heavy bulletproof vest. Sweat began to run down my temples.

Fifteen minutes later we stopped on a hill that was thickly vegetated. Peering over the crest of the hill, we could see a rice paddy a hundred meters wide and a wooded hill on the far side. Sergeant Turner and I were the only ones concerned enough to climb to the top of the hill and look over. The other four men just dropped in their tracks, especially the radio operators, who were each carrying an extra twenty-five pounds of radio.

Sergeant Turner said, "Sir, our objective is on the next hill. We were supposed to be in position fifteen minutes ago so we're cutting straight across the rice paddy." We scanned the area with our starlight scopes and night vision goggles and it looked clear.

This patrol obviously became non-tactical from the instant we got off the truck. I knew that cutting across the open rice paddy wasn't a very sound decision because North Korean Guard Post 224 had a direct line of sight to us but I wasn't the patrol leader.

"We're late. They hate late patrols more than anything else. We're cutting across." It sounded like Sergeant Turner was trying to convince himself that it was the right thing to do. I thought, *Better late than dead.* I couldn't imagine a late patrol would be hated one billionth as much as a dead one.

"Saddle up." (His favorite line.) We spread out five meters apart and walked single file across to the small finger of land that was our objective. Sergeant Turner was leading the way. I was the fifth man back, next to last. When we reached the hill, we closed the gap a little more between us because the vegetation was surprisingly thick. The Ranger file began to snake its way through the dead underbrush. After five minutes of roaming around in the woods, Sergeant Turner told the radio operator to call in that we were at the ambush site, which of course, we weren't.

The call was made and we continued our search. I thought that we were looking for a good place to set the ambush. I was looking for a spot with a lot of cover and concealment but still having good fields of fire. After two more minutes of walking around I found what Sergeant Turner was looking for. It wasn't the ambush site. It was a yellow sign thirty-nine inches by twenty inches that denoted the Military Demarcation Line, that imaginary line that separates South Korea from North Korea. The sign had letters on it, written in Chinese and Korean, which meant only one thing; the patrol was in North Korea. We were on the wrong side of the sign.

"Freeze!" I yelled in a gruff whisper. "We're in North Korea."

I had stopped walking when I noticed the sign in the dark but I still went three feet inside North Korea. I took one giant step and placed myself on the opposite side of the sign, in South Korea where the words on the sign were written in English and Korean. Every man was tiptoeing back to my position. Each man made his way safely into South Korea and in two minutes, I had a four-man perimeter with me in the middle. Of all people, Sergeant Turner did not make it back and was still somewhere in North Korea.

I went over to the primary radio operator, the next highest-ranking man. I told him to wait here for us and if we didn't come back in ten minutes or if he heard shooting of explosions, stay tactical and call it in for further instructions.

I pulled out my stiletto and began to probe my way back into enemy territory. I was terrified that there might be a minefield lining the North Korean side of the MDL. Duck walking with an M-16, starlight scope, flak jacket, helmet, grenades, ammunition, and other assorted gear is virtually impossible. I mostly waddled along and dragged half the gear on the ground behind me.

I probed down the heavily vegetated trail, twenty meters into the bush. I felt relatively safe until I passed the point of the patrol's furthest penetration. I was now pioneering my own path. A few meters further and Sergeant Turner came into view. He was sitting at the base of a small tree, leaning back against the trunk. He had his helmet off and was smoking a cigarette.

His mind is gone, I thought to myself. Within a couple of seconds, I had probed my way up next him.

"Put that butt out and let's get out of here," I whispered.

"Ya know, this is all fucked up," he said in normal conversation volume.

"Don't talk so loud. You know we're inside North Korea, don't you? Put that butt out and let's go back." I spun on the balls of my feet in a squatting position, but he made no motion like he was going to follow me back. I turned around and stood up. I towered over him as he remained in a sitting position with his knees drawn up. I put the sole of my boot up to the side of his face and shoved with all my might. His face went to ground like a bolt of lightning. His head bounced off the turf and his cigarette went flying.

"Get up, soldier."

He sprang to his feet. We stared at each other for a moment. I thought I might have to fight him. Then he reached down and picked up his weapon and put his helmet on his head. I led the way out with an uneasy feeling that I might get shot in the back.

Sergeant Turner was back to "normal" when we reached the rest of the patrol and he took charge immediately after we linked up. Unbelievably we set up an ambush ten meters inside the South Korean boundary, a really ineffective position, but I will give him credit for continuing the mission.

When the claymore mines were set up and the fields of fire were established, we sat back to wait and watch. It only took me a few minutes to realize that the cold weather was too much to try to fight. After running a couple of miles in full combat dress and duck walking around in North Korea, sweat was soaking through my clothes from the inside out.

We tried to lie in the ambush site as still as possible, but one of the members began to cough and another started to tremble violently and then he threw up. Our ambush was an atrocity. The ambush site that the patrol leader picked out was on the "down" side of a hill. It was more like a death trap for us than an ambush against the enemy. The guy who was coughing was making so much noise that he could be heard at least a quarter of a mile away and the vomit smell filled the cold, dead air for several acres. My nose was running badly and I tried to keep it wiped with my sleeve, but I couldn't keep up with it, so I just let it run. I didn't want to make a bunch of loud sniffing noises. "Silly me."

Every now and then I actually scanned the kill zone of the ambush with my starlight scope, but it really took an effort. Any infiltrators would just avoid the ambush because they could hear, see, and smell us for miles. After four very uncomfortable hours of remaining silent and immobile, the patrol leader called off the ambush with the words, "Saddle up!" We rucked-up very quickly and moved out. Everyone was thankful that we were humping through the bush again. We were making quite a bit of noise. The man was still coughing and I decided that it would be okay to go ahead and sniff and snort my snot back into my nasal cavity.

The man who threw up, begged us to stop after about a mile. He said he thought he was going to crap in his pants if we didn't stop. We set up a small perimeter and let the man take a dump behind some bushes. I couldn't see him in the dark but I heard him grunt, groan, and curse a bit. Three minutes later we were humping down the trail again. We called in our bogus checkpoints on the move and reached the pick-up point with ten minutes to spare. We called for the extraction vehicle and loaded when it arrived.

We were sitting in the blackness of the enclosed truck bed and I'm sure everyone was as cold as me. I was trying to wipe all the snot off my face before we got to the Southern Boundary of the DMZ. About two minutes into the trip back, one of the soldiers let out an exclamation, "Gawd-a-Mighty! What's that smell?"

I couldn't smell anything with my nose running so badly, but I was curious. There was a moment of silence and I kept inhaling trying to smell whatever it was the soldier had smelled. Finally, the soldier I had left in charge back at the ambush spoke up.

"Hey Shortbread, did you shit your britches?"

A voice came out of the darkness that I assumed was Shortbread's. "I couldn't get my pants unbuttoned in time." Shortbread had in fact, shit his pants.

The inside of the truck was filled with alternate rounds of insults and laughter. I had to start giggling to myself. I felt sorry for the guy. I'm sure his buddies would never let him live it down. They'd make up stories for months about how Shortbread got so scared that he shit his pants.

We cleared the Southern Boundary and reported to the bunker for debriefing. The patrol leader said he didn't see anything or hear anything. He described the patrol as routine. When asked about voices yelling the word "stop" several times, the patrol leader lied very easily and denied hearing anything. I sat back and watched and listened. When Sergeant Turner left the room, the other soldiers came over to me and begged me to do something about Turner. I assured them that they would not have to worry about Sergeant Turner anymore.

It was very late in the night when we finally left the debriefing room. I racked my weapon and headed for the sack. The quarter mile winding road to my hooch seemed awfully dark and long. The only movement I saw was that of the perimeter guards. As I walked, I wondered just how close we all had come to getting killed. How many more feet or inches did we have to spare before we hit the belt of North Korean antipersonnel mines. I made a mental note that I would talk to Sergeant Turner's Company commander and get him relieved of any further important responsibilities for the rest of his tour, which was synonymous with ending his career.

I stood on the concrete slab of the porch in front of my hooch and looked out over the river. *Still frozen,* I thought, *just like me.* As I shut the door to my hooch, a loud thunderclap rang out that shook the windows. I'd finally gotten used to the "explosion."

When I reported to the bunker the next morning, Captain Starns greeted me with a question, "How'd it go?"

"You wouldn't believe it," I said.

"Who was your patrol leader?"

"Sergeant Turner."

Captain Starns grabbed his stomach and made a retching noise. "I've been on patrol with him before," he said.

"Yeah," I said.

"He's messed up."

"You're tellin' me."

"Did he get you lost?"

"Continuously," I said. "It was a disaster from the start. We should have called it off from the minute we reached friendly front lines."

"Oh?" said the captain.

"We were let off at the wrong place, about eight hundred meters off target. We got lost goin' there and double timed all the way. I nearly died of heat stroke and when we stopped, I nearly died of hypothermia. Two guys got sick; pukin' and coughin'. One guy even shit his pants."

Captain Starns started laughing. I didn't know if he was laughing at my experience or reminiscing about his own. I continued, "When we dismounted the truck, believe it or not, one guy got stuck on the bumper and got drug two hundred meters by his ass."

I let Captain Starns revel in the laughter for a moment longer, then I dropped the bomb.

"We also went twenty-five meters into North Korea."

Captain Starns sobered instantly.

"How do you know?" he queried immediately.

"Because I walked up on the MDL marker, from the wrong side."

"Don't tell anybody," he emphasized the word "anybody"

"Are you kidding?" *They wouldn't believe the whole story anyway,* I thought. There was a pause. "Damn, I hate this place," I said.

"And you're just getting started, Turtle."

That sentence changed the subject and the "lost ambush patrol" was forgotten forever. I could have been twenty-five meters into the Twilight Zone and no one would have known the difference and they damn sure didn't care.

CHAPTER 6

Party

Patrol after patrol went out and came back without incident. The days in February rolled on and we quickly approached the time when we would hand off the DMZ mission to another infantry battalion for the spring and summer. The battalions taking the mission from us stayed in tents for three months. Since we had semi-permanent buildings for billets (Quonset huts), we got the mission during the winter months. It made sense but we really got tired of freezing our asses off in the field.

As the 28th day of February dawned, I realized that it was leap year and I fell into that twenty-five percent group of soldiers who actually had a year and an extra day to serve on their one year Korean Tour, 366 miserable fucking days instead of 365. Eleven months and a wake up to go.

I'd been in Korea for a month now and only two-thirds of my baggage had arrived, or since I was a pessimist and always saw the glass half empty, one-third of my baggage was lost. The box that contained my guitar was missing and a ring that I had given my high school sweetheart and of course she gave back (actually she threw back at me) was also missing. Most importantly, the box with my winter clothes and parka was gone. To make my start in Korea worse, I didn't get paid for January or February, and before it was over, March would be added to the list. The cherry on top of all was the injury to my leg after only eight days of being in country.

I had a history of having bad luck with new assignments. In Alaska, the tour I had just before coming to Korea, I was a brand new second lieutenant and was nearly in culture shock arriving in Alaska in the middle of January. I was assigned to Fort Richardson, which is near Anchorage and is supposed to have a maritime climate. I guess it did, if you consider ten degrees your concept of a maritime climate. I had just come from assignments in Georgia, Arizona and a leave in Texas. It was a fifty-degree change and needless to say, I was a little apprehensive about the cold. I attended a three-day cold weather course and became a little more familiar with cold weather operations. After completion of this course I was sent to my unit that was conducting a field exercise at Fort Greely. Fort Greely was about 300 miles north of Fort

Richardson and it had a real Arctic climate.

I found my new boss at the Fort Greely snack bar. He looked burned out and was eating a Twinkie. I sat down at the table with him and we discussed my brief career. He told me to take a jeep and drive around the thirty-three mile loop and get a closer look at the training area.

My driver was a Spec/4 named McGuran. We got in the jeep and quickly turned on the heater because it was minus twenty-three degrees. We drove off the small main post and went down the major highway for a couple of miles to a point where the Alaskan pipeline came close to the road. At the pipeline, we went into the southern entrance of the thirty-three mile loop. It was a frozen one-lane road that had a bulldozer run down it to open about three-fourths of the one lane. Ice was still covering the surface and mounds of snow were piled up about six feet high on each side of the open lane.

I unzipped my parka because the jeep heater kept it very toasty. We made two fairly sharp curves and I reached in the back seat for a map so I could follow our progress around the loop. As I turned my head to get the map I caught a glimpse of an object in the road out of the corner of my eye.

We hit it! Things went yellow for me. Any time I got hurt, especially when I had my bell rung really hard playing football, I would see yellow. My best friend, Jim Locke, would sometimes see Dairy Queen Signs. I preferred yellow. Everything was brilliant yellow now, nearly as bright as sunlight, then I opened my eyes. It was still yellow around the edges.

"Did we hit it?" I asked, foolishly. Of course we had.

I felt a hand run through my closely cropped hair—

"Sir, you've got to hold your head up!" I heard a strained voice. My eyes focused a little more clearly. The object I had seen magically appear in front of us was an engineer's five-ton dump truck with a ton and a half of block ice in the back. Our little quarter ton jeep took it squarely on the hood, a head on collision, with the force of the blow concentrating on my side. I was thrown forward and my face impacted on the 'dash' of the jeep. Actually there was no real dashboard in the jeep, but there was a metal cylinder that housed the windshield wiper motor. The bottom of my chin landed on the motor and I actually 'kissed' the metal frame holding the windshield in place. I hit it hard enough to make everything from my nose down feel crushed. Besides the pain, it all felt out of place.

I saw two soldiers getting out of the truck and walking towards us. One of them came up to my window and asked if I was okay. McGuran answered for me, "Hell no," and then McGuran placed a four by four inch gauze pad on my nose and lips and instructed me to hold my head back and keep the compress in place. I weakly put a hand up to hold the bandage on my injury. I put my fingers on the gauze covering my lips and nose and hooked my thumb under my chin and squeezed my fingers together, pinching my lower face. As I did this, my thumb slid into my mouth and touched what I thought was my tongue. There was a tear in the flesh under my chin that went all the way into my mouth.

I motioned for one of the engineers to come over to me because I wanted him to get another compress. I couldn't talk too well but he finally understood what I wanted and placed another bandage under my chin. Meanwhile, McGuran was assembling a radio from the wreckage of the jeep. The jeep engine was smashed so badly that it wouldn't run and the dump truck couldn't get around the wreckage. It was thirty-two miles back to garrison by taking the thirty-three mile loop the long way. The dump truck would have taken at least an hour to get back. McGuran called over the radio for a medical helicopter and I just sat quietly, concentrating on running my tongue around my teeth to see if they were all still there. They were, but I felt something loose inside my mouth. My imagination ran wild. I reached up with my free hand and scraped a wad of gum out of my mouth with my index finger. I had forgotten that I was chewing it and was relieved to see it was gum instead of God knows what.

I looked down towards my stomach, trying to see part of my mangled face. All I saw were icicles made of my blood stretching from my chin to my chest. I was fascinated: bloodcicles. It was still minus twenty-three and McGuran suggested, after seeing my frozen blood hanging off my chin, to move me to the truck since it was unharmed by the accident and its heater still worked. The two engineers grasped me firmly by either arm and assisted me like a drunken sailor into the truck cab and I lay down on the seat. I was getting warm and I think I fell asleep because the next thing I remember was hearing the *wop-wop* of the Medevac chopper. The truck doors flew open and a sea of hands were grabbing at me. I was half carried and half walked to the small OH-58 helicopter, which wasn't a real medical chopper. It just happened to be flying in the area and heard McGuran's distress call. One of the engineers flew back with me in the helicopter to a field aid station. I somehow managed to ask him how I looked. He turned his head away so he wouldn't have to look at me and said, "There'll be a little scar, Sir."

We landed twenty meters from an all-purpose-medium tent that I figured was the aid station. I got out of the chopper and was ushered into a waiting jeep. For an instant, I thought that we were going to drive off somewhere far away, but the jeep only drove me to the front of the tent, fifty feet away. I couldn't help but think how stupid was that. I could have walked but it was probably Standard Operating Procedure (SOP) to be driven.

I lay down on a table and a female aid came over to me and started washing the blood off my face and hands. She asked me how it happened, just like a dentist does when he gets your mouth crammed full of instruments and cotton. Here I was bleeding profusely from the chin, lips, mouth and nose and she wanted to have a conversation. I tried my best to accommodate her but didn't do too well. I managed to get the idea across that I "hit my face on a truck."

She returned, "Yeah, it is slippery out there." To this day, that woman thinks I slipped on the ice, fell down, and hit my face on a truck bumper. It bothered me that she thought I held a black belt in spastic.

The doc, a real doctor, the brigade surgeon, came over to look at me. He probed on my face a little and asked me several questions. Then he told me that I was very lucky not to have lost any teeth. He said since the injury was on my face, he'd take me back to the big clinic to suture me up.

Once back at the clinic, the doc asked me if I wanted to see it before he fixed it, so I could really appreciate the good job that he'd do. I nodded my head and the nurse held a mirror in front of my face. I wish I hadn't seen it now. I was split open from under my chin, through both lips and up through my left nostril. I looked like something out of a horror movie. I had the appearance of a corpse with the flesh half rotted off. It made me feel nauseous. I wasn't extremely vain but I didn't look very good then and I had my doubts about the future. The blood I swallowed began to churn in my stomach and I was really beginning to feel sick.

The doc flushed out the wound with a saline solution. The salt water burned all the way into my sinuses and I ripped at the seams of my fatigue pants fighting the pain. He deadened me after the irrigation. *Thanks for nothing, doc.* Then he began to sew. Thirty-four large stitches and several butterfly bandages later I was closed up. I had big blue sutures hanging out of my face.

It was not a good start to my previous tour in Alaska or my current tour in Korea.

I'd grown a moustache to cover some of the scars on my lips. I'm not sure anyone would really notice or not, but I was quite conscious of it. That little fold of skin that separates one's left and right upper lip was completely destroyed. I had a smooth lip, giving it the appearance of being overly large. However, no one gave a damn in Korea what happened at my last assignment and rightfully so. Here, we had to concern ourselves with the issues at hand and that was transferring the DMZ mission to our sister battalion.

The takeover of the mission wasn't going anything like planned. There were guidelines and SOPs set up to guarantee a smooth transition but the incoming battalion wasn't meeting the standards. I was supposed to get face to face with my counterpart, the S-2, twenty-one days prior to takeover. The first time I saw him was three days prior and then it was for only thirty minutes. During the next few days, I saw him every now and then floating around north of the river. I knew from experience that it took a hundred percent effort at all times to have a successful and safe mission but the incoming battalion was taking the DMZ mission too lightly. I offered as many suggestions as I thought were necessary but they seemed to think they knew everything already. I didn't like to be unprofessional but I got to the point that all I wanted was for them to take the mission and be done with it. If they botched it up, it'd be no skin off my nose, because I'd given them every available opportunity.

Finally the day came when we surrendered the DMZ Mission to 'our summer help,' as we called them. It was the Vernal Equinox, March 20, 1980. We were glad and we showed our joy by planning a party in the Officers Club.

In our Officers Club we have bronze plates that have the unit crest in the center and have the officer's name on the edge. The plates are hung on the walls in order of assignment to the unit. When you first get there you are "hailed" by drinking the "fire of the Manchu dragon," and your plate is hung in the very last place. As people are "farewelled" and rotate out, their plates are taken off the wall and everyone else's moves forward a space. Your tour progress is marked by the place that your plate occupies on the wall. The very last place before you go home is over the fireplace and that space is called "on the range." When the ranking combat arms officer in the club decides to, he can "open the range," similar to opening a rifle range. Once the range is open, the officers in the club are allowed to throw things at the brass plate "on the range" over the fire place. It sounds childish but when done properly, it's quite hilarious.

The plate on the range generally gets banged up. Mostly the thrown objects consist of smashed beer cans but sometimes the firing party gets carried away and throws saltshakers or silverware. A dinged up plate is an indication of a well-liked officer. Our beloved Executive Officer, Major Winston, "the Grinch," was a very popular man. His decisions were fair and he had a good head on his shoulders. Everyone liked and respected him. Major Winston's plate, unfortunately hung "on the range" for quite some time. At first, Major Winston stood guard on his plate by taking the closest table to the fireplace, because it was indeed a grave transgression against the brotherhood of Manchu Officers if someone were to be wounded by a misfired beer can. Also, Major Winston was usually the highest-ranking combat arms officer in the club, always choosing never to open the range.

Unfortunately for Major Winston's plate, he was a fine and deserving officer and was promoted to lieutenant colonel, and then immediately had his tour extended on the DMZ for thirty more days. There were few things more terrible than being extended on the DMZ, erectile dysfunction and death were among them. Because of the extension, the new lieutenant colonel's plate hung "on the range" for an extra thirty days.

Shortly after the news of Lieutenant Colonel Winston's extension spread throughout the compound, a very serious transgression against the brotherhood occurred; the plate was stolen. No one really knew who did it or cared because within twenty-four hours the plate was returned. However, it had been brutally shot to death with two blasts from a high-powered rifle. Two days after the "murder," an electrical cord was woven through the two bullet holes. Lieutenant Colonel Winston couldn't figure it out until they told him that it was an *extension* cord in honor of his thirty-day extension on the DMZ. Also, one night, Lieutenant Colonel Winston's plate was adorned with a small pair of hot pink lace panties. A file label was stuck on it that read "Top Ten Best Dressed." The final insult came just before the general arrived for dinner at the Officers Club. One of the Company commanders found some semi-wild marijuana plants near the perimeter fence by his Company's billets. He picked the weed and laced the plants through the bullet holes along with the extension cord. We laughed until we cried when the general saw it. The general never made a comment but his eyes widened like saucers when he glanced up over the fireplace.

When the day arrived for Lieutenant Colonel Winston to leave, the plate was in pretty poor shape. It had been transformed from bright shiny brass into a brown, dirt-colored aberration, with green mold growing out of the intricate folds of the unit crest. It was dented in a few places from hits by large objects and was dog-eared on one side because it was knocked off the range and smashed against the brick hearth in front of the fireplace. It was shot twice, dressed with panties, and laced with marijuana and an extension cord. Outwardly, it appeared to be a dismal display of esprit de corps, but from within, it was a thing of pride.

The parties up on the Z came few and far between so we had to make the most of them. Our Company commanders were very efficient at bullshitting women. Thus they were tasked with sending out personal invitations to all available American females. The party was set for a couple of days after the handoff of the DMZ mission. Very little work got done during those interim days because anticipation of the upcoming party overshadowed the need to get ready for the annual General Inspection.

Party night was Saturday night. At least a dozen women consented to come, maybe more were waiting in the wings, but it couldn't be confirmed. Many a heart can be broken in Manchu land when you get thirty lonely men and a dozen adventurous women on a veranda overlooking a mysterious river on a moonlit night with a dash of chill in the air: love, lust, and laughs are inevitable.

The party was scheduled to start at 1800 (6 PM). I didn't quit working until 1900 (7 PM) that night. I figured that every woman would already be taken by the time I got there. I took a quick glance around the bunker to see if all the classified material was put in the safe. I turned the inside light off, the fire light on and closed the Greenleaf lock through the three-fourths inch thick iron hasp.

PARTY TIME! I rushed back to my hooch to change clothes, hoping that there would still be a woman somewhere for me. I hadn't even seen or spoken to an American woman for over a month. I tried not to get my hopes up because arriving an hour late cut my chances by about a million percent. I had to walk by the "O" Club to get to my hooch. I heard music and gayety coming from within. As I got closer, I heard a loud thump and the sound of broken glass, then a roar of laughter. I assumed that someone threw a saltshaker or beer glass at Lieutenant Colonel Winston's plate on the range.

I walked into my hooch and went to the latrine. The only shower was belching forth an absolutely blinding veil of steam, immediately fogging up my glasses. Using the Braille method, I fumbled my way to the single commode, put the seat down, and closed the door of the stall. As soon as I positioned myself comfortably on the throne, the shower turned off. I started to say something to whoever it was, but they were out of the shower and I could just barely see the feet under the stall door through the steam. The feet were about size five and a half with painted nails. It was one of the women. I didn't know if I should say something or just hope she didn't see me. How embarrassing it would be to meet my first round-eyed women in over a month while I was sitting on the pot. I said nothing, sitting motionless with my pants around my ankles trying not to make any bathroom sounds. Seeing me through the tiny cracks of the stall in the man-made fog would have been virtually impossible. She never noticed me as she finished drying off and went to the next room.

I concluded my business and was standing in front of the sink looking into the steamed up mirror when she and her friend came back into the latrine. Both women were wearing tight, shift style dresses. They were probably average looking women but they looked great to me. We stared at each other for a moment; then I broke the silence.

"Do you need to get in here?"

"If you don't mind?" they said.

The girls began putting on makeup and blow-drying their hair. One was blonde, blue eyed and five foot two. The other was brunette, brown eyed, and five-five. I looked down at their feet, the blonde had painted toenails, the brunette did not.

We socialized a little, the *who are you? where you froms? what d'ya dos?* were exchanged. They asked if I was going to the party. "Yes I am, as soon as I change clothes." They made their final primp and finished dressing in the visitor's bunk room then left the Quonset hut for the Officers Club. I showered and changed clothes as fast as possible.

I was nearly afraid to enter the club. It sounded like it was full of caged animals. Miss Yi, the pretty young waitress, ran by me in a fret. I called to her but she just ran off into the darkness. The club looked like shit; two tables were overturned, food, napkins, empty bottles, and glasses were everywhere. One of the officers was asleep on the bar, several couples were dancing, some talking and a threesome was making out in the corner.

I was overdressed. I had on slacks and a tailor made shirt. Most officers had on blue jeans. The women looked really nice but women always overdress. I purchased a diet cola and began to mingle. I didn't see the blonde with the painted nails. I was afraid that she was already snatched up even though it had only been fifteen minutes since I saw her last. Within half an hour I'd met every woman in the club. There were eleven of them; two intelligence officers from Yongsan-Seoul, five nurses from the 121 EVAC Hospital and four schoolteachers from the dependent school system in Seoul.

There were two nice looking girls, three if you counted the blonde that was missing, five average looking girls for the civilian world and two average looking girls by Army standards and two that were butt ugly no matter how you looked at them. These two poor girls only looked average if you compared them to each other. I had this fear that I would end up with one of them. I would try, at all cost, to avoid it.

There was a wager among the men to see who could get laid first. The motto for the night was "go ugly early." I think the bet had already been won by the time I'd gotten there.

I was sitting with a fellow officer when Miss Yi came back into the club. It was obvious that she had been crying. I asked her what was wrong.

She said, "Some man not nice."

"Who?" but she wouldn't tell me.

She went back to work and I started to walk around nervously eating the hors d'oeuvres. I felt like a fish out of water. Going out on the veranda with my diet cola and cream cheese celery stick, I stood by the rail, looking down, one hundred feet to the river. It was really a little too cold to be outside in just a shirt but I didn't care. I thought, *I might as well practice being miserable.*

Finished with my celery stick and drink, I turned to go back inside. The blonde with the painted nails was standing right behind me. I never heard her walk up.

"It's lovely out here," she said and folded her arms to keep warm.

"Are you cold?" I asked.

"Not if you hold me," she said.

I think I went stupid.

She came closer and stood with her hands on the rail next to me. I moved behind her and wrapped my arms around her waist. She was tiny and smelled so good that I nearly reeled backwards.

"This is the way it ought to be," I said.

"What ought to be?" she asked as she turned around to face me, still in my arms.

"A visit to a foreign country should be like this, a romantic venture, not..." my words faded.

"You guys must have it rough up here?"

"Not really, it's all what you make it and right now you are helping me make the most of it." I thought I was being irresistibly charming.

"Oh, yeah?" she said. Her head fell back, her eyes closed and her lips parted over so slightly. For a moment, I just stared, drinking in every detail. Then, I lowered my lips to hers. We pulled apart slightly and I felt her warm, sweet breath against my cheek. I kissed her neck, ear, and lips again and again and she kissed me back. Some women really know how to be with a man and she was one of them. She responded so well, when I caressed, she caressed back, when I hugged, she hugged back and when I kissed, she kissed back.

"This only happens in dreams," I whispered. I don't think I really meant to say that out loud.

"I'm real," she said.

We were lost in another embrace when a loud crash from the club startled us. It was the communications officer. He'd flown through one of the plate glass windows diving for a Ping-Pong ball. The doc ran out the back door, still holding a Ping-Pong paddle in his hand. He made sure the young commo officer wasn't cut to ribbons. He didn't have a scratch on him and most of the guys were disappointed that there wasn't at least a bucket of blood on the porch.

Linda, my new significant other, and I went inside to join the reverie. We danced closely and held each other tightly. Once or twice we kept dancing when the music stopped. It was embarrassing, but good to be lost in a world so different from the DMZ. The songs played on and we drifted further away from Korea. She laughed at my jokes and always smiled at the perfect time. I decided that this girl was either made especially for me or she was just a vicious delusion and would morph into Godzilla before the night was over.

At 2300 (11 PM) the club began to clear out. Four women and six guys were left, not counting Linda and me. She asked if I liked to play backgammon. After I recovered from the strange question, I told her that I did like to play and I just happened to have a backgammon board in my room. We left the club immediately and headed for my Quonset hut. Before we entered my room, she said she wanted to change into something more comfortable. "Sure, go ahead."

I sat on my bed with the backgammon board in front of me. I was playing craps with myself while Linda changed clothes in the spare room across from the latrine. It was packed with bunks for our visitors. So far, not a single bed had been touched. I heard a door shut and the sound of wooden shoes coming down the hall. I acted as nonchalantly as possible.

She surprised me. She was wearing a black baby-doll-half-see-thru nightie with black high-heeled slippers. She closed the door behind her, leaned back against it and said, "Make a wish."

I went stupid again.

"If you beat me at backgammon," she said, "your wish will come true."

She came over to me and lay down on the bed in the sexiest fashion that I could ever imagine. Her slippers fell off her feet and she buried her toes under my thigh.

"You go ahead and roll," she said.

"That's not fair," I said, "I can't think clearly."

I threw the dice, double sixes! This was going to be my night. The game didn't progress fast enough for me. We each had a few markers sent back but it soon became apparent that I was going to win. A half dozen rolls would put me out but she insisted on playing until the bitter end. I watched her slender fingers handle the dice. I know she was average looking but compatibility and willingness to please was way off the chart on the high side. I even caught myself trying to think about love. I must have been lonelier than I thought or I was still stuck in stupid.

"Three more rolls and I'll win," I said.

"That's good because I'll get what I want too," she said smiling.

Yes, Sir, this is going to by my night. I couldn't believe that this woman was in the same Army as me. She was a lieutenant, in intelligence (of all things) back in Seoul. I didn't care what she did, she could have been a garbage collector.

I rolled the dice, double fours. "Puts me out," I said, as the phone rang. I jumped up automatically reacting to the ring.

"Don't answer it," she said. "Please," she begged as I stood up.

"It may be important," I said.

"You're not on duty now. Let someone else take care of it," and she spread her legs slightly, "Come here," she emphasized it by putting her hands to her inner thigh.

"I have to be there if someone needs me." I turned toward the door.

"What could be so damn important at this hour?" she said indignantly.

"Are you really an intelligence officer? I don't think you understand the first thing about this place." I ran down the hall. As I answered the phone, she slipped past me in the hall and went into the room prepared for the women and slammed the door.

Well, I screwed that up, I thought.

"Lieutenant Osterhout," I said into the phone. The electronic voice on the other end was the staff duty officer. "Dave, we've got a problem down at the bridge."

"What is it?"

"The bridge platoon has reported gunfire within two kilometers, coming from the northwest."

"Has this been passed up to brigade?"

"No, not yet."

"Don't, until you hear word from me or a field grade officer," I paused to think a moment. "Call the ROKs and see if anything has been reported to them. Maybe an ambush was triggered. Send the jeep up here to get me at my quarters. I'll tell the commander from here."

"Roger, anything else?"

"Yeah, you spoiled my trip down paradise lane."

"What?"

"I'll explain later," and hung up.

I hollered through the closed door of the bunkroom, "Linda, I've got to go down to the bridge. There's been a shooting incident."

"So," she said back.

"I've got to go," I said.

"Well, go then, but don't expect me to wait for you."

"I don't ever expect anything," I said as I walked out the door of the Quonset hut. I left my room open, hoping she would change her mind and wait for me there.

I ran up the steep hill to the parking lot of the Officer's Club just as the jeep rounded the corner. I climbed aboard and we sped toward the bridge. I didn't like being out after curfew, especially north of the river. The ROKs were a lot more lenient than we were with their shooting policies; after all, it was their country. We had to pass the largest ROK compound in the area to get to the bridge. They often set up ambushes and I figured that the shooting may have been an ambush being triggered. I hoped that we wouldn't trigger one on the way to the bridge.

The jeep skidded to a halt at the guard hut on the north end of the bridge. I jumped out and asked the guard what was going on. He said that he couldn't see anything from the north end but he heard several dozen rounds being fired and at least two explosions.

"Call the south end and tell them I'm on my way over," I instructed the guard as I got back in the jeep. The bridge was a scary thing by itself. It was large and rickety and had the appearance of a long, foreboding tunnel. The experts say that the bridge didn't play a large part in the Korean War but the number of bullet holes in the superstructure told me a different story. I imagined scores of souls parted with their bodies in battles over this bridge.

I reached the far end and told the driver to turn around and stay in the jeep. The sergeant of the Guard greeted me and began to lay out the situation. He pointed to a section of black shore on the north bank and said that several hundred meters inland from that point was where the shooting took place. He told me that he was checking the guards when all hell broke loose. He described it as "ten seconds of thunder." The explosions, two of them, came first and then the rifle fire. "I think I heard a machine gun too, Sir," he added.

"Did you see anything?"

"Yes, Sir, a flare went up and burned about twenty seconds."

"Did you see anything else?"

"Yes, Sir, a couple of red tracers flew up in the air. One came pretty damn close to the bridge."

"I see that you've got two men extra on the bridge?" I stated as a question.

"Yes, Sir, I thought I'd scramble an extra two men to help keep watch."

"Okay, that's fine but I want three men at the north end. If the ROKs did set off an ambush and that's what it sounds like happened and they didn't kill everybody, then there may be a couple of infiltrators running around over there and I don't want that guard post under strength. Do they have a can of ammo up there?"

"Yes, Sir."

"Okay, I'm going back to the Headquarters. You've done a good job, sergeant. I want to talk to the men on the bridge so I'm going to walk back. Call the other end and tell them I'll be walking down the planks in civilian clothes and not to shoot me."

"Yes, Sir," and he snapped a sharp salute.

Good man, I thought as I began walking.

The first guard challenged me. He knew who I was all the time but was scared that he might get reprimanded if he didn't do what he was supposed to do. He and I talked for about five minutes. He talked about the Korean women and the varieties of oriental liquors. I politely listened and then instructed him to remain alert.

I walked on down another one hundred meters and a dark form stepped out of a shadow and halted me with such a business like tone that I felt uneasy. I identified myself and began to chat with the next guard. He told me that he had never seen a river like this one before. It kept flowing backwards at times throughout the day and night. I tried to explain to him that it was close to the ocean and the tide caused the river to flow backwards. He just stared down at the black water hoping the answer would come up from the bottom.

The third guard walked over to us. He was a KATUSA soldier and had been a guard on the bridge for six months. He knew every whirlpool and sandbar like the back of his hand. He spoke very poor English but he could communicate his thoughts fairly well. He was a smart guy, probably smarter than the two American soldiers I'd just talked to. He said that he thought the shooting was an ambush. I agreed with him and told him to keep a sharp lookout for movement on the north bank.

I moved towards the north end and met up with the fourth man at the searchlight. I explained that I wanted him to stay with the guards at the north guardhouse because if the ROK ambush didn't kill everybody, there may be a few infiltrators running loose. He was a real macho guy and said that he wished they'd show their faces because he wanted to get a body count.

I thought, *you dumbass.* "Nevertheless," I said, "don't take any chances, and don't get trigger happy."

I met the other guards and explained the situation. They weren't fools like Mr. Macho and had a look of genuine concern.

"Do you think they'll come to the bridge?"

"I really don't think so," I said. "I think they'll try to get back into North Korea since they've been discovered. Call the south end and have my driver come on back." One of the guards gave the other end a ring on the field phone and we could see the jeep lights heading this way.

At that moment, a ROK field ambulance pulled up to the north end guardhouse. We had to hold it up until my jeep could get across since it was only a one-lane bridge. As we were waiting, I told the guards to check every vehicle thoroughly. We didn't want Joe Chink to get a free ride to the south. The three guards went to look the ROK ambulance over. A KATUSA guard was talking to the driver and Mr. Macho went to check the back while the other guard positioned himself in front of the vehicle.

I stood by the guard hut waiting for my jeep when I heard a gurgling cough come from the back of the vehicle. For an instant I had the awful feeling that Mr. Macho had just gotten his throat cut. I went racing around to the back of the ambulance not knowing what the hell I was going to do. I didn't have a weapon and I didn't look very tough in my party slacks and tailored shirt. As it turned out I didn't need a weapon. Mr. Macho was on his hands and knees puking like a sick drunk. I felt weak when I saw it too and I was even prepared for the ugly sight of a man with his throat cut.

The macabre vision in the back of the ambulance was beyond comprehension. On the stretchers on either side of the ambulance, were two piles of body parts partially covered by Army blankets. There were at least three bodies because that's how many heads were on the floor. There was a boot with a leg sticking out of it and a left arm from the elbow down which was floating in the two-inch thick pool of blood that sloshed in the floor of the ambulance. The smell was suffocating. It reeked of the sweet smell of rotten fruit. It was the smell of blood. I stepped up on the bumper to get a better look inside just to make sure that what I was seeing was what I was really seeing.

"Jesus Christ let 'em go," I said and climbed out of the back of the ambulance taking a couple of deep breaths of fresh air. Never had I seen anything like that before. I've come upon a couple of car wrecks where the victims were hurt and I helped pull them out but they were whole people. The "bodies" in the back of the ambulance weren't even human beings anymore.

As the ambulance drove off down the bridge, Mr. Macho was just standing up and wiping his mouth. I asked the KATUSA what the driver told him.

"Not to alert, there is no danger," the KATUSA said.

"Bullshit, you guys stay alert!" and I got in the jeep and the driver and I rode silently until we reached the first gate.

"Where to, Sir?"

"Hell, I don't know. Take me back to the Officer's Club." As we drove up the final hill, I told the driver to tell the duty officer to hang tight and I'd give him a full report in a few minutes.

"Sorry to spoil the party for you, Sir," said the driver.

"It's not your fault. I wasn't getting anywhere anyway." My nose should have grown.

"Keep up the Fire, Sir," the driver yelled the unit motto as the jeep sped off into the night.

"Keep up the Fire!" my voice chased the jeep into the darkness.

I went back to the club. There were only two drunk guys rockin' their brains out. I left and walked down the hill to Lieutenant Colonel Winston's hooch. He wasn't a married man and I was afraid that he might not be alone. My fears proved wrong. He never mentioned anything about being awakened time after time in the middle of the night. He was a professional. He just sat on his bed and listened to my story.

"Sir, the ROKs triggered an ambush about a half a click from the north end of the bridge. I saw the results of it about forty minutes later. An ambulance came across the bridge with the remains of at least three bodies in the back."

"Attractive, huh?" he queried jokingly, "and there's blood on your pants."

I continued the story as I wiped at my slacks, "The ROK ambulance driver told us not to go on alert, that everything was taken care of and there was no danger."

"What do you think, Dave?" he asked.

"I agree. I think a ROK ambush fired up everything in their kill zone whether it was friendly or foe. There are two extra men on the bridge just in case. They'll remain there until sunrise but I really don't think anybody was left alive."

"Have you reported it yet?"

"No, Sir, not yet. I was afraid that brigade might alert the whole battalion and half the officers are so drunk they can't find their own rooms, let alone lead men in combat."

"Okay, I'll tell the commander in the morning. If there's any repercussion, I'll take the heat."

"Thanks, see you in the morning, Sir" and I left hoping that Linda would be waiting for me, asleep in my bed. It was three in the morning and I was tired but always very capable of performing my manly duty.

The door to my room was still unlocked. I slipped in and tiptoed over to my bed. I could see a lump under the covers in the dark. *She must be there.* I grabbed a towel off the mosquito rack at the foot of the bed and went to the shower to clean up. I was probably an infection control disaster with a five-inch swath of blood on my pants from brushing up against the bumper of the ambulance.

The shower was invigorating or was it the excitement of what awaited me in bed. I dried off and wrapped the towel around me and walked down the hall to my room. Out of curiosity I went back to the room prepared for the women and stuck my head in the door. All but two of the bunks were empty. I chuckled to myself. Evidently most of the women were spending the night with our officers.

I eased the door open to my room and dropped my bloody clothes in a pile on the floor. I sneaked over to my bunk reached for the covers and began to pull them back.

"Wait a minute," it was a man's voice.

I ran back across the room and turned on the light. I went stupid again, but this time for another reason. It was an officer from Alpha Company with a fully morphed naked Godzilla.

"What are you doing in my...bed?" I asked the Alpha Company Lieutenant, feeling fairly uncomfortable with only a towel wrapped around me.

"Let me explain," he became defensive immediately. "I have a roommate back at Camp Liberty Bell and the Alpha Company vehicle had already gone so I just borrowed your room. It was open."

"And what's your story, Linda?" I asked.

She made a point to sit up and let the covers fall off of her, showing complete frontal nudity. "You had to go off and play soldier so ... I found somebody else."

The Alpha Company lieutenant looked pathetic, just sitting there ready for me to make the next move. I momentarily thought that he and I should fight to settle this but the vision of us wrestling around on the floor; both of us completely naked instantly drained my desire to exact any revenge.

"That's okay, all's fair in love and war. You got the love and I got the war. I'll sleep down the hall." I exited with the towel still wrapped around me and went to the room prepared for the visiting women. I opened the door and tried to sneak into an empty bed, after all there were ten of them

"Get out of here you horny son-of-a-bitch!" came an angry voice from a dark corner.

"Sorry," I jumped back into the hall as my towel fell to the floor. I pulled the door shut. "Fuck me naked" I said under my breath. I don't know where I got that expression but I smiled to myself when I said it because I was standing in the hall, naked. I went to sleep on the wooden bench in the shower with a towel wrapped around me. What an end to a ridiculous rollercoaster night.

CHAPTER 7

Commander's Leave

Part I

The North-Of-The-River-After-The-Mission-Debacle at the None of the Above Inn came to a close as we waved goodbye to the girls from the front door of the club. "None of Above Inn" was the official name of the Officer's Club. Some years ago there was a list compiled of fifteen potential names for the club. The list was passed around to all the officers for them to select a name. When the ballots were returned to the Adjutant, the near unanimous choice was number sixteen which was "None of the Above." The name stuck.

In the cold light of day, after a raging party, nobody looks very impressive and the same was true with these women. I suppose the dark of night and carnival atmosphere helped give the impression that they were better looking because in the early morning they all looked like they had been rode hard and put up wet. I'm sure they were also asking themselves, "What was I thinking?" because most of us looked ridiculous in our high and tight hair cuts, crisp, close cropped moustaches and me with my best pair of black horn rimmed military issue glasses. Short hair in 1980 was not exactly the cutting edge of fashion.

In a day or two, we discovered that two-thirds of the officers got laid that night, averaging two guys per woman. However, we decided that one of the more capable women carried the brunt of the action. Four days after the debauchery, the doc confirmed that at least one of the women had associated with eight officers because they were lined up in front of the clinic with a dose of the clap, eagerly awaiting the magic of modern miracle medicine. The line in front of the infirmary was not the place an officer, or anybody else, wanted to be.

When the battalion was healed from the DMZ mission and then recuperated from the celebration, the battalion commander decided to go on leave back to the States, Washington, D.C. to be exact. He had family in D.C. and there was no sense wasting time trying to finagle another assignment. He might as well get right to the heart of the matter. The Army guarantees thirty days leave a year, except for soldiers in key positions, they only get seventeen days. I fell into that category along with the battalion commander and several other officers in primary command and staff positions.

Lieutenant Colonel St. John handed off the command to the Executive Officer and the longest two weeks of my life began. Immediately, the Executive Officer called a command and staff meeting just to run over the ground rules while the battalion commander was away. It lasted until 2100 (9 PM). We adjourned to the None of the Above Inn which was unofficially changed to North of the River Inn by the Executive Officer. I ate a plate of rice with two eggs on top and retired early to my Quonset hut. The phone rang twice that night: once to tell me that there were suspected infiltrators crossing the DMZ and again to tell me how many people were dead.

The first call came after midnight from our bridge guards. They had heard unusual noises in the water. I called the staff duty officer and asked him to send the jeep to get me. The procedure had become a familiar one to every lieutenant who had ever pulled the duty.

The sergeant of the guard led me out to the darkest spot on the bridge and pointed into the black water twenty feet from the north bank. The sergeant said, "I heard a noise like someone breaking brush and then a splash. I turned the searchlight on but whatever it was had already disappeared in the water."

I just stood for a minute looking into the void. The sergeant waited impatiently for instructions. "Who else heard it?" I asked.

"Two others, Private Kim and Jim Bob."

"I'll have to get statements from them. Call them over."

I pulled out a pen and paper and began to write down all the details. Each person had a little different story. Private Kim, an outstanding guard, was very concerned that swimmers might reach the pylons and destroy the bridge. I tried to assure him that keeping the bridge intact would be more advantageous to them. A more feasible scenario would have the infiltrators surreptitiously killing the guards and gaining control of the bridge. Besides the truth in that, I said it to inspire the guards to remain awake. Jim Bob, Private Olan, was almost incapable of speaking an intelligible sentence. The sergeant had to help him by putting words in his mouth making his report totally unreliable.

I copied times and actions in a chronological order so brigade would be able to tell "Who shot John" later on. When something went wrong, half the time the Army didn't try to correct it, the Army tried to figure out who screwed it up. We called this, finding out "Who shot John." I finished the notes and told the guards to report any noise or movement to the shift leader. "Use the searchlights a lot," I said, "from far off it gives the appearance of being alert or suspicious, and they may abort their mission." They all assured me that they were ready for anything.

"Be careful," I said, and went to deliver my report to HQ. The staff duty officer had some shocking news for me when I got to the Headquarters: a shooting incident had taken place in the American sector of the DMZ less than an hour before the bridge reported noises. "Well, pass this report up to brigade and watch us all go on alert before you can say 'on your horse in the motor pool.' Anybody hurt?" I asked.

"No, didn't get a body count. Those idiots couldn't hit the broad side of a barn." Referring to our sister battalion, the summer help, who assumed the mission from us.

I went to tell the XO who greeted me with a familiar grunt as he sat up on the edge of his bed. I explained the situation and concluded with, "I can't tell if the bridge noises and the DMZ shooting incident are related. However, the DMZ Battalion is on alert."

To my relief he said, "I think one battalion on alert is enough."

I went back to my hooch and stood on the concrete porch staring into the muddy water a hundred feet below. I was just about to go inside when I heard a noise on the other side of the Quonset hut. There was a concrete foundation that extended four feet from the building, making a walkway connecting the porch by my door to the porch by the door at the other end of the hut. Next to the walkway was a steep cliff leading down to the perimeter fence and the river.

I eased up to the far edge of the building and peeked around the corner. I could see a very dark blob on the otherwise light colored concrete but I couldn't make out what it was. I turned and went into my hooch and got a hellaciously big bowie knife weighing several pounds. It was reasonably sharp but could more logically be used for knocking someone out. Whether used as bludgeon, cleaver, or knife, I felt safe with it. I grabbed a flashlight and headed off to do battle. I eased up to the corner and the spirit of the bayonet filled me. "What is the spirit of the bayonet? To kill!", I remembered from my early training days. I stepped around the corner and planted my feet squarely on the walk and challenged the blob in my best military fashion, "Hey!"

It stirred. I took a step closer and shined the light directly at it.

"Turn the damn light off," the blob said. It sure didn't sound like a North Korean infiltrator.

"Joe?" I said.

"Yeah, is that you Dave?"

"Yeah, what the hell are you doin' out here in your sleepin' bag?"

"I'm trying to sleep."

"Of course, how stupid of me, but why?"

"Oh, I don't know, I just felt like it. What are you doing up at this time of night?" Joe wiped his eyes as he asked.

"Aw there's been a little trouble up on the Z. One of the American patrols had a small firefight with some suspected infiltrators. About thirty rounds were fired, no casualties on either side."

"Good shootin'," Joe added sarcastically.

"Yeah, that's what I said. The bridge guards heard some noises an hour after the incident so the two may be related. The DMZ Battalion is on alert but the XO doesn't want to alert us."

"Why not, I'm ready," and Joe pulled a Browning nine millimeter automatic pistol out of his sleeping bag.

"Where the hell did you get that? You know private weapons are supposed to be registered and kept in the Arms Room."

"Yeah, I know, but it wouldn't do me any good in there."

Joe was the battalion communication officer. He's the one who flew out of the plate glass window during the party. He could make any piece of junk communication gear work. One time while we were out in the field, he rigged up a telephone that we could use to call home, all the way back to America. In 1980, that was magic. He was a true wizard with commo equipment. We talked for an hour about the Korean people and the strange customs. Joe had been in Korea longer than I had but he'd been on the DMZ a shorter time.

There was no moon out and the sky was clear and cold. It was the kind of cold that crept up on you and made you shiver. After shivering twice within a short period of time, I decided that I'd better go in and get some shuteye. I said goodnight to Joe and locked myself in my room. I placed the knife and flashlight next to the bed and read a few short passages in the Bible. Then I glanced through a seven-year-old Playboy magazine that had been handed down from generation to generation of Manchu Soldiers.

I turned off the light and had just settled in when I got this eerie feeling. Something wasn't quite right. I turned the light back on and searched the room with my eyes. Nothing. I went to the closet and looked behind the hanging uniforms. Nothing. I opened the room door and looked down the hall. Nothing. I opened the door of the Quonset hut and saw Joe standing in his under shorts on the edge of the porch with his pistol in his hand.

"Joe, do you hear something?" I asked without moving.

"I don't know," he said.

"Then what is it?" I asked as I walked out of the building, also in my underwear.

"Down the river," he said and pointed. "Do you hear it?"

Several hundred meters on the far side of the bridge, flares went into the air and the quiet chatter of automatic weapons fire rushed across the water.

"Combat," Joe said as he stared. He wasn't talking to me.

I ran back into my room and came out with a pair of field glasses and focused them on the dying flares.

"I can't see anything," I said.

"You don't need to," Joe said deadpan. "You can feel it."

"Yeah, I know. I knew it was going on while I was in my bed. I felt it, but I couldn't recognize the feeling."

The whole affair lasted about ten minutes. I called the duty officer before he called me. He reported that the bridge was witnessing a firefight of some sorts. I informed him that I was on top of the situation and he should go through ROK channels and find out what happened. "Call me when you have the story straight," and I hung up.

I went to see the XO again. It was becoming obvious that we weren't going to get any sleep. The XO and I hashed it out for a while and decided to wait on orders from brigade. In a few minutes, the duty officer called the XO and told him that brigade had radioed our operations center and said to "Take necessary precautions."

"What the hell does that mean?" the XO asked himself as he hung up the phone in disgust. "To alert or not to alert, that is the question," he then said in a more lighthearted manner.

"Why not one company," I suggested.

"Better yet," said the XO, "let's roll the Recon platoon. Their jeeps with M-60 machine guns should discourage any infiltrators." He thought for a minute. "Get the battalion maintenance officer to open the motor pool and the arms room to issue the weapons. Work out a plan to secure the compounds. I'll get the combat support company commander up and get him to light a fire under his platoon."

The recon platoon leader would love this job. I went to his hooch and briefed him on the situation, as he got dressed. Then I explained what I wanted his guys to do: "We have six gun jeeps to work with. I want one at the bridge, one at Camp Liberty Bell, two at Camp Greaves, and two to rove the four miles between the compounds. I want the radios of each jeep set on the battalion command frequency so the duty officer can listen to the traffic. Your command jeep can go anywhere you think is necessary. The duty officer will log in a status report every thirty minutes. The report should come from you personally. If there's trouble, all jeeps will converge on the location of the trouble. Everyone else will go on alert at that time. The jeeps at the compounds should rove within the limits of their respective compounds."

The recon platoon leader said that this was going to be great. He finished tying his bootlaces and reached into the top drawer of the chest and pulled out a .357 magnum.

"Not you too?" I said as I saw the revolver.

"What do you mean?" he asked as he strapped it on.

"Forget it. Your platoon was alerted the same time you were so they should be dressed. The combat support company commander is getting the motor pool guys rousted out." The recon platoon leader made a final check of equipment. "Good luck," I said and we left his room.

I walked back up the hill to the XO's hooch and found him making coffee. One of the other company commanders was up and anxious to find out what was going on. I ran down the whole series of events. It was 0315. I told the XO that I was going to get some sleep and left.

Joe was still sitting on the ledge when I walked up. "Are you going to bed?" I asked.

"No, I don't think so," he said.

"Well, I am, Gung Ho Joe" I said instead of good night. The nickname stuck, Gung Ho Joe.

I was asleep for an hour when the phone rang again. It was the duty officer informing me that First Corp Group had called us and spread the word that three frogmen of North Korean extraction were killed as they exited the waters of the Imjim River 900 meters from our Freedom Bridge.

"Are there any details?" I asked.

"No, just that they were killed pretty good."

"What's pretty good?"

"They were shot over a hundred times," the duty officer said.

"How did they ever recover the bodies, with a squeegee?" I asked half heartedly.

"Their wet suits were the only thing holding them together."

"No kidding. Are the reports coming in from the Recon?"

"Just like clockwork."

"Okay then, I'll see you in a couple of hours at breakfast."

An hour and a half went by and the alarm clock jarred me awake. My head throbbed and felt swollen. Even my hair hurt and my tongue felt fuzzy. I wished I hadn't gone to sleep at all. It would have been more comfortable to stay awake all night. I slept a total of three hours, all in about one-hour intervals. "Another fine day in the R-O-K," I said out loud realizing that I was talking to myself. I got dressed and headed to breakfast. Gung Ho Joe was still asleep, leaning against the side of the Quonset hut with his pistol in his lap. I was afraid to wake him up so I just left him there.

The breakfast was marginal, as always. However, the new bread cook made some excellent biscuits. As I was leaving the mess hall, Denny Johns, one of the finest lieutenants in the outfit, met me, "Dave, we've got to run a patrol."

"Good morning, Denny, now tell me something funny."

"Honestly, the brigade commander wants us to recon the north bank of the Imjin River several hundred meters on either side of the bridge."

"When?"

"At daybreak."

"That was thirty minutes ago!"

"I suggest we hurry."

I finally caught on that Denny was serious and that we'd better get moving because the brigade commander would be calling us back in a few hours to get the results. I made a mad dash through the bunker and arms room grabbing equipment, weapons, and ammunition. Denny and I were ready in twenty minutes. The duty vehicle took us to the bridge where we linked up with six guys from the Bridge Platoon.

We set out on our trek through the jungle on the north bank of the river. The banks of a tidal river are perpetually muddy and the Imjin was no exception. To get anywhere close to the water meant slipping ass-deep into the mud.

Denny was a former Green Beret and was scuba qualified. The brigade commander insisted on sending a scuba-qualified officer on this patrol. He thought that would give us a better chance of discovering the presence of enemy frogmen. I didn't really get the logic, but he was a colonel and I was a lieutenant.

We stumbled around in the mud and bushes for forty-five minutes. There was no bush left un-stabbed with a bayonet or rock left unturned. I was convinced that there had been no infiltrators near the river within the last few hours. However, last night, a regiment could have come through and the tidal action would have washed away the footprints. If we were lucky and the infiltrators had been unprofessional, there might have been a lost piece of equipment or pile of feces left behind.

Once, a small pile of feces appeared near a guard post inside the DMZ. The daily perimeter patrols swore that it wasn't there on the previous day. With a little obvious deduction, we surmised that the dung was laid during the night. I dispatched a patrol to secure the area around the pile of shit while a photographer was ordered out from brigade Headquarters to take pictures, which were developed into eight by ten glossies. When the photos reached the G-2, who was the highest intelligence source available, he wanted another patrol sent out to bring the crap back.

It was extremely difficult for me to brief the patrol and keep a straight face at the same time. But dutifully, the patrol captured the shit, bagged it, and handed it over to me. All was done without casualties, even though we laughed so hard that we nearly needed stitches.

We sent the bag of shit off to the lab back in the United States. It was stamped SECRET and sent by special courier. The lab could only tell if it was human or animal and if it was human, they could discern if it was a person who ate on the Korean economy or one who ate in American chow halls. It didn't much matter because we never heard about it again.

Buried in the mud, a soldier found an en electronic gadget of some kind that was attached to a long wire. We didn't know what it was and we never found out because it was sent off to higher Headquarters in a bag labeled SECRET and it went the way of the bag of shit.

I spent the rest of the afternoon inventorying storerooms. There was a CONEX across the small parking lot from the Headquarters building that had to be inventoried monthly. In the CONEX there was nothing but old web gear, ancient World War II packs, dozens of canvas cots, old hammocks and several cases of Korean maps that were made before the Koreas were divided. Standard Operating Procedure required me to conduct the monthly inventory because the maps were considered to be essential equipment. I sent my sergeant to inventory the CONEX because I just couldn't face such a riveting good time again this month.

Within minutes after the sergeant opened the CONEX, the whole thing was engulfed in flames. The sergeant was a smoker but he wouldn't admit to lighting up during the inventory. The obvious conclusion was a mystical spontaneous combustion or, more likely, the sergeant set the son-of-a-bitch on fire because he hated inventorying the damn thing more than I did. The Executive Officer stood in the parking lot and just watched the big box burn to the ground. During the hour it took to burn, the XO must have saluted two hundred soldiers who came by.

During the Boxer Rebellion in China, around 1900, the 9th Infantry commander was mortally wounded and his last dying words during the battle were: "Keep Up The Fire," obviously referring to the volume of rifle fire directed towards the enemy. Ever since those dying words were uttered, the Regimental motto has been "Keep Up The Fire." The motto is verbalized when Manchu soldiers (another nickname from China) salute one another. The Executive Officer was forced to stand in front of the burning embarrassment and salute every single soldier, each one screaming at the top of his lungs "Keep Up The Fire." He was royally pissed off for the first fifty salutes and then his whole demeanor changed and each time he returned a salute with an echoed "Keep Up The Fire," he and the soldier both smiled. I, on the other hand, had to write a wickedly long report about the fire and explain how we could ever possibly get along with so much essential equipment all burned up. Thank God that bitch was gone.

I knocked off early and went to the Officers Club at 1800 (6 PM). I spoke a few kind words to Miss Yi. She was the hottest thing I'd seen all day and I just witnessed a fire hot enough to melt a metal CONEX container. I always wanted to "date" her but she was too discreet to do anything like that. I ate a plate of rice and went to the Quonset hut early. I was listening to the Armed Forces Korean Network radio station when I heard the announcement that a nation wide practice blackout would take place at 2100 (9 PM), two hours away. I made a mental resolution to remain awake until then and observe the blackout as I would an eclipse of the sun.

At 2045 (8:45 PM), I was sitting on the concrete walk behind my Quonset hut with my legs dangling over the bluff overhanging the perimeter fence and the river. I had a small pitcher of Tang next to me. It was the last of my ration for that month. Gung Ho Joe came out to watch the blackout also. He had a steaming cup of hot chocolate. Even though it was still early in the month, I'd long since used up my ration of cocoa. It's funny how I never really wanted Tang or cocoa until they told me I couldn't have it anymore.

As the moment of the blackout approached, we were joined by the chaplain, drinking part of his ration of beer; the S-4 Supply Officer, drinking his ration of whiskey and smoking his rationed cigarettes and finally the Assistant S-3 (AIR) appeared with a six-pack of rationed Coca Colas.

We were all sitting ducks in a line with our feet hanging over the concrete edge of the building foundation. We synchronized our watches and waited for the lights to go out in the village across the river. Gradually they began to fade, one house at a time and a section of streetlights, here and there, until the village was completely dark. Our Quonset hut lights went off, the compound lights extinguished and then to everyone's surprise, the bright security floodlights on the bridge went black. We sat for a few seconds. The only light was the quarter moon and it was low in the sky and partially obscured by clouds. I could barely see my buddies sitting next to me.

"Damn, it's dark," someone said in awe.

"I don't like this. How long is this supposed to last?"

"Infiltrator heaven," another one said.

"Don't start that shit," said the S-4.

"I wonder if the Bridge Platoon knows about the blackout or do they think something's wrong?" I asked no one in particular.

"Sshh—did you hear it?" someone said.

"Don't start that shit," said the S-4.

"No fooling, I heard something in the bushes on the river bank."

There was complete silence for a moment as we all listened.

"Don't start that shit," the S-4 said for the third time.

Just as the S-4 spoke, I thought I heard something move and so did the chaplain because he shushed the guys again and said, "I heard it."

We all stood up in unison. Gung Ho Joe's cocoa spilled over the edge and splattered on the ground near the fence.

The assistant S-3 (AIR) said, "Listen," and I was aware of a quick motion as if he threw something towards the river. Within seconds, we heard a crash near the river as the full can of Coke, that the S-3 (AIR) had just thrown, fell through the trees and became buried in the tidal mud. We heard a secondary rustle of the bushes. It was impossible for the thrown Coke can to make the second noise.

We all used our favorite swear word, including the chaplain who dropped the F bomb. The S-3 (AIR) gave the intruder no time to recover from the first hurled can. He ripped off the next five from his six-pack and threw them in quick succession. The frenzy caught on as I heaved my glass of Tang and then the pitcher. The chaplain's beer and S-4's whiskey glass followed suit. Gung Ho Joe was pissed that he'd dropped his cocoa cup and didn't have anything to throw.

We went inside and made a few calls to see if everything was secure. I phoned the XO first and found out that the Companies had all been alerted that there would be a blackout; however, the bridge had been overlooked. I called the sergeant in Charge of the bridge to tell him that it was just a practice blackout and to put an extra man on the north end because we thought we heard something on the north bank.

Glancing at my watch, I noticed that the lights had been off for six minutes. My watch had a luminous dial for just such occasions. I heard a dull thud and a grunt come from the porch. I didn't know who it was but I could tell what had happened just from the sound. Someone had fallen in the concrete drainage ditch. These ditches varied in size from six inches deep to seven feet deep. The one outside my Quonset hut was only two feet deep but caused one hell of a jolt when it was stepped into accidentally. They call these ditches "turtle traps." When the new guy on the block falls into them, the turtle is considered trapped. Only new guys are allowed to be trapped, lest they be ridiculed severely.

I ran outside to see who was caught in the turtle trap. To my chagrin, it was the XO. He'd just "dropped in" to see if everything was under control. The XO limped to the door. "Are you hurt?" I asked.

"No," he said, "but I spilled my beer."

"You'll live."

We talked a few more minutes and I told him about our assault on the intruder. He made a joke about being arrested for black marketing; after all, we had thrown half a dozen rationed substances over the fence into the hands of Korean Nationals. Suddenly, all the lights came back on. With the illumination, the XO managed to make it safely back to his hooch.

I hit the sack at 2200 (10 PM) on the dot. I had an alarming dream about a man with a muddy face, slithering out of the river, crawling on his belly up to the perimeter fence with a jar of Tang in his hand. I was struggling to understand why the infiltrator's jar of Tang kept ringing. After the fourth ring, I woke up and realized that it was the hall phone. I heard someone answer it and I prayed that it wasn't for me. I glanced at my clock; it was 0100. It must be for me, *only I get calls in the middle of the night*. Sure enough, it was for me. It was the duty officer, who told me that the ROKs to our right killed two more infiltrators. I was supposed to "get on top of the situation" and brief the XO as soon as I had all necessary information compiled. "I'll see you in a minute," I said as I hung up the phone.

I got the shooting story details confirmed and went to the XO's hooch to make my report. Again, I had to wake him up in the middle of the night. I unfolded a map. "Long story short," I said, "a ROK ambush patrol was sent out to site Alpha-one-one, which is here," I pointed. The XO cocked his head so he could see a little better. "They killed an infiltrator who was wearing a uniform of a South Korean Army sergeant. There was a chase and they caught up with a second infiltrator. They wounded him and a third infiltrator is believed to have made it across the MDL into North Korea. Final tally, five South Korean soldiers killed, two wounded, one North Korean killed, and one wounded. First Corp thinks it was an isolated incident and so do I."

"How far away was this from us?"

I pointed on the map and made a few crude measurements with my fingers. "About thirty kilometers away," I said.

"Well, what in the hell are we doing up in the middle of the night?"

"The higher command wants us to take necessary precautions," I said.

"Then take precautions," he said, "use a rubber, and go to bed."

"Yes, Sir," I said with a smile and went to the rack. At 0330, day two of the commander's leave thankfully ended.

CHAPTER 8

Commander's Leave

Part II

Day three of the commander's leave started like normal, a 0530 wake-up and a splitting headache taking over where sleep left off. I was hoping that the last two days were not an indication of how things were going to go until the commander returned.

My job today was to inspect two Company arms rooms and a third Company for crime prevention. It should be a kick-back day. I needed a goof off day after two sleepless nights. I just finished inspecting Bravo Company arms room when I got a call from my office. Alpha Company, which was out in the field, had found a body. The duty jeep was sent for me and I was off to examine the remains. After a bumpy three and a half mile ride, we came upon the bivouac site of Alpha Company and I was greeted by one of their lieutenants.

My first thought when I saw the body was, *I wish I had a camera*. A perfectly preserved, medical textbook quality skeleton was sitting in the bottom of a foxhole. His clothes, except the boots, were long since rotted away. A leather bandolier of ammunition was slung across his chest from left to right and a rusted Type 97 rifle lay across his legs.

"How'd you find it?" I asked.

"The platoon was digging in but Sheridan, being the lazy ass that he is, found himself an already dug hole. It was dark and he just climbed in to go to sleep. When he woke up this morning, that", he pointed to the skeleton, "was sitting right next to him."

I stood at the edge of the fighting position staring at Mr. Bones. I couldn't figure out what killed him. The bones appeared to be intact, head bone connected to the neck bone and so forth.

"What do you want us to do with him?" asked the lieutenant.

"Does he have any grenades around him?" I asked.

"No."

"Then bag him up, ammo and all. I'll take him back with me. His weapon and cartridges appear to be the type used by the North Koreans back in the day. He's probably been down there for thirty years. We're giving the frogmen back to the North Koreans tomorrow at Panmunjom, maybe we can give this guy back too."

"I don't care where he goes," said the lieutenant. "Just get him out of here. Every time I walk away and come back, some asshole has stuck a cigarette in his mouth and they won't quit teasing Sheridan about sleeping with a boner."

Two anxious soldiers helped me bag up Mr. Bones. Our makeshift body bag was a double thick Hefty trash bag. I took it back to my Quonset hut and put it in the corner of my bedroom.

Right before I went to bed that night, I moved the bag of bones to my closet and shut the door. Anybody ought to be able sleep with a skeleton in the closet, right? Not me, two hours later, after not sleeping a wink, I moved the bones again to the latrine. After only fifteen minutes I was afraid that someone would find them and call me to do something about it so I decided to put them in the turtle trap outside. As I was transferring the bones to the turtle trap, I took a mental snapshot of myself. Here I was standing on a cliff overlooking the Imjin river, in a foreign country, in the middle of the night, in my underwear and flip flops, with a trash bag in my hand filled full of human remains. You just can't make this stuff up, it happens only in Korea. Another late night, purely self-inflicted.

On day four of the commander's leave, there was a layout of the dead frogmen and their equipment at the Joint Security Area's Headquarters building at Camp Kitty Hawk. None of the equipment could be traced to North Korean origins. The wetsuits were US Navy and the weapons were Czech made Skorpion machine pistols. There were about a dozen miniature claymore mines that were the size of a foot powder can. They could explode with the force of about two twelve gauge shotgun shells. There were also Japanese flashlights, German knives, civilian clothes, floats, medical supplies, and bags of rice. The bodies of the three mutilated frogmen were lying in a row wrapped in real body bags. My garbage sack of Mr. Bones was at the corner of the display. No one asked what it was and I guessed no one cared.

After I toured the weapons/equipment/body layout, I spent the rest of the time around the battalion area. The battalion was on standby, just in case there was trouble at Panmunjom. The North Koreans eventually stormed out of the negotiation leaving the mess for us to clean up. The frogmen bodies were subsequently buried on South Korean soil in unmarked graves. Their weapons were turned over to a museum that the South Korean government had erected. The museum displayed war relics and kept an account of all North Korean hostile actions. Not buried with the frogmen and never seen again, Mr. Bones is considered to be missing in action.

At 1700 (5 PM), I was in the Officer's Club talking to Miss Yi. She had just brought me a diet soda when I asked her about her family. She blushed a little and bowed her head. Another officer came up and ordered a beer and Miss Yi walked off quickly.

"What's wrong with her?" asked my companion.

"I don't know," I said sipping my drink, "I just asked her about her family when she clammed up."

"It's kind of a jaded story," Miss Yi returned with a beer as my friend became silent for a moment. When she went to another table, he resumed talking. "I think she's married to an ex-ROK soldier. He was hurt somehow and lost one leg or both, I don't know which is true, but you know how the ROKs are. They'll use you up and then throw you away. It's a real shame, just use you up and throw you away, ya know," he said again as he took swig of the beer.

"Yeah, just use you up and throw you away," I repeated to no one in particular as I stared at Miss Yi across the room.

"You know," he paused for effect, "one of the frogmen was carrying an automatic pistol with a silencer on it?" He waited for my reaction. I gave a dramatic pause myself and then said, "That's classified," and gave him a wink.

For some reason the club was filled with rowdy officers. I guess since the battalion commander was gone, the guys all knocked off early. When the officers were at the peak of rowdiness, the senior combat arms officer "opened the range," and a hail of beer cans ricochet off the XO's plate over the fireplace.

At 2230 (10:30 PM), the management ran all the stragglers out of the club. We moved the party down to the company commanders' hooches. Someone managed to scrounge up a projector and three somewhat dubious "training films" (really old porno flicks).

"If you won't fuck, then you won't fight," was one philosophy that floated around the military. We'd been trained to fight all our careers. These films were to enlighten us on the different techniques of fucking. We saw all the techniques too. Each position seemed more comical than the first. We saw your basic man on top, woman on top, side by side, dog style, lazy dog style (that's where you doing dog style and fall over) two on one, three on one, two on two, oral, anal, and the proverbial toe fuck.

The old films didn't have a sound track. All that could be heard was the clicking of the projector. Officers yelled out dialogue. One officer, with absolute perfect timing, said, "Excuse me Ma'am, you have a smudge on your nipple, let me get that for you." At that precise moment, the actor in the film bent down and began sucking and slobbering all over the female actress's breast. It was hilarious. It's one of those *you had to be there* situations but it was the lighter side of the battalion commander's leave. At 0200 the party broke up and the officers began to meander back to their respective hooches to sleep. As always, the telephone rang and startled the whole populace of the Quonset hut awake.

Day five began when I answered the phone and discovered that there had been another shooting somewhere on the coast. The ROK Navy was involved and I was supposed to get the details. I got dressed and found myself in my office at 0530. I started dialing the phone, contacting half a dozen agencies and no one had any answers for me. Brigade snubbed me, division told me to go through brigade. The ROKs didn't give up information very easily so they were of no use. I called the Combined Field Army, the new name for First Corp Group. They told me that there had been a SCUNK boat incident down at Pohang Harbor.

"Do you have any details?" I asked hopefully.

"None, but you can call the Navy Department at the Combined Forces Command."

"Okay, I'll do that. By the way, where is Pohang?"

"Well," the telephone voice answered, "it's the asshole of the rabbit."

"What are you talking about?" I asked.

"Do you have a map of North and South Korea handy?"

"Yes."

"Well take a good look at it. Doesn't it look like a rabbit?"

"Yes."

"See that little spot that sticks out and makes the tail?"

"Yes."

"That's Pohang; the tail of the rabbit is Pohang."

"You're right, now one more question."

"Sorry, I don't have time."

"What's a SCUNK boat?" I yelled into a dead telephone.

As I hung up the receiver, I looked at the map intently and sure 'nough, the Koreas looked like a rabbit. My compound was located just about at the forepaw armpit. *It figures, the armpit is about par for this place.*

I called the Combined Forces Command and got someone who directed me to 8th Army Headquarters. I called there but they told me to call Combined Forces Command. I called them again and I got a sailor on the other end of the line. I got passed around the Navy Department for a few minutes and then ended up with a Naval captain. He explained that a SCUNK boat is an acronym that stands for Surface Craft, Unidentified, North Korean.

At noon I reported to the XO at the staff meeting and began the briefing.

"At 0240 this morning, a ROK Navy gunboat pulled up beside a small fishing trawler flying the South Korean flag. The trawler fired a rocket-propelled grenade into the hull of the ROK gunboat just above the water line. The SCUNK boat took off at a high rate of speed. The ROK gunboat tried to pursue but it was unable to continue because of the extensive damage to the hull. Two more gunboats were dispatched but were hours behind the SCUNK boat. At daylight, ROK Navy planes were sent out to locate the SCUNK boat. At 0620, the ROK Navy planes reported finding a fleet of fishing boats and attacked them. Two boats were sunk by rocket and machinegun fire from the airplanes. When the gunboats finally caught up to the fishing fleet, they found a man in a small dingy. He said that he had three other men with him but the planes killed two, who were found dead in the bottom of the boat and the third, had fallen overboard. A search of the dingy revealed that there were ten hand grenades hidden under the seats. The unidentified sailor has been taken into custody and is being interrogated at this very minute," I concluded.

The XO sat there as if he hadn't heard a word I said and then he asked, "What's a 'SCUNK' boat?"

Several officers in the briefing felt compelled to answer, "It stinks." "It's black and white." "It's supposed to be powered by squirrels but this being the Land of the Not Quite Right…" Everyone laughed.

I told the XO that it stood for "Surface Craft, Unidentified, North Korean." Then I asked, "Did you know that Korea looks like a rabbit?" Everyone cracked up again. It took fifteen minutes to defend myself by producing a map and outlining the rabbit.

After the meeting, my time was taken up with writing an SOP for patrolling at the bridge. Since Denny Johns and I slithered our way around the north bank, I discovered that we had broken every rule in the patrolling book so I was in the process of rewriting the book. An arduous task that took all day.

The sun was beginning to set over the North Korean Mountains. Where we lived on the DMZ, *The sun never set on South Korea.* I should sell that slogan to the tourist bureau. On the other hand, they say, *It's not hell, but you can see it from here.* I don't think they would go for that one.

I answered the phone on the second ring. It was my Korean security guard platoon leader inviting me to a party in my honor tomorrow. I graciously accepted because it's extremely hard to refuse Korean hospitality.

I headed to the club at 1930 (7:30 PM). I ordered a hamburger instead of rice. Miss Yi was in fine form that night. She switched from winter uniform, long black pants, to summer uniform, short skirt with black stockings. Every soldier who came into the club that night commented on the fact that her legs just came right up and made an ass out of themselves. Her face blushed continuously. She was just setting my two hamburgers and fries on the table when Miss Kim called me to the phone. I made a growling sound as I got up to get the phone.

"Poor lieutenant Oh," Miss Yi said. She couldn't pronounce my last name, but most Americans couldn't either.

I threw the phone down and flew out of the club screaming, "Where's the XO?"

Someone yelled, "He's in his hooch," as I went careening down the hill. I found him in the shower.

"Sir," I yelled over the running water, "the bridge has spotted some frogmen. I don't know any details. I'm on my way down in the duty officer's jeep. Yours is on the way."

"I'll be down in a minute," I heard him say as I ran off up the hill.

I reached the bridge in a matter of minutes. There were a dozen guys on the bridge with rifles and bandoliers of ammunition. My jeep roared up and skidded to a stop on the wooden planks. "Who's in charge?" I yelled as I dismounted.

"I am, Sir."

"And who are you?" I couldn't see him in the dark.

"Sergeant Henderson."

"What's the story?" I walked to the edge of the rail, and the sergeant began his report.

"Not much to it, Sir. Private Kang saw a frogman swimming up river...."

"Up river?" I interrupted. That was headed back towards North Korea and more surprising, against the current.

"Yes, Sir, Private Kang raised his rifle to fire but the swimmer went underwater. I saw him for an instant myself. Second shift was alerted and we've been watching closely."

The sergeant stopped talking. "I want to talk to the KATUSA who saw him first?" I said. He was standing right next to me but I didn't know it. I asked him to explain to me what he saw. The KATUSA started to speak the best English he knew how. It was hard for me to interpret but when he started making the motions of a swimming man, I understood completely.

Within minutes the XO bounced to a halt in his jeep just behind mine. He stepped out and asked the same questions I did and got the same answers. It was the Army way. The XO stood, bewildered, in the middle of the bridge.

"Has it been reported to brigade?" asked the XO after some time.

"Yes, Sir," I said.

"Who authorized it?"

"I told the duty officer to report it?" I said rather weakly.

"I think that it might have been a bad idea." he said a little agitated.

"Sir, the general is coming to Camp Greaves tomorrow. When he passes over this bridge and one of the guards tells him about seeing a frogman and hearing that we didn't do anything about it, he'll fire us, court marshal us and then send us some place worse than the DMZ."

"Yeah, you're probably right. Well hell. Let's get it cleaned up. I'll call Colonel Lee, the 4th ROK battalion commander, and get him to alert his troops. Get me a full report and brief me in my hooch in one hour."

I'd done the same old drudge a dozen times before, alerting guards, checking facts, and writing a chronological report. I could nearly do it blind folded, asleep, and with one arm tied behind my back.

An hour and fifteen minutes later I was briefing the XO in his hooch when the duty officer called. I sat quietly as the XO spoke into the receiver, "When?" he asked and then, "Okay, I'll meet him there." Hanging up the phone, he said " Well, that will stretch your rectum." I couldn't help but laugh.

"What's the deal, Sir?" I asked.

"The brigade commander wants us on the bridge in thirty minutes. He's driving up from Camp Howze."

We met the brigade commander on the bridge. He's a man of few words and generally conveys himself in a reserved manner. He was true to form and said very few things to us. He just paced up and down on the bridge with his hands behind his back, helmet strapped down tightly on his head, and flak jacket pulled up snugly around his chin. The XO and I stalked along behind him, hoping he would dismiss us. But he didn't. We just paced up and down with our hands behind our backs, looking like the Marx brothers.

"I think I'll spend the night at Camp Greaves," he said.

"Shit," I heard the XO say under his breath. I just smiled.

"The general will be here in...." the brigade commander looked at his watch, "... in two and a half hours. I want you and the lieutenant to meet him here then."

"Shit," I said under my breath this time.

It was 0300. The fifth and sixth days of the commander's leave were quickly flowing together. Back to my room, I knew better than try to sleep, so I wrote letters and read the seven year old Playboy. The jeep came for me at 0500. The XO was already in it.

"I feel terrible," I told him and climbed into the back seat.

"Did you sleep?" he asked.

"No."

"Me either," and we drove away.

We were twenty minutes ahead of the general's party. The XO and I were standing on the north end of the bridge and the brigade commander was on the south end. We got a call from the south end informing us that the general's party was headed to the middle of the bridge and they wanted us out there. We walked to the center of the bridge to meet the three generals: two, two-star generals and one, one-star general.

As we approached, the XO said, "Am I seeing stars or what?"

"If you are, I am."

We popped about a half dozen salutes apiece. If you had seen us from a distance we looked like we were swatting flies or fanning farts. Luckily our division commander, one of the major generals (two-star), was just showing the other major general around. The brigadier general (one-star) was our assistant division commander (for support) and was going to perform a semi-annual inspection of some kind. After we explained what happened last night, which took five minutes, we were dismissed.

"What was the big deal?" I asked.

"I can't believe I stayed up all night for that," said the XO.

I was back in my room at 0615 trying to figure out what to do next. I thought, *I'll just lie down and think about it a while.* Immediately, I feel asleep. I became a little conscious when Mr. Yi, my houseman, opened my door.

He asked, "You no workee today?"

I don't remember what I answered but he left in a huff.

At 0800 on the dot, the hall phone started to ring. I was in a deep slumber and I didn't realize that the phone was ringing until the fourth or fifth ring. I jumped out of bed to run for the door. I must have been lying on my wounded left leg in a strange way because it was asleep, completely numb. At the high velocity that I shot out of bed and with one numb leg, I was totally out of control. I immediately listed left, bounced off my desk, which was in the exact opposite direction from the door, and then I fell, head first, into my open closet. On several occasions I've succeeded in embarrassing myself, even when I was the only one around. This was one of those occasions.

I scraped myself off the back wall of the closet and limped down the hall to the phone. The call was my sergeant wanting to know if I overslept.

"Yeah, I guess I did," I told him, if you consider lying down for one hour and thirty minutes sleeping.

After preparing for the day I made a quick walk through the Headquarters building before going into my bunker. I didn't see the XO anywhere. I told my sergeant about the generals and the bridge. He apologized for calling me and said that he wouldn't have done it if he had known I'd been up all night.

I had little work to do, thank goodness. Mostly, I sat around, holding my head in my hands. I got word at midmorning, as soon as all of the brass left, the XO was reported to be temporarily KIA (killed in action) in his bedroom. At 1100, I told my sergeant that something exciting better happen or I'd fall asleep.

"Why don't you go take a nap? I'll cover for you here," he said.

"I think I'll go get a haircut and then eat lunch in my hooch…maybe lie down for a minute or two."

"God idea," said my sergeant, "wish I thought of it." He smiled at me.

I walked into the barbershop and I'll be damned if the XO wasn't sitting there with a green mudpack on his face asleep in the chair. I just smiled and sat down beside him in the middle chair. Miss Pae came over to service me. I ordered a deluxe and laid back to enjoy. Somewhere between the mudpack and facial massage, I heard the XO say, "Goodnight S-2," as he walked out of the door.

Fifty-three minutes later I was clean-shaven, massaged, mudpacked and had my haircut. I went to my room to sleep.

Two hours later the phone rang. It was Sergeant Pettit, "We've got a sergeant from the mortar platoon, Combat Support Company, who needs to talk to you."

"What about?" I asked.

"He's found some mines—"

I cut him off, "I'll be down in a minute." I threw my fatigues on and headed for the bunker.

A dirty, rock-hard looking sergeant was waiting for me. He explained that his mortar firing pits were within ten meters of two anti-tank mines stacked on top of each other. "Some old Papa-san must have piled them up," he said. We lit out in the sergeant's jeep.

Someone had definitely been fooling around with these mines. Luckily, the fuses appeared to be removed. The sergeant and I walked around a little and saw at least ten more mines in the tall grass, which was more than enough for me. We went back to the Headquarters and I reported to all the company commanders that there was an unmarked minefield near firing point 501.

I called my buddies on the EOD team (Explosive Ordinance Disposal). They couldn't make it up to the Z until the next day, so I had to wait. I just hoped no one would kill themselves until the EOD guys arrived. I checked my charts and this minefield was considered to be cleared. The fuses may have been removed but high explosives were still in them.

Once back in my bunker, Sergeant Pettit reminded me that I had a party to go to that night. I'd forgotten all about it. "I don't know if I can stand it. I'm beat."

"I think you can muster the strength," said Sergeant Pettit, smiling. He smiled at me a lot.

It was 1700 (5 PM) and the second in command of the Korean Security Guards came in and reminded me to attend the party. He said he would pick me up at 1900 (7 PM) at the front gate.

I said, "Okay," and he left. I laid my head down on the desk and rested. I think I actually fell asleep for about 20 minutes. The phone rang. I never got a break. Sergeant Pettit answered it.

"Yes, Sir, He's here. Just a moment."

"Who is it?" I said.

"It's the XO."

I answered the phone immediately. "I'll get right on it," my last words into the phone. "Sergeant Pettit, there's been a shooting at the bridge. I'll be down there for a while." I picked up my flak jacket, changed my mind, and let it drop to the floor.

I couldn't find a vehicle, so I double-timed to the bridge. It took me ten minutes. It was only a short mile, but there's a real heartbreak hill in the middle and my leg hurt a little.

An E-5 sergeant named Zok met me at the north end of the bridge. Sergeant Zok was the heavyweight-boxing champion of Fort Bragg, North Carolina. Fort Bragg is the home of the 82nd Airborne Division and they all think they're a bunch of bad asses. You have to whip a paratroopers pride before you can whip him and that's hard to do. However, Zok managed to whip them all, he was undefeated. I asked Sergeant Zok what happened.

"We fired a warning shot at a boat."

"Which one?" I asked.

"It's the one going around the bend, red sail, two men in it."

"Okay, tell me exactly what happened," I pulled out a pad of sweaty paper and a pen. Forty-five minutes later I had all the information I was ever going to get. Now all I had to do was account for the one expended round of ammunition.

At 1815 (6:15 PM), I was in the FBSP (Freedom Bridge Security Platoon) barracks talking with the armorer about the missing round that had just been fired. When I inventoried his ammunition and checked it with the paper work everything indicated that all of the rounds were accounted for because his platoon sergeant slipped the armorer another round of the same lot number within minutes after the shot was fired. I called the platoon sergeant in and gave him a good talkin' to about proper procedure. He let it go in one ear and out the other as most platoon sergeants did when staff lieutenants talk to them that way.

The Platoon phone rang and it was for me so I cut my lecture short by saying, "Do the proper paperwork tonight before lights out." I answered the call and Sergeant Pettit told me that brigade had called and wanted to know what the shooting was about.

"I haven't reported it yet," I said. "How did they find out?"

"I don't know," said Pettit, "but they also want a description of the boat and people in it and all the other particulars."

"Hold 'em off for me. I'll be back in fifteen minutes with the answers."

I hung up the phone and ran out the door jogging around the bend in the road and started up the hill. My knee began to throb, then burst into waves of pain. I actually had to double up to fight the urge to scream. A minute went by and the pain subsided enough where I could walk the rest of the way.

The second in command of the Korean Security Guards was waiting for me at the front gate. *Hell, I'd forgotten all about the party.* I explained to him that it would be a few minutes. He said okay and waited.

I went to the XO's office and explained what happened at the bridge. I told him that we had a snitch who was reporting directly to brigade and I needed two hours off the compound this evening to go to a party.

He was taken back a little as it all soaked in and then he said, "Find the son-of-a-bitch who doesn't report through channels and have him report to me tomorrow morning at 0800," he smiled and then he said, "Have a good time at the party."

I went back to my bunker and called brigade. It took me twenty minutes to give my report because there was a Spec/4 on the other end copying everything I said down word for word. I asked him who initially reported the incident. He said a sergeant from the Bridge Platoon. I called the bridge and had all the sergeants E-5 to E-7 standing in a line for when I got there. I was in civilian clothes and my mode of transportation was a Korean security car. Most Korean cars were made by a company called Hyundai, commonly called "High and Dries." In 1980 these cars were a piece of crap and I was sure that they would never catch on any where but Korea. I got my Korean Security Guard to pull over his piece of crap Hyundai Moonbeam, or whatever the hell it was, at the bridge while I went to interrogate the sergeants. After a short cross examination, the platoon sergeant I'd just chewed out about not doing the proper paperwork for the expended ammunition, confessed to calling brigade.

"Report to the battalion XO at 0800 tomorrow," and I left.

The party was in Munsan, the largest town within ten miles of the bridge. The second in command of the Korean Security Guards drove like a bandit. I think we hit a case of oranges on the side of the road by a vendor's stand. We went completely through town and stopped at a small building that resembled a hotel. We got out and entered a reception hall and I began to converse in broken English with some of the guards. They all looked like dirty old Korean men when they were in their civilian clothes. The Korean Security Guard uniforms gave them a more distinguished look.

The adjacent room was a dining room with a long table and cushions on the floor. The kitchen was the second room over where the women were milling around. All of them were dressed in traditional Korean dresses. The dresses were extremely colorful, but they didn't do much to accentuate the figure. There was a strap that went around the breasts that smashed them unmercifully flat.

After thirty minutes of conversation, we were seated. We sat man-woman-man-woman. I, being the guest of honor, had a rather plump Korean woman sitting directly behind me. She was there so I could lean back on her and use her as a pillow. What a wonderful culture.

Dinner was served. Drinks came first, both hands were used to pour, and the other person used both hands to hold the glass. Some nuts and dried fish were brought out next. Then they brought out three huge bowls of vegetables, an enormous bowl of rice and a plate of bulgoki, a cooked beef similar to teriyaki. Then a whole cooked fish was served to each man at the table. The girls on either side of me made sure that I didn't lift a finger. All I had to do was lean back on the plump woman while the other two fed me and gave me drink. The plump one would massage my neck and shoulders between bites and swallows. The food wasn't too bad although I passed up my portion of kimchee. Kimchee is cabbage that's been buried in the ground for months, fermented and peppered to an unbearable height of sour heat. The Koreans loved it. After eating kimchee, one can smell a Korean's breath a hundred feet away. If there were an unfavorable wind, two hundred feet!

It was getting pretty late, about 2130 (9:30 PM). The last military bus ran north of the river at 2200 (10:00 PM). I had thirty minutes to get there but the Korean head honcho wouldn't let me leave. He picked out a girl for me and led me to a hotel room. I entered with the girl; assuming that she was to sexually satisfy me. It took her ten minutes to untie all the strings on the yellow traditional dress and let it drop to the floor. I was astonished to see that she was wearing a form of long-johns underneath. She removed them quickly and reclined on the only piece of furniture in the room, a mattress.

I removed my clothes and moved towards her. She pointed to the light switch and I turned out the overhead bulb. It was completely dark in the windowless room. I groped around a little bit until I found the mattress. Then the rest was by memory and instincts. It took the girl longer to undress than it did for me to finish. It was a pretty much slam-bam "comsamnida" (Korean thank you) ma'am. I turned on the light and started getting dressed. It was eight minutes until the last bus. I pulled out my wallet and flipped her a ten-dollar bill. She grabbed it up and clutched it to her breast. "For me?" she exclaimed in what I thought was genuine excitement. She must have already been paid for her services. The ten was just a tip. I imagine she only got paid about a thousand Won, the going rate for Koreans who paid prostitutes. Being American, I would have to pay ten times that amount which I pretty much just did.

I went flying out of the hotel, running towards the street. The Korean Security head honcho was standing at the corner waving me on like a third base coach. A taxi was waiting and I slid into the back seat with a grunt, "Take me to the bridge." The head honcho doled out a couple of thousand Won bills, said good-bye and I sped away through the narrow streets to the highway. I sat back and reminisced about the evening. Sometimes I wondered why I hated this place so badly.

We came to the bridge and I was greeted by some of my guards. Korean taxis were not allowed to cross the bridge and soldiers were highly discouraged to walk across the bridge in civilian clothes. Anyway, I didn't want to emerge on the other side in front of the ROK compound after dark wearing suspicious looking attire. I gave the staff duty officer a call.

"I missed the last bus. How about sending the jeep down to get me." It was my good buddy, Denny Johns. He said he'd come down in a minute because he had to check the bridge anyway.

The guards I'd been talking to told me about an incident with the MPs that had occurred a couple of hours before. The MPs evidently came across the bridge going north without ever stopping. It was a stupid thing to do. It could have gotten someone killed or it could have caused a traffic jam on the one lane bridge. Since they were "real" MPs, they felt that they didn't have to stop for anyone.

Lieutenant Johns showed up at 2230 (10:30 PM), the same time the last bus came from the north to the south. I told Denny about the MPs and he said that when he talked to the guards at the other end of the bridge, they said that the MPs shot them the finger and called them pussies. Denny looked at me,

"Have you got a few minutes?" he asked.

"Sure," I said, "What've you got cooked up?" He just held his finger up to indicate wait and see.

Denny went into the guard shack and made a couple of phone calls. Then we waited. At 2300 (11 PM), the guards at the other end of the bridge called and said that the MPs were there. I heard Denny say, "Okay, just hold them there." There was a pause, "Until I tell you to," he concluded. The MPs sat at one end of the bridge, six hundred meters away and we sat at the other end. Forty minutes went by and this time, the MPs called us. Lieutenant Johns talked to them, "The bridge is closed for security reasons," I heard him say and then he hung up. He came out of the shack shaking his head.

"How much longer do you think they'll wait?" I asked.

"Probably not much longer."

At the stroke of midnight, headlights popped on and started moving towards us. The phone rang simultaneously and the north end guards said that the MPs just took off through the barricade, without permission. Denny and I scrambled into our jeep and sped towards the center of the bridge, meeting them halfway. Since the bridge was only wide enough for one vehicle at a time, we made them back up on the narrow railroad ties for three hundred meters. We all got out of our jeeps and met for a Pow-Wow. The MPs were very pissed off. They started to voice an opinion when Lieutenant Johns cut them off. He asked, "Why did you cross the bridge?"

"We're MPs, we can do what we want." Of all the things he could have said, that was about the worst. Lieutenant Johns called over five of our guards, armed with M-16s. He told the MPs, "You are under arrest for disobeying an order and causing a serious breach in our security." He then pulled a little card out of his wallet and started reading, "You have the right to remain silent..."

"You can't arrest us, we're MPs."

"SHUT THE FUCK UP!" and there was silence.

"This is Lieutenant Osterhout," continued Lieutenant Johns, "he's in charge of security north of the river. He's a plain-clothes intelligence officer and knows that you didn't really have a mission up here. All you did was take your buddy on a tour with a military vehicle, which is another violation. Lieutenant Osterhout was in the middle of an important surveillance mission that you just screwed up and by screwing up that mission, you screwed up the plans to expose a spy ring." I just kept quiet and tried to keep a stern look on my face, which was a pretty tough job considering all of the bullshit that Lieutenant Johns was spouting.

He finished reading the two MPs their rights. "Sergeant," he said to one of our guards, "take their weapons and tie them up until the MPs can come take them away."

"But we are the MPs," one of them said.

"I'm talking about the Korean MPs," said Lieutenant Johns and the two American MPs faces blanched white. Korean MPs would beat the hell out of them for no reason except the shear enjoyment of beating someone. One of our bridge guards went into the shack and called the south end of the bridge and pretended like he was talking to the Korean MP Company.

"Wait," one of them said. As the bridge guards started to tie up the MPs.

"Please wait?" one MP begged. He was a private first class and had probably been out of Military Police School for all of two weeks.

Lieutenant Johns asked, "What do you want?"

"You're right, Sir. We've screwed up everything. We apologize, don't we?" he looked over at his buddy who was either pissed or sick, I couldn't tell which one, but he looked a little green.

"Yes, Sir, we won't ever come north of the river again unless we have a valid mission. I swear it, Sir."

"Well," said Lieutenant Johns, "I don't know. You disobeyed my orders and misappropriated a government vehicle for personal use but you ruined his secret mission," Lieutenant Johns' pointed to me. "I don't know if I can let your inexcusable actions go without some sort of punishment."

"It won't happen again," blurted the sick looking MP corporal.

"You're damn right it won't, because you're going to be in jail or under the bridge with the Korean MPs next time. I'm getting tired of you. Now get the hell out of MANCHU land! North of the river is ours, gentlemen, do you understand that?"

"Yes, Sir," said in unison.

"Get their names and cut them loose, sergeant," Lieutenant Johns instructed the bridge guards, "and call the Korean MPs and tell them that we won't need them anymore." Lieutenant Johns gave me a wink.

It was 0100 when I finally hit the sack. My alarm sounded at 0530. I turned it off and sat up wondering, *what the hell happened.* I couldn't believe that I had slept all night long (if you call four and a half hours all night long) without a single interruption. I dressed and went to the chow hall. Breakfast wasn't half bad either. The cooks somehow came up with some fresh oranges, a real treat. I went to my bunker and was joined by my staff. I took great lengths in explaining how good the previous night had been. I guess the most impressive things were the fat girl that I got to lean back on and the uninterrupted four and a half hours sleep.

After the staff briefing, I was in the Headquarters building and saw the platoon sergeant from the bridge standing in the foyer. He waited a moment and then knocked on the XO's door and entered. I waited patiently for eighteen minutes. The sergeant emerged from the office a different man. He saw me and walked over.

"Sir," he said, "I'll get that bridge squared away it if's the last thing I do."

"I'm sure you will," I said and he left. I don't know what the XO did or said, but it was extremely effective. I went back to the bunker experiencing a great degree of satisfaction. Next on the agenda: taking the Explosive Ordnance Disposal Team (EOD) to the minefield.

CHAPTER 9

Commander's Leave

Part III

At a little after 1000 hours, the EOD guys came into my office. We'd become fairly good friends in the last couple of months. They said that my unit had found more stuff for them to blow up than any other unit in Korea. I beamed like a new daddy. I was proud of my guys. I could send them out on a patrol inside of the DMZ and they'd come back with a treasure chest of policed up items; shoes and boots, clothing, half eaten food, four different types of barbed wire, half a dozen pictures of footprints, propaganda leaflets and about a dozen other things that I thought were absolutely fascinating. My guys were great!

I saddled up with my flak jacket and helmet. The EOD sergeants laughed at me.

"Where you goin' with that stuff on?" one of them asked.

"Same place you are," I said.

"We're not wearing any of that junk."

"That's okay by me," I said, "When you hit one of those mines I don't plan on taking any shrapnel."

"We're not planning on hitting a mine," the other laughed.

"You're not going to embarrass me into taking this off," I said with a smile.

We got in the EOD jeep with red lights on top and drove to the suspected minefield. As we approached the bridge spanning the nearby creek, I got the driver to slow to a dead crawl.

"There are minefield signs and fences on the left," I pointed to the red triangle signs as we went by. "But I don't see any on the right. My charts show that it should be on both sides of the road." We all stretched our necks and looked back and forth several times.

"I don't see any markers out there," the EOD staff sergeant pointed to the right.

"That's why you're here," I said. "It's packed full of mines." We pulled off the road and parked the jeep near the creek bed under the bridge.

"Tell Headquarters that we'll be calling in every thirty minutes," the EOD staff sergeant instructed the driver.

We all went to the mortar pit with the two mines stacked up together.

"Have you ever seen this kind before?" I asked.

"Yeah, they have two fuse wells, one for the pressure fuse and one for the anti-handling fuse. Since somebody piled these bastards up, I assume that they don't have anti-handling fuses. As you can see, the main fuse well is empty." He ran his finger down a hole on top of the mine.

"Do they still have the explosives in them?" I asked.

"They appear to," he picked one up, "they weigh about right."

We began to look around.

"There's one."

"Here's another."

"There's two together."

After it was all done, we had found forty. That's over six hundred pounds of explosives lying on the ground.

"Hey, come here and look at this."

I walked over to see. It was a cylindrical piece of metal about the shape of a medium size cigar. It had three prongs sticking out of one end.

"It looks like a contact fuse," I said.

"It is," said the sergeant, "but this fuse is for an anti-personnel mine. These other mines we've been finding are anti-tank mines."

"Isn't that how mine fields are set up?" I asked. "Two anti-personnel mines for every anti-tank mine or something like that?"

"That's right. I was hoping that we wouldn't find any of these."

The staff sergeant said, "Let's spread out and see if we can find some of these anti-personnel mines."

"Okay," I said, "I'll spread out over by the jeep. You experts can comb the tall grass."

"What's wrong, not your cup of tea?" the sergeant asked jokingly.

"You broke the code," I said, "Can't we just get some Bangalore torpedoes or something and shove in here and clear the whole place?" I asked.

"Let us make the recommendations. You just take it easy by the jeep. You're the officer, you know."

I got half way to the jeep when I heard something that sounded like a firecracker going off. I whirled around in time to see the sergeant caught in a white tuft of smoke and then he slumped to the ground. The other EOD man ran over to him.

"What happened?" I yelled.

"It's alright!" the sergeant returned. I saw the two men stand up and start to walk out. In a minute they were next to me.

"What happened?" I repeated my question.

The sergeant said, "I stepped on a discarded fuse. It scared me so bad that my knees buckled. It felt like someone hit me in the bottom of my foot with a sledge hammer."

"And you wonder why I wore my gear," I said adjusting the helmet on my head.

"I've seen enough," said the staff sergeant. "I saw at least two small round anti-personnel mines called toe poppers. They're designed to maim not kill."

"Good name," I said, "now that we know what's in there, what are we going to do about it?"

"I suggest you turn it over to the engineers," said the staff sergeant. "They will probably blow them in place."

We drove in silence the rest of the way back to Camp Greaves where I said goodbye to the EOD team. I entered the bunker and called the engineers assigned to support us. They were billeted twelve miles to our rear and would need a day notice before they could get up to the Z. I talked to Lieutenant Grimes who was a platoon leader in B Company 2nd Engineer Battalion. He agreed to meet me at the Headquarters building at 1000 hours the next day. I told my sergeant that I was going to take a long lunch and I would be in my hooch if anyone wanted me. It was a bright, clear, warm, spring day. I should have been on a baseball diamond or on a lakeside, fishing instead of at the edge of the DMZ.

I decided that I'd take a quick bowl of ramen at the KATUSA Snack Bar. The snack bar was constructed for our KATUSA soldiers so they would have a place to go to hang out and eat native foods. It was open to anyone as long as they could pay the price. As I passed the barbershop, I stuck my head in and said, "Hello," to the barbershop girls. I paid my thirty cents for a bowl of steaming noodles and devoured it quickly. I felt stuffed but I'll be damned if I wouldn't be hungry again in an hour.

I went to my room and sat at my desk flipping through my little black book trying to figure out who I could write. Halfway through the first page of a letter, the phone rang and I crushed the sheet of paper into my fist and dropped it into the trashcan on the way out to get the phone.

"Hello."

"This is Captain Benson."

"Yes, Sir, what can I do for you?"

"Listen, my guys found another body. Can you take care of it for me? I'm pinched for time."

"Yes, Sir, I sure will."

"Could you see my first sergeant at my orderly room?"

"Yes, Sir, I'll be right up there."

"Thanks, LT (lieutenant)."

It was the Alpha Company commander. The boys had scrounged up another body. I locked my door and headed for the bus stop. Digging through my pockets, I came up with a bus token for the Myung Jin bus company. Altogether, it took fifteen minutes to get up to Camp Liberty Bell. I went to the Alpha Company orderly room and found the first sergeant.

"Sir, I'm glad you're here," he said.

"What's the problem, Top (first sergeant)?"

"Let me tell you the damnedest thing."

"Alright," I said.

"I got a squad up on that ridge where we have Local Dispersal Areas. They're digging a small perimeter of fighting positions and sandbaggin' 'em. We had this KATUSA in the bottom of one position with a pick." The first sergeant paused just long enough to spit a mouthful of tobacco juice into the trashcan.

He continued. "Well, this KATUSA took a pow'rful stroke like ol' John Henry and broke through something hard." The first sergeant laughed a bit, "He thought it was a tunnel and jumped out of the hole and shagged ass down the hill. The squad leader ran after him and tackled him in the middle of the road. He was stark raving mad so the squad leader punched him in the face, twice, before the little bastard calmed down." The first sergeant spat again. "That KATUSA went back to work in the hole with a shovel. He cleared away a couple of boards that were on the bottom of the hole and continued to dig. Three shovel's full later, up come a skull on the shovel." The first sergeant roared with laughter. "Gawd Damn, Sir, that KATUSA jumped fifteen foot straight up and hit the ground with his short legs a-churnin'. I mean everybody looked like they was backing up compared to him. It took the whole squad to catch him this time." The first sergeant let out a great big Haw-Haw and continued his conversation. "Sir, could you go up there and see what you think about 'dem bones?"

"Sure," I said chuckling at the story. I walked out the main gate of the small compound. The Local Dispersal Area was only a couple of hundred meters away but I had to walk three quarters of a mile around a suspected minefield. It was marked, but last year about this time, five ROK soldiers cut across the field. Two came out completely unharmed, one remained in the middle of the field without either of his legs and the other two pretty much just disappeared and returned to the soil. Dust to dust.

I walked up on several guys digging a fighting position and filling sand bags. The KATUSA in question was sitting on a small hill twenty meters away. He was talking to himself. I had to laugh. *Poor son-of-a-bitch is ruined.*

The guys continued to dig as I walked up. Nobody spoke. A pile of bones lay disheveled at the edge of the foxhole. The bones weren't very impressive, not like the first skeleton anyway.

"Who's in charge?" I asked.

"Right now, I guess I am, Sir," a black Spec/4 said.

"Put those bones in a couple of bags and rebury them down the hill a little ways."

"Yes, Sir."

"You don't need to tell a lot of people about digging this guy up. Let's just let sleeping dogs lie."

"Yes, Sir."

I decided not to catch the bus and started walking back to Camp Greaves. I wanted to think for a while. It had been a very busy and sleepless seven days since the commander went on leave. The afternoon was warm and the sweat started to soak through my fatigues. Halfway through my hike, I wished I had waited on the bus.

When I got back to my bunker, I sat behind my desk and relaxed. The frozen ground from the winter made the bunker stay cool until the middle of summer. The bunker was naturally air-conditioned and everyone who walked in was surprised to feel the coolness. In the evenings, the bunker was cool enough for me to wear a field jacket. After leaning back with my feet propped up on the desk for ten minutes, I thought I better get busy. I pulled out a map of Korea and began plotting all the activity that we had in the last week. I put a little plastic flag at the location of every incident, the SCUNK boat, the frogmen, the ambush, the chance contact, the minefield, the skeletons, everything. The map was littered with flags when I finished. The purpose of the map was to brief the battalion commander when he returned from leave.

"Sir, I've got Staff Duty tonight, so I won't be in tomorrow," my sergeant interrupted the silence.

"Well, that's okay," I said. "You can handle all the bullshit that comes up tonight. Don't call me unless they're in the wire."

"I'm going to go and get ready then."

"Okay, I'll see you day after tomorrow," I paused. "The rest of you guys knock off too." The room cleared immediately.

At 2000 (8 PM), I made the final check of the bunker and locked it. It was deep into twilight, my favorite time of day. Instead of going to the hooch or to the club, I walked up on top of my bunker where the helipad was located. I sat down in the middle of the concrete helipad and laid back, looking up at the sky and relaxed.

I began to daydream about a particular incident that happened when I was seventeen, my first and only drunk. I'd just graduated from high school and my friend and I decided to camp out so we wouldn't get caught. We sent out to the local bootlegger for some wine, and presto, within the hour we had a half-gallon of Spanada and a fifth of Pagan Pink Ripple wine. We drove our second-hand pick up truck out to a campsite, consisting of a small fire pit and pup tent. We didn't exactly know what serious drinking was about but we got down to doing our version of it. We drank a whole half-gallon of wine in sixty-four consecutive shots. In a half hour, my friend and I looked at each other through rose-colored eyes and asked, "Are you drunk yet?"

"No, I don't think so."

We pulled out the fifth of Pagan Pink Ripple wine and began to pour some more shots. We drank twenty something more consecutive shots.

"Are you drunk yet?"

"Uh," I didn't have a response this time.

"Let's go swimming," he suggested.

My mind said "Hell no," but my body just went along with it.

The swimming hole was a good quarter-mile away, across an oat patch. It wasn't too hard getting there but when we undressed and jumped into the water, the wine hit us both...even harder than before. The water was only chest deep in the deepest part but we damn near drowned, numerous times.

I remembered standing waist deep in water and showing each other pictures of our girlfriends that we had in our wallets. Somewhere along the way we finished swimming, more like not drowning. Both of us were naked as jaybirds. I was too drunk to notice but it had become night. I crawled around the entire pond on my hands and knees and couldn't find my clothes. My buddy and I were lucky to find each other again. We got side by side and headed back towards the tent.

There was one medium sized mesquite tree between us and the campsite. One tree in the whole damn field and I walked right into it. The largest limb struck me just above the right eye and knocked me down. My friend walked on for a couple of minutes before he realized I wasn't walking next to him anymore. It took five minutes for him and me to get linked up again. A full hour went by before we got to the tent from the pond.

The tent, through drunken minds and in the dark, was a formidable foe. For the life of us, we couldn't figure out how to get into the thing. There were two zippers holding it together, one for the outside flap and one for the mosquito screen, but our combined IQ's were about two above rock and the zippers proved to be smarter than we were at the time. We gave up and collapsed on the top of the tent and went to sleep, (passed out would be a better description).

During the night I woke up once and realized that it was raining and I tried to cover the firewood with a piece of canvas. It also proved to be too difficult so I went back to sleep on top of the tent.

The sun woke us up about 0830. We were cold, wet, tired, sick, and naked. What a stupid feeling, to wake up in the middle of broad daylight, totally nude on top of a tent, right next to another naked guy waking up on top of the tent. I also think there was a dead fly in my mouth. We ran the quarter mile to the pond with our little white bottoms getting switched by the tall oats. Our clothes were still in piles where we had left them, soaking wet. We dressed as hurriedly as possible, giggling and cursing the whole time. Once dressed, we ran back to the tent.

I had to be at work in an hour so we were a little pressed for time. We readied the tent, sleeping bags and uneaten food for loading in the truck. The truck was parked on the edge of the creek and it had become partially submerged because the rain caused the creek to rise. We thought we could drive it out but there was a flat on the left front. We couldn't begin to get it rolling. For the time being, we forgot about the truck and concentrated on getting the other equipment rounded up, namely the guns we had hidden earlier so we wouldn't kill ourselves in a drunken fit. The problem was, we couldn't remember where we hid them. We never found them but we suspected that the swollen creek washed them away.

I decided to walk to a nearby farmhouse so I could call my Mom to come and get me for work. What a loser. As I was walking, I found half of my glasses in my pocket. They were broken right down the middle. The other half was Lord knows where.

I felt in my back pocket and my wallet was missing. I vaguely remembered having it out the night before but I didn't have time to look for it. I got to the farmhouse and called home. I vowed that I would never get drunk again. We lost our guns, woke up naked, tore up our tent, submerged the truck, had a flat, broke my glasses, lost my wallet, bumped my head, called my mother to come get me and on top of it all, I felt like death warmed over.

"Yes?" I said as I sat up on the concrete. "What?" I said looking around. I'd fallen asleep on the helipad on top of the bunker. The Korean perimeter guard came over to me and said something in Korean. We went back and forth smiling at each other not understanding a word the other said. I gathered that he thought it was funny, me sleeping on the helipad. It was midnight or there about. It was pretty good sleep because there wasn't a phone around to wake me up.

I yawned and stretched, still sitting on the concrete slab. *I better check in, just in case someone has been looking for me.* I went to the Headquarters, trying to rub the kinks out of my back. The coast was clear, no hits, no runs, no errors, and no one left on base. "Adios," I said to the operations center officer, "I'm heading to the hooch."

CHAPTER 10

Commander's Leave

Part IV

Lieutenant Grimes and I linked up and were out at firing point 501 before 0930. He was a really young 2nd lieutenant, twenty-one years old.

He said, "I'm going to want you to help me put out these stakes to mark the mine field perimeter. Now, if you don't want to, I'll understand."

"Sure, I'll help." *My God, what did I just say?*

We grabbed a small pile of stakes and flags from the jeep trailer.

"Let's start where the two mines are piled up and we'll work in opposite directions. Do you have a probe?" asked Lieutenant Grimes.

"Just my knife," I pointed to the Gerber hanging from my web gear.

"I imagine that it will be okay. This minefield looks older than when they began using metal contact detonation devices."

"Well, that sure doesn't help my confidence," I said meaning every word.

"You think you can handle it?"

"Of course." I said in an even more unenthusiastic tone.

We started methodically working our way around the perimeter of the minefield. I'm afraid that I was cheating a little bit. Every time I saw a mine, I only probed to within ten feet of it and put up a flag, making the minefield appear larger than it really was. I'm no hero. I can promise you that.

I had the most difficult section to start off with. It was packed with tall grass and weeds. When I walked on it, I never really touched the ground. It was a solid mat of bent over stalks and vines.

I'll have to admit that it was thoroughly exhilarating work, even though my back was getting a cramp from the weight of the flak jacket, my eyes were filled with sweat and my helmet made my head itch intolerably. Every step was a new adventure, to paraphrase a philosophy, "You are never so much alive, as you are when death is near." Our Recon Platoon had this painted on the side of their Quonset hut.

An hour passed and I had three flags set out. The flags were placed at each bend with a straight shot between markers.

"How're ya doing'?" hollered the engineer lieutenant.

"Okay! How 'bout you?" I asked.

"Outstanding!"

Yeah, we're out standing in a minefield. I stood up being sure not to waver from my stance. "Hey, you got anything to eat in your jeep?" I yelled.

"Yeah, we'll eat in a minute. Let me finish up a few more meters."

We both squatted back down and resumed our fine-tooth combing of the field. In thirty minutes, the engineer walked over to me with a C-ration can of tuna fish and a can of crackers. "Is this okay? I had a can of turkey but the driver's eating it. I got 'beef and shrapnel' so you're not so bad off."

We moved over ten meters and sat with our legs outstretched in the shade of a tree and opened the C-ration cans with our P-38 can openers. I had the open can of tuna on one thigh and the open can of crackers on the other thigh. I was digging around in my web gear trying to pull my canteen out when my tuna fell off my leg and landed upside down on the ground. I picked it up quickly, pulled the grass out of it and tried to brush off the dirt, but I just ground it in. "What the hell," I said and ate it anyway.

The C-ration tuna was terrible to begin with but the dirt made it sub-Army quality, which was absolutely disgusting. However, after gagging it down, I was no longer hungry. I guess the dirt was good filler but I drank at least three quarters of the water in my canteen trying to wash it down. In twenty minutes we were ready to get started again.

The hours dragged on as we made our way around the minefield. At 1630 (4:30 PM), we linked up on the other side, sat under a tree, and surveyed the area that was enclosed by the seventeen red and white flags.

"Smoke 'em if you've got 'em," the young engineer lieutenant said as he lit up a cigarette. He offered me one.

"No thanks," I drank my last swallow of water. "I'm glad that's over with."

"Yeah, it was a bitch wasn't it?"

"How are going to get rid of these mothers?"

"Oh, I think we'll just string det-cord (basically explosive rope) over the whole mess and get them all in one big boom."

"Is that standard operating procedure?" I asked.

"Well, we've done it before but the minefield wasn't this big."

"Are you going to burn it off first?"

"We may, but it's hard to control a fire, especially if mines are blowing up from the heat unexpectedly. If the fire gets away from us and spreads to those marked fields over there", he pointed, "we'll be hard pressed to stop it. It may burn all the way to the North Korean capital before it stops. What the hell's the name of that place again?"

"Pyongyang," I said.

"Yeah, that's it."

We sat in silence, listening to the spring breeze rustle the tops of the trees. I unzipped my flak jacket and laid my helmet down beside me running my fingers through my sweaty hair, massaging my scalp.

"Grimes, this sucks," I said.

"I used to dream about stuff like this," he replied.

"What? Diggin' around in a minefield?"

"Naw, livin' an adventurous life."

"Yeah, that's what I said, 'diggin' around in minefields.'"

"C'mon, you know what I mean. Didn't you ever play soldier when you were a kid?"

"I played soldier but I never thought I would be one," I said.

"I always wanted to be a fireman," Grimes said. "I loved fire. It fascinated me."

"So you became an engineer instead and now you blow things up."

"Close second wouldn't you say," he smiled.

I leaned my head back against the trunk of the small tree and closed my eyes. I heard Grimes light up another cigarette. I looked at him and he had the butt of one in his right hand and a fresh one in his left.

"What are you trying to do, suffocate yourself?"

"I like to smoke when I'm in the field."

"It's a bad habit," I said, as he flipped the short butt to the ground. A ghostly sliver of smoke trailed up from the grass where the butt landed. I put my helmet on, strapped it down, and zipped my flak jacket up to the top.

"Are you ready to go?" I asked Grimes.

"Yeah, another day, another Yankee dollar."

I walked over to the smoldering butt on the ground and took a step to crush it out so it wouldn't start a brush fire and blow all of our hard work to Kingdom Come.

"STOP!"

I did, frozen in midstride.

"Put your foot down right next to your other one."

I did.

"Look next to the butt."

A green disc of some kind was barely distinguishable through the grass.

"I don't know the real name of that," said Grimes, "but it's a toe popper. It's an anti-personnel mine designed to—"

"I just heard about these just yesterday. Why is this little bitch outside of our perimeter?" I asked.

"Because I fucked up."

"Do you think there are any more outside our flags?" I asked knowing the answer.

"Does a Korean squat to shit on a city street?" Grimes said.

"Yes, he does"

I pulled out my stiletto and began to probe around a little and asked, "Which way do you want to go to get out of this mess?"

"Hell, I don't know. Let's go toward the road. We know it's safe there."

It was about 150 meters to the road. We worked smoothly, side by side on our hands and knees for about thirty minutes.

"This is getting old," I said. "How long have we been doing this?"

"Three days" Grimes said sarcastically.

"Have you seen anything that even resembles another toe popper?"

"No, what are you getting at?"

"Do you think it's safe to get up and walk?"

"I'm game if you are," he said.

"Hell no, I was just momentarily delirious. Although at this rate it will be dark by the time we get out of here. I know I don't want to be in here at night. I'm a restless sleeper. I'll roll around all over these son-of-a-bitches," I said.

"What son-of-a-bitches? I don't think there are any mines over this far."

"Are you saying the little piss ant popper back there was the only one?" I asked.

"No, don't pay any attention to me. I'm just getting delirious too."

"Well, cut that shit out and let's pay attention to what we're doing."

An hour later we were fifty feet from the road still side by side, crawling along, sweating like warthogs and we hadn't found another mine. The sun was just about to dip below the horizon and our driver looked remarkably comfortable, asleep in the jeep.

"I can't see a thing," said Grimes.

"Just keep—" I was cut off in midsentence by an explosion.

I could feel the heat against my face. Dirt and rocks stung me all over. Luckily my eyes were protected by my glasses, but I was temporarily blinded by the flash.

"Grimes!" I screamed. "Grimes!" I screamed again. I felt something chewy in my mouth.

"Yeah?" he said.

"Are you alright?" I scraped at the lump inside my mouth with my tongue.

"Yeah, my hand hurts a little."

I spit out a piece of slime. It was part of Grimes' finger.

"Let me see." I spit again. His blood tasted like salty tomato paste. Grimes held his hand up for me to look at. All fingers and the thumb were intact but there were serious burns and large chunks of flesh missing. I know that for a fact because one of the chunks was temporarily in my mouth.

"Jesus Christ," I said.

The driver fell out of the jeep screaming, "Do you need a Medevac?"

"No, I don't think so," I yelled. "Turn the jeep around and put the lights on us the best you can."

"Yes, Sir." The driver started maneuvering the jeep.

"Grimes, we're going to get out of here." I spat again. Real finger food tasted like shit.

Grimes lay down and I began probing frantically but carefully, finally reaching the road. I had marked the trail and went back to get him. I put his arm around my shoulder and his bloody hand hung next to my ear and slapped against my face as we hobbled out of the minefield.

In a moment Grimes broke the silence, "What'd ya say we come back tomorrow and finish up?" I thought he was serious for a moment but then he smiled.

"You fuck-head," I said.

As we neared Camp Greaves, Grimes asked to go back to his own compound for treatment.

"No," I said. "I outrank you, so let's get your ass up to the infirmary."

"Please," he said. "I'd like to keep this hushed up as much as possible. They'll take care of me at my place. I'll tell them that I did it on a gasoline stove or something. Don't tell anybody?"

"Why don't you want anyone to know?"

"No one will let me live it down. Can't lead men if you're a fuck-up."

"You're no fuck-up," I said, "You're a fuck-head." Grimes drove off leaving me at the Camp Greaves main gate. As he drove off I heard him threatening to revoke the driver's next three overnight passes if he didn't keep his mouth shut.

It was late and I thought I'd go up to the O-Club and grab a bite to eat. The tuna fish a la dirt was beginning to wear off. The club was semi-full of officers. I sat down with my friend Denny and began to talk.

He asked, "What's on your face?" I went to the latrine and washed off the blood.

In a minute the waitress brought out a pizza and someone hollered "Manchu Pizza!" which meant everyone was entitled to a slice.

We all rushed the waitress grabbing for a slice. I got a good hold on one piece but someone jerked half of it out of my hand. To prevent the other half from being scavenged, I crammed it in my mouth. I turned my head away from everyone and spit it all back up as my gag reflex brought tears to my eyes. Gooey warm cheese and tomato paste tasted just like the chunk of Grimes' hand that flew into my mouth.

"I'll see ya later, Denny," I said and ran out the front door. I stood at the entrance of the club and sucked in a couple of lungs full of fresh air. I spit a few more times.

"Jesus, help me get through this," I said under my breath.

Miss Yi, the pretty, young waitress came out to speak to me.

"Lieutenant O, are you well?"

"Miss Yi, you have perfect timing."

She blushed and touched my arm. I had my head bowed so she bent over a little to look up into my eyes. She raised her eyebrows as if to say, "Tell me what's wrong."

"Miss Yi," I said, "I nearly got killed today." I don't know if that was exactly true but somehow, it felt like it right then.

"Oh!" She put her hand to her mouth.

Then after an awkward moment of silence I said, "I'm going to bed. Maybe I'll have a good dream."

"Have beautiful dream, Lieutenant O," she said.

I walked away down the hill to my hooch. For no reason, tears welled up in my eyes and I thought I might start crying. I wasn't sobbing or sniffling or anything like that, but tears were forming and if I blinked hard, they would have rolled down my cheeks. "Sissy-ass bitch," I said to myself and went to bed mercifully ending the eighth day of the commander's leave.

The first thing I did the next day in the office was call the Engineer Battalion to find out about Lieutenant Grimes. Surprisingly, he answered the phone himself and said he was doing fine. His doc believed him about a gasoline burner blowing up. However, his commander made him the ondol stove inspector for the village of Yongtori as punishment for being careless. We had a good laugh and then I made him promise to blow the hell out of that minefield within the week.

Two shooting incidents occurred during the night, however, neither was very significant. Both took place off the East Coast, about 145 miles from our compound. I stuck little pins in my briefing map for the battalion commander. I ran out of pins and got mad at my sergeant for not having any more. Obviously I was very irritable. Sergeant Pettit suggested that I get laid to relax me a bit.

I apologized to my sergeant. He responded with, "Sir, you need to relax. I'm serious, get laid."

I chose to ignore him, "What's on the agenda today?"

"We got a butt load of security clearances, you have a class on Rules of Engagement to teach to Charlie Company and you are supposed to meet with the S-4 about someone stealing gasoline out of the motor pool."

I went to the theatre at 0900 with my box full of training aids. I taught the Rules of Engagement class at least twenty times during my tour in Korea. There were six or seven rules that basically had to be memorized. The easiest one, and the one that every soldier wanted to exercise was "Kill anyone in or on the river at night," simple and direct, easy to remember. All the other rules had different stipulations about time of day, location, and if the personnel in question were unidentified or not.

There were always one or two guys who liked to stay after the class and shoot the bull. I usually made them help me clean up and carry the training aids back to the Headquarters. There was a corporal on this particular day that stayed to help me. His name was Corporal Sargent Major, if you can believe that. I asked him if he'd ever read Catch 22. He didn't know what I was talking about.

"Sir?" he started to ask a question.

"Yes," we stopped putting the projector up for a moment.

"Are there tunnels under the DMZ?"

"Yes, quite a number of them I would imagine," I really knew exactly how many had been found but he didn't need to know.

"How did they get there?"

I did a slight double take at the question. "Pardon?" I said.

"How do those tunnels get there?" he repeated.

I gave a smile with half the side of my face and said, "They're dug by the North Koreans."

"Yeah, that's what I thought."

"Why do you say that?" He had my curiosity thoroughly aroused now.

"I heard them digging."

Tunnels are not taken lightly on the DMZ. There have been three major tunnels found so far, one of them cropping up a mile away from the movie theater where we were now standing. It was the latest one found and was six feet high and six feet across. It was as deep as one hundred feet at one point. We were very lucky to discover it.

The 8th Army TNT (Tunnel Neutralization Team) had been looking for this particular tunnel. They would make a best guess as to where a tunnel would most likely be located and then the TNT would drill a bore hole straight down several hundred feet hoping to hit a cavity. They would drop a listening device down the hole to see if it would pick up sounds of enemy drilling or blasting.

The TNT drilled a borehole about every ten meters and it just so happened that a North Korean tunnel was being dug right between two of the boreholes. The North Koreans planted charges to widen their tunnel. When detonated, water, smoke, and small chunks of debris came shooting out of one of the American boreholes.

Our astute TNT workers, while eating sandwiches during a lunch break, noticed that "water, smoke and small chunks of debris" were shooting out of one of the boreholes. Even the dimmest of TNT workers thought this to be quite unusual. They reported it to their boss and within minutes, the whole country was on alert and major plans were started to intercept the tunnel. It took a while but the forces of good and righteousness were well on their way to thwarting the forces of darkness and evil, a hundred feet below the ground. Another communist plot had been diverted.

It wasn't all flag waving and bands playing. The North Koreans released nerve gas up the borehole. One man died and another man was never the same. As with all the tunnels that were discovered, the North Koreans left behind mines to kill and maim the courageous men who went into the tunnel to meet the enemy face to face. Through careful detection procedures, all the mines were discovered in this particular tunnel, without any further injury. We weren't so lucky in other tunnels. A while ago, a colonel was killed in one, while getting his picture taken as the first man in.

I asked Corporal Sargent Major, "What noises did you hear and where did you hear them?" He pulled a folded map out of his back pocket and pointed to a spot near the south end of the bridge.

"I'm not the only one who heard it. Some of the bridge guards heard it too."

"Heard what?" I asked even more curious.

"The whining of a drill under ground."

"When did you hear it?"

"Usually in the early mornings, about dawn."

At the office, I called the bridge and talked to the sergeant in charge. He didn't know anything about it. I told him to find out. An hour later he called me back and told me that twenty-one of the forty-seven soldiers he canvassed had heard the whining noises. That was twenty-one soldiers too many to be a coincidence.

I got a description of the noise from no less than a dozen soldiers and everybody's description was reasonably matched: "A faint high pitched whine, heard loudest at the south end of the bridge during dawn and predawn hours." Then I made the dreadful mistake of telling the bridge guards to call me when they heard the noise again.

I then, through a series of telephone and radio calls, got in touch with Major Bailey, the Tunnel Neutralization Team commander. He was a big burly guy, kind of soft spoken but wouldn't turn down a cold beer with you. He had a moustache that was at least twice regulation size but so was he, so no one said anything about it. He agreed to meet me in my office for a chat about his operations and my problems.

I thought Major Bailey would think that I was crazy but he took it all in stride, writing my story down in a little note pad that he carried in his pocket.

"Here's my phone number at the site," he said, handing me a piece of paper.

"What am I supposed to do now?" I asked.

"Wait."

"I'm going to report this to brigade," I warned him.

"Well, it won't be long then. I usually wait for official instructions, rather than do something on my own and then have to do it all over again when the top tells me to do something else. It won't be long, I promise."

"You're probably right," I said and he smiled from underneath his unruly moustache and departed.

I composed a report for brigade, which I decided to deliver in person, giving me a chance to socialize in Bong Gil Chon, the village outside the brigade Headquarters.

I commandeered a jeep and a driver from the motor pool and was on my way south. It's about a thirty-minute drive to the brigade Headquarters so I relaxed a little and enjoyed the countryside. If it wasn't for the fear of a collision with the ever-present taxi or the old Papa-san walking down the road with his A-frame pack, I might have even been able to doze off. I liked riding in jeeps. Our jeeps had roofs but no doors so we could escape easily if we were ambushed.

At brigade, I left the report with the S-2 sergeant and said that I would be back in three hours. I told my driver to hit the snack bar or go to the mess hall if he was broke. I walked out the front gate and into the village.

Most of the shops were closed. It was a little before noon and the majority of the businesswomen were still asleep. Only the ones with small children were up at this hour. I stopped at a grocery store and bought a half pint carton of room temperature banana milk not knowing what possessed me to do it. It was pretty sickening but I drank it anyway.

I walked from one end of the village to the other. I didn't see any action anywhere so I decided to create my own. I went into a courtyard and started knocking on the hooch doors. When someone answered, I told them that I was inspecting the ondol stoves, just like my buddy, Grimes. They usually believed me and let me in. If they weren't businesswomen, I made a cursory glance around and gave them an, "Okay." If it was the hooch of a businesswoman, I took a long time to make the inspection and tried to strike up a conversation.

I'd been doing this for about an hour when I finally hit pay dirt. A woman answered the door who had the biggest tits that I'd ever seen. They started at her collarbone and ended at the waist. She didn't have a chest, she just had tits. They were hidden behind a sweater and ensnared in a bra that must have been made out of an old parachute. This is it. This is where I wanted to stay for the next two hours.

I tried to talk to her but her English was extremely broken. I went through the motions of inspecting the stove and when I got finished, I sat down on her bed, which was unusually like an American bed. It had a headboard and was raised off the floor. It was a little short, but she was only 4'11" or shorter

In Korea, you can walk into a club, put a ten-dollar bill on your forehead, and instantly make all the female friends that you could possibly want. I reached in my wallet and pulled out a ten and laid it on the bed.

"Are you a businesswoman?" I asked. She smiled with a gleam in her eye. I knew that she was without her ever saying a word.

"What you want?" She asked out of the corner of her mouth.

I was trying to think of a way to say, "I want to see your tits," in a language that she would understand. I just pointed to them meekly. She gave me a grunt as if to say "Stupid GI" and believe me I was beginning to feel the part. I reached over and tugged on her sweater and said, "Take it off. I want to see." The sweater was skintight and with a great effort she got the sweater pulled up around her neck, one arm in, one arm out. I heard her gag a little from strangling herself. I started to laugh. She choked some more and spun around in a circle, flailing. It became uproariously funny and I laughed like a hyena. She started to curse in Korean and frantically tried to get the sweater over her head. She finally wriggled the sweater off and threw it in the corner. She stood upright immediately, straightened her hair, posed with her hands on her hips, and tried to look dignified. Her chest (I should say tits, she didn't have a chest) heaved heavily from the effort.

I suppose my continuous laughing was not appropriate because she said, "What matter? You no likey? You cragee something?"

"No, no," I laughed again. It was hopeless; I couldn't keep a straight face. I tried to regain composer but I just couldn't

She began to unsnap her bra. The snaps were in the front. It was really wide or I guess I should say it was long. The industrial size bra went from her armpits down to the top of her pants and it was reinforced with staves of some kind. The little metal clips keeping the bra hooked had a lot of pressure on them. There were seven clips holding it shut. I'd never seen a seven-clip bra before. Each one became increasingly more difficult to undo. The pressure was inversely proportional to the number of clips left unbuttoned. I instinctively put my hands to my face for protection. I was really afraid that one of those things might pop off and put my eye out.

She finally got the bra removed and the next two wonders of the world were loosed. I'll have to admit that I was embarrassed. Her tits were so large that she didn't have nipples. They were stretched completely smooth, only a slight discoloration of the skin gave away the position where the nipples were supposed to be. I always heard that anything more than a mouthful was a waste. Negative, not applicable, anything more than a heaping double handful was wasted with this girl. She stood with her hands on her hips proudly displaying them. I reached out and touched one. I tried to lift it up with my right hand but it was like trying to pick up a gigantic half filled water balloon. Most of it just slipped through my fingertips. I reached out with both hands and attempted to lift it. *Ten pounds* I mentally assessed, *maybe more.*

If I'm lying I'm dying … She bent over, keeping her legs straight, ankles together and touched her tits to the floor. She could put her arms down between them and shove them around behind her. She could lift them up and lick the place where the nipples were supposed to be without bending her head. Hell, she could damn near walk on them. She got down on her hands and knees and no matter how hard she tried, she couldn't keep them from dragging on the floor. I wanted to take her back up the Z and show all the guys.

Through the whole affair I hadn't even begun to feel a tingle of an erection. So when she started to take off her pants, I stopped her.

"What now?" she asked.

"That's it," I said, "job well done."

I gave her the ten and thanked her for the show and left feeling stupid and small. I went back to the brigade S-2's office but he was out so I went down to the snack bar to look for my driver.

It was nearly dark when we arrived at the bridge. I got out of the jeep and talked to a couple of the guards on duty. I told them to be sure and call me if they heard any strange drilling noises. Through the course of conversation with any soldier the subject of women invariably crops up and I told them about the girl I'd just seen in Bong Gil Chon.

"You ain't never seen her before?" a guard asked.

"No, that was the first time I'd ever been there."

"Was she at the Lucky Seven Club?" he asked.

"I don't know. I just saw her in her hooch."

Two more guards came over when they heard us talking about women and I relayed my experience to them.

"You didn't fuck her, did ya, Sir?" one of them asked.

"As a matter of fact, I did not."

"Cannonball's got every type of disease there is and probably some there ain't too."

"Her name is Cannonball?" I asked.

"What else could it be? What would you call someone who had bowling ball size tits?"

One of the soldiers in the back quipped, "Bowling Ball."

"Well, I'm glad I didn't do anything," I said.

"Did you get a blow job?"

"No, I said that I didn't do anything."

"Well, I got her to suck me off and I squirted cum on her tits."

"Impossible to miss," someone said in the dark.

"Go ahead, be blunt, I can take it," I said.

"What?" he said not understanding.

"Go on, I was just making a joke," I said,

"Well, it took me seven weeks to get my dick to quit dripping."

"Did you learn anything?" I asked.

"What do you mean?"

"Never mind," I hopped in my jeep and headed back to the compound.

The bunker was locked. I started to go in and do some work but decided not to. Whatever work there was would wait until tomorrow. Maybe if I put off my work long enough, we'd get attacked and then I wouldn't have to do it. I went up to the club to chow down and watch some of the Armed Forces Korean Network TV. I could never remember what came on but I could be assured that it was terrible, whatever it might be. I sat down by a Bravo Company lieutenant named Clark. His nickname was Moose. He had a moose puppet that fit over his hand that would say some of the most vulgar things but it was funny.

"Hey, Moose," I greeted him. "You'll never guess what I just saw down in Bong Gil Chon?"

"What?" he said as he took a swig of beer.

"A woman with the biggest tits in the world."

"Yeah, that's Cannonball. She gave half my platoon the clap and the other half the crabs."

"I must be the only person up here who didn't know about her."

"You didn't fuck her, did you?"

"No, I just looked at her tits."

"I didn't know you had a two day pass." I must have looked dumbfounded, because he felt compelled to explain. "It takes that long to inspect them because they are so big," he whispered loudly in an exaggerated manner.

"Eat me," I said, "I must not be a very good intelligence officer. I don't know anything about what's going on down range. I think I'm the only one in-country who didn't know about this girl"

"You don't know anything anyway," another lieutenant from Bravo Company walked in and sat down with us.

"I was just telling Clark about this girl down in Bong Gil Chon with tits the size of watermelons."

"That's Cannonball. You didn't fuck her, did you?"

"I can't believe this!"

"She gave one of my guys a chancre sore that took four weeks to heal up and gave another one the big H."

"Herpes?" I asked.

"Yeah, and it doesn't heal."

"I'm glad I didn't fuck her. I just looked at her tits."

"Did you have two hours to kill or what?"

"Two days," I said, and looked at Moose. He chuckled.

I ate a plate of rice and watched a stupid sitcom about Robin Hood and then went to my room. There was a note thumb tacked to the door. Immediately every imaginable piece of bad news ever conceived crossed my mind. I snatched it off the door sending the thumbtack sliding down the hall. I unfolded the note and read:

The colonel is my shepherd

I shall not want

He maketh me to lie down in

green rice paddies.

He leadeth me beside the MDL,

He restoreth my ammo.

He sendeth me on recon routes

for the S-2's sake.

Yea, tho I walk through the valley of

the shadow of the North Korean guard posts,

I will fear no evil ...

For my radio art with me

My map—my compass

they comfort me.

Thou preparest a briefing before me

in the presence of my patrol

Thou annointest my face with camouflage paint.

My rucksack runneth over

Surely the TOC will follow me by checkpoint

All the time of my patrol

And I will dwell north of the

Imjin River . . . forever

It was unsigned but was entitled The DMZ Prayer. I figured that the chaplain must have had something to do with it. He was always doing that kind of stuff.

Stick a fork in me, I was done and jumped in my bunk as day nine of the commander's two-week leave passed into history.

CHAPTER 11

Commander's Leave

Part V

Five minutes after lights out, I was dead asleep. Then the phone rang, ruining everything. I went careening down the hall, racing the S-4 to the phone. We both made a grab for it on the third ring and the receiver clattered to the floor. I fielded it in one bounce and discovered that it was for me. The S-4 went back to bed.

The bridge guards reported hearing the drilling sound. The staff duty officer sent the vehicle for me and we drove out on the bridge where I saw a small group of soldiers. The XO was one of them.

"What are you doing out here, Sir?" I asked.

"I got a phone call from the brigade commander. He gave explicit instructions for me to personally handle this. I told the staff duty officer to call you after I was notified."

"You could have skipped me altogether and I wouldn't have minded," I joked.

"We've got to figure out what this noise is. I haven't heard it yet. How about you?"

I stood perfectly still for a moment and listened. "I don't hear a damn thing," I said.

"Me either," said the XO.

"Who heard it first?" I asked looking around.

An American guard confessed and he tried to imitate the sound when I asked him what he heard. The sound he made could have very well been a drill but it could also have been a bee, mosquito or hair lipped cat.

The XO said he would stay the first part of the night and I would come on and relieve him at 0330. Boy, was this going to be rip-roaring fun. I love getting up at 0300 and working twenty-hour days. The harder pressed I am for sleep the harder it is for me to fall asleep. By the time I got back to my hooch,

I only had four hours that I could sleep. I laid down for one, tossed for two, and got back on the bridge an hour early.

The XO was still out on the bridge, relatively in the same spot that I left him but a little less alert.

"You're an hour early," he said.

"I couldn't sleep, knowing that the earth we walk upon is infested with communist assassins."

"What?" he asked.

"I think it's pretty late, Sir."

"You're damn right it's late."

"Have you heard anything yet?" I asked.

"Private Kim broke wind but that's all," the XO half way pointed over his shoulder at a KATUSA soldier standing behind him.

"I'll take over now."

"Let me know if you hear anything. Let me rephrase that, anything short of Private Kim passing gas."

"Don't worry, I'll squeal like a pig at the first sign of a drill, a blast or a pick axe in the sod."

"Good man," said the XO.

I snapped a salute and he kind of gave a wave in my direction and then I was alone. I listened intently for ten minutes, then I just paced back and forth fighting sleep and boredom. I heard a faint trickle of water. "Shoot anything in or on the river at night," the rule of engagement popped into my head. Then I realized it was one of the Korean guards pissing through the bridge rails into the river. An hour later, the trickle of water the others heard was me pissing through the rails.

A false dawn was lighting the sky. I think a false dawn is nothing more than soldiers on the night watch hoping really hard that morning hurries up and gets there and then imagining that it is. It was a little before 0500 when I heard an unexplainable splashing noise. I looked over at Private Kim standing next to me. He said, "Pishy." My astute command of Pidgin English allowed me to interpret that as "fish."

164

At 0540 the XO showed up.

"A little early isn't it, Sir?" I said.

"I didn't sleep a wink. Did you hear anything?"

"Pishy," I said.

"Lieutenant!" hollered a guard at the south end.

"Yes!"

"I heard it!"

The XO and I broke into a double time. "I don't hear it now," said the guard as we arrived at the south end. I was thinking the worst as all S-2's do. If the noise could be heard on the south end of the bridge, then the tunnel was already under the river.

We listened. We waited. Then we heard it. We cocked our heads back and forth trying to put our best ear forward. It only lasted for a fleeting second and it just didn't sound right. I looked over the rails. "I think the sound's coming from the wires," I said as I pointed to a series of electric and telephone cables stretched under the bridge.

"That's what I thought too," said one of the guards.

"But there's no wind blowing," said the XO.

I noticed way down from us, there was a flock of black and white birds sitting on the wires. I think they were called magpies but we called them Heckle and Jeckle birds. "Maybe it's an electrical hum or maybe it's those birds chirping and causing a hum, but I'm nearly positive that it's coming from the wires."

"Are you willing to tell the brigade commander that it's...humming birds," asked the XO.

"Let me listen a little longer."

"That's what I thought." The XO was smiling to himself. I think he thought his humming bird joke was funny.

We waited a little longer.

"Who's going to report to brigade?" I asked as we were driving back to the compound.

"I'll call the brigade commander. You call the brigade S-2," directed the XO.

I couldn't help but think that it really was those damn birds chirping on the line that made the ringing sound and we were just wasting our time.

At midmorning I was nearly comatose at my desk. I hadn't had a solid night's sleep since the battalion commander went on leave. I think he cursed us somehow before he left. I hoped to write some papers for the upcoming inspection but gave up when my vision blurred.

"I got to get out of here before I fall asleep," I said to my sergeant. "I'm going to walk around the compound." I didn't make it through the second security door of the bunker when Major Bailey, the TNT commander, walked in.

"I told you that it wouldn't take long to get orders from the top," he said.

"One day for Eighth Army is pretty damn fast. I suppose that you are here to consult with me about something?" I asked.

"I just wondered if you wanted to ride with me over to Echo Site to pick up an SLD."

"Sure, but I don't know what an SLD is. Do I need a weapon?"

Major Bailey laughed, "No, I don't think so."

As we were driving through the ROK sector by Echo Site, Major Bailey explained to me that an SLD was a Seismic Listening Device which is a machine composed of three main parts: a microphone, a geophone, and a tape recorder. They are designed, through the process of elimination, to determine if tunneling activity is taking place.

We drove through three gates with armed guards, over two bridges spanning tank pits, through one tank wall with a tank drop and in between two marked minefields. We pulled up into a small ROK compound on the edge of the DMZ frontier. Major Bailey and I dismounted and walked toward the South Barrier Fence.

The hurricane fence had river stones stuffed in the links. If someone scales the fence, the stones would fall out. It was a fairly effective after-the-fact detection system. There was also a cleared area about ten feet wide near the fence that looked like a baseball warning track. The track was raked daily and if footprints were discovered on the track then it was proof that someone came that way. Another good after-the-fact system

The ROK soldiers had fighting positions constructed about every fifty meters along the Southern Boundary. I was told that they man those holes every night. To my dismay, the third position that we walked by was occupied by a scarecrow with a fatigue shirt and a plywood M-16. I stopped Major Bailey and pointed to the dummy in the bottom of the hole. "There's our main line of defense." We walked a little further and found that every third position had a scarecrow and plywood rifle.

We finally reached the SLD site between the compound and the huge Namsan hill mass. The hill was bristling with gun barrels but in light of the fact that one-third of the guard forces were dummies, I wasn't sure how many gun barrels were steel and how many were plywood. The major whacked at the ground with the hand pick he was carrying and uncovered the geophone. He checked the tape and all was used, indicating several hours of activity. The major grunted something that I didn't understand and he slipped the tape into his fatigue pocket. I carried the rest of the SLD back to the jeep.

Some of the ROK soldiers were washing their clothes in tubs of creek water. They washed themselves in the same creek and believe me, during the dead of winter, a lot of Korean soldiers became rather gamey smelling. I would too if I had to bathe with ice cubes. The Koreans shouted to us as we drove away. "Hello! Hello!" The only English word they knew.

We quickly sped through all the obstacles and barriers back to the north end of the bridge. The major and I got out and I told the guards to call everybody in the world and tell them that we were going to be walking on the north bank. We waited ten minutes for the word to disseminate through the ranks, especially for the ROKs on the south side. When enough time lapsed, the major took his fist steps down under the bridge.

"Sir, I've heard there are mines down here," I said.

Major Bailey stopped so fast that he nearly fell over.

"Just kidding," I said. He raised his eyebrows at me. Although I knew there weren't supposed to be mines down there, Major Bailey and I both slowed way down and kept a sharp watch because, after all, we were in the Land of the Not Quite Right.

We stopped at a place just outside the dragon's teeth. The ground was firm and we were well away from the tidal action of the river. I watched the good major bury the geophone and mount a fresh tape. We got back to the jeep and drove the length of the bridge and repeated the process at the south end.

The major took me back to the compound and left for the next subterranean adventure. I went to chow: meatloaf, peas, and something mixed with noodles. Sometimes there was soft ice cream but the machine was broken. The alternative to ice cream for dessert was brown peaches floating in runny Jell-O. I passed.

At 1300 (1 PM), I found myself back behind my desk with a three-inch thick pile of papers stacked up in front of me. I was just deciding how to tackle it when I was saved by the bell, the phone rang.

It was the XO, "I'm sending some people over to talk to you. I want you to give them full cooperation, understand?"

"Yes, Sir," I said into the transmitter.

I had no idea who to expect. I spruced the office up a bit and stood waiting at the door. In a moment I heard voices and then a knock. Immediately, I knew that it wasn't anyone too important or they would have just walked right in.

"Come in!" I said in a stern voice.

It was a captain and a second lieutenant.

"What can I do for you?"

"Well," said the captain, "I'm Captain Sanchez from Division G-2 and this is Lieutenant Spivey. He's the new S-2 of the DMZ Battalion."

"That's not fair," I said. "I can't believe the DMZ Battalion gets an assistant S-2 and I don't."

"They don't," said the captain. "I said he is the new S-2 of the DMZ Battalion, the former one was relieved of duty and Lieutenant Spivey is his replacement.

"What the hell did he do or didn't do, to get relieved?" I asked.

"He screwed up royal," said the captain.

"Well, can you tell me what he did so I don't do it too," I halfway joked.

168

"He scheduled patrols too close together."

"What do you mean? Time wise or distance wise?" I asked.

"Both, they were at the same place at the same time. They fired each other up!"

"Was anyone hurt?" I asked.

"No, thank the Lord," said the captain as he crossed himself, "but the general took a high interest in it and needed a head to roll. The S-2 got the axe. Career over in a 30 second shoot out"

"When did this happen?" I asked.

"Last night, about 0300 in the morning."

"Why didn't I hear about it?"

"They shut it up tighter than a frog's ass during monsoon."

"I guess they did. I usually hear just about everything," I said.

"Yeah," said the captain. "I want you to go over the ropes with Lieutenant Spivey. I'll be back in a couple of hours. Where's the steam bath?"

"We don't have one here, Sir," I said with a smile.

"Damn, and no village either?" the captain semi asked.

"No there isn't," I smiled again. "Welcome to North of the River."

"What do you guys do for relaxation?"

"What's that?" I said still smiling.

"What kind of place is this?" he said as he walked out the door.

"He's only been here five minutes and he's already crazy. I've been here..." I started counting on my fingers, "too long," I said. "My name's David."

"Greg," the lieutenant said as we shook hands.

"What do you want to know?" I asked.

"I don't know shit. I just got out of the intelligence school two weeks ago."

"You've got to be kidding me," I said.

"No, honest."

"Are you planning on being a career officer?"

"West Point," he said and held up his hand with the college ring on it.

"Why did you pick intelligence instead of a combat arms branch?"

"They assigned me to it. I think it was because I didn't score so well on my PT tests."

"Well, don't hesitate to call me, anytime night or day. Nobody else minds what time they call, so you shouldn't either, okay?"

"Okay," said the new lieutenant.

"I guess we'll start with the map."

For two and a half hours I orated to the new DMZ S-2. He took detailed notes and asked dozens of questions, all of them pertinent. This guy was sharp, and as bad as I disliked West Pointers, he seemed amiable and professional from stem to stern.

Several hours later, Captain Sanchez came back into the office. I could smell beer on his breath.

"Well, Sir, I see you found out what we do up here for relaxation."

"If you mean drink like a fish, that's exactly what I've been doing'."

"Oh," I said. "I was talking about playing basketball at the gym."

The captain just grunted. "Let's go, Spivey."

"Good luck," I said to Greg.

"Thanks, Dave." We shook hands and a bond was formed instantly. I liked this guy. However, six months later, Second Lieutenant Gregory H. Spivey went home. Both of his legs were rendered useless. He was run over by a M-113 Armored Personnel Carrier during an exercise in the Chorwon Valley.

I found out that Captain Sanchez, from Division, was ordered to stay on the DMZ with Lieutenant Spivey for a month. Being plucked from Division rear and ushered up to battalion front, could drive any man to drink and I think Captain Sanchez and Mr. Bud Weiser were already intimately acquainted.

Drinking was a big problem north of the river. Alcohol was rationed from the Class VI Store (liquor store) but purchases were unlimited over the counter at the club. One of the sergeants who was being "farewelled," drank an enormous amount of 151 proof rum. His buddies put him to bed and left him. When they came to wake him up and shove him aboard his freedom flight, they found him dead. He had drowned in his own vomit. He died the day before he was supposed to go home. How do you explain something so senseless to his wife and children?

The actual business day came to a close and I sent my sergeant's home but I remained behind to single handedly tackle the stack of paperwork. What bullshit, a bunch of crime prevention inspections, Korean Security Guard reports, arms rooms inspections, security clearances, SOP's and the request by Combined Field Army for us to revise our war plans. I had to write the threat portion. It only took about an hour and a half to get it ready because I just made it up. I locked it in the safe, locked the iron doors behind me and went to eat chow at the O' Club.

I felt like eating something different for supper instead of the usual plate of rice so I ordered a deluxe cheeseburger. A deluxe cost about twenty cents more because you got a slice of tomato and a piece of onion. However, there was never-ever any lettuce the whole time I was over in Korea.

At 2000 (8 PM), a three-day-old sports event, a baseball game, was coming on the television. I wasn't bored enough to watch already played sports so I went to my hooch and took a long hot shower. I steamed up the latrine really good.

I thought about the last time I saw the latrine full of steam. Linda was standing right where I was then. Ah, what a good-looking gal. Her looks got better as time passed. It's a shame that I messed up that night. I'd never get another opportunity like that. However, she was really a bitch for what she did. Her bitchiness also increased with the passing of time.

After a moment in a trance, I stepped out of the stall and dried off. I went to my room and put on a jogging suit. Putting my feet up on my desk, I began reading the seven-year-old Playboy, which I'd probably looked at fifteen times before. It was the only light reading that I had on hand.

There was a knock at the door. "Yes," I said.

"It's the chaplain."

"How do I know?" I said just kidding.

"Because I have a ten-pound box of fudge brownies from my wife."

In a flash I opened the door, "Name your price," I said.

He held a large box out in front of me and then pulled it back just when I reached for it. "I want to borrow your TV tomorrow to watch the game." I had a thirteen inch black and white TV that I brought over in my household goods.

"You got it."

I've never eaten a particular food up to the point of feeling absolutely gut wrenching, throwing up, puking sick, but I did that with these brownies. I ate more than half and the chaplain ate the rest. The chaplain was a much smaller man than me so his quantity was probably statistically bigger. After the last swallow and a couple of deep breaths the chaplain took my TV and waddled back to his room. I just sat on the edge of my bed. I think I was about to go into a hyperglycemic coma of some kind.

The phone rang. I sat there in a stupor. The phone rang again and then again. "Please don't be for me," I kept repeating. It rang again and then a fifth time. I heard the chaplain's door open and the sound of his slippers shuffling across the floor. On the eighth ring, he answered it. He didn't call me so I assumed that it was someone else's problem.

I slowly fell over on the wool army blanket and curled up in the fetal position. My mind was blank. I was thinking with my stomach and it wasn't thinking good thoughts at all. I fell asleep with visions of sugarplums doing a war dance in my head. They were mean sons-of-bitches too.

I woke up, abruptly, a few hours later. I found myself making a mad dash to the latrine, not totally sure which end fudge brownies were going to come out of first. As I burst through the latrine door...

"Chaplain?"

"What?"

"Do you have the shits?" he was sitting on the one commode.

"Yeah," he grunted in an excruciating way.

"Well, hurry up, I've got 'em too." I was actually grabbing my ass trying to prevent something from coming out.

"Unk," the chaplain grunted again and I heard a rush of liquid surge against the porcelain.

"Chaplain, you better hurry up or I'm going to shit on the floor." Now I'm dancing and grabbing my ass.

The chaplain could care less what I'd just said. He had problems of his own. I was swaying back and forth, pigeon toed and knock kneed, then bow legged trying to pinch it in.

"Hell with it," I said and went galloping outside, banging the Quonset hut screen door behind me. I found myself straddling a turtle trap, crapping and puking for all I was worth. It was by far one of the most disgusting things that I'd ever done. I was in a half squat, gathering in my warm-up suit, all the while projectile squirting out of both ends. After I thought I was finished, I waited another minute or two checking to see if it was really over and to try to figure out what to do next. Holding my warm up suit between my legs and still squatting, I hobbled my way over to a single small tree in our 'backyard' and plucked the leaves off it. I thought, *here I am, an officer in the United States Army, reduced to wiping my ass with leaves ten feet from my own hooch.*

After rubbing myself raw with the scratchiest damn leaves in Korea, I slowly walked, almost limped, back into the latrine. The chaplain was still on the commode.

"Hey, you want some more brownies?" I asked in my best devil-may-care style.

The chaplain just grunted a return answer.

Well, if you do," I said, "I've got some out in the turtle trap. Two varieties of already-been-used, homemade fudge brownies. What will it be, Sir, oral or anal?" The chaplain was still working hard to purge himself.

"Wait until I see my wife," he said, "I think she tried to poison us."

"Us!" I said. "You! I was just an innocent bystander."

We sat in the latrine for about thirty more minutes, alternately taking turns on the commode, wooden bench and in the shower. When we finally parted company for the rest of the night, the chaplain shook my hand and said, "It's been a delightful evening. We must get together and 'shoot the shit' again sometime."

I had just closed my room door behind me when the screen door to the outside of the Quonset hut made a creaking sound. I stood quietly behind my door.

"Which one is it?" I heard a voice say.

I opened the door. "Who are you looking for?" I asked.

"Lieutenant Oster-something, the S-2."

"Well, you found him," I said expecting the worst.

"Sir, I'm the Staff Duty driver. The bridge called and said they heard the water running out of the river or something like that."

"I have no idea what they are talking about but I guess I'm supposed to go down there."

"Yes, Sir," said the driver.

"Give me five minutes to get a uniform on." Right outside the door, I heard the driver ask, "What's that smell?" I was hoping that he wouldn't go over to the turtle trap and feel compelled to ask me questions later. When I had it all together, I went up the hill to the jeep. It was a quiet night. Of course, at 0300 in the morning, the only thing that breaks the silence is gunfire, explosions, or an alert siren. Or if you are really unlucky, you'll hear someone shitting and puking in the turtle trap outside your window.

The night scene at the bridge was a familiar one: searchlights helter-skelter across the water and a lot of phone activity from either end. The bridge guards were trying to tell me that there were some unnatural whirlpools in the river. I tried my best to convince the troops that the whirlpools were formed by the tidal action of the river but they wouldn't hear of it. Finally I just told them to call me if anything bubbled up from the holes in the river. I thought to myself, *I bet the battalion commander planned this crap to happen to me while he was on leave.*

The sun was rising. I got the driver to take me to the dining facility (DFAC). We weren't supposed to call them mess halls anymore. The DFAC is part of the new Army, but still, they served more messes than they did dinners. The XO was at breakfast and I told him what happened last night, the part about the whirlpools, not about getting the shits. He just shrugged his shoulders knowing immediately that it was nothing and he didn't even miss a bite of biscuit.

At midmorning, Major Bailey came to my office with four rolls of film for my camera. "Next time the soldiers see a whirlpool in the river, have them take pictures of it."

Without our knowledge, the ROK MPs at the bridge reported an embellished version of the whirlpool story through their channels. The whirlpools, when translated up the Korean chain of command, came out as a collapsed tunnel under the bridge. A ROK entourage consisting of a brigadier general, two full colonels, a major, a captain, and a first lieutenant converged on the bridge at midafternoon. We retaliated with two lieutenant colonels, a major, a captain and me, a first lieutenant. If nothing else, the guards on the bridge were impressed by all the brass and it reinforced the idea that something was wrong, making rumor control impossible. I ran to the bridge every night for the next three nights always too late to see the whirlpools. We never had any conclusive proof of anything, although the Seismic Listening Device did come up with a couple of minutes of something that sounded like drilling. Of course, the tapes had to be sent to Japan for analysis. They are probably next to a lost bag of shit somewhere in an archive.

The bridge was the greatest headache I had the entire tour. The job of maintaining the platoon of men on twenty-four hour guard duty, who lived in a separate compound a mile away, was hard enough. Additional investigations of the infiltrator sightings, frogmen, defectors, shootings, tunnels and various other things that go splash in the night was an added migraine. Even the tourists gave us trouble.

There was a national shrine at the south end of the bridge. Tourists would flock to the national monument on holidays and Sundays. There was a line painted on the ground halfway between the edge of the park and the start of the bridge security area. Tourists believed that the line represented the line between North and South Korea and they would come up and put a foot over the line or start walking across it to see how far they could get before we turned them back.

As a general rule, the soldiers just ask the tourists to get back and stay behind the line. One overzealous tourist, a Korean National, was showing off for his fiancé and walked right up to the guard shack and started to take a picture. The guard shack was a good fifty feet behind the 'do not cross' line.

My south-end sergeant in charge, Sergeant Zok, the heavyweight boxing champion of the 82 Airborne Division, knocked the little bastard and his camera into the next time zone. They had to retrieve him from the coy pond twenty feet down the hill. After being hit, the Korean tourist crashed through a small wooden rail fence that hasn't been repaired to this day. Sergeant Zok was the best crowd control device we had, although he wasn't very good in the public relations department.

As afternoon approached, I was visited by a member of the CID (Criminal Investigation Division). He came to interrogate me about my involvement with selling drugs, of all places, on the bridge. He read me my rights just as a precaution and I called the XO in as a witness. The CID man then promptly accused me of selling lysergic acid diethylamide or in a more common acronym, LSD.

I started to become angry and then I could do nothing but smile. It was a big smile too. The XO just stared at me. I sat upright behind my desk and tried to look as serious as possible. "I have a confession to make," I said as the CID agent pulled out a pad of paper and pencil and began to write. "Yes, I'll have to admit, within the last week I've put no less than two SLD boxes near the bridge."

"You mean LSD?" corrected the investigator.

"What the hell are you talking about?" asked the XO.

"Sir, the Seismic Listening Devices that Major Bailey and I emplaced at the bridge are called SLD's," I explained.

"Jesus H. Christ," swore the XO, as he walked out of my bunker. As far as he was concerned the case was closed. The investigator was a little harder to convince but eventually he left. His parting words: "We're gonna' keep an eye on you."

The only other unusual thing that happened that afternoon was a visit from a Private Pobnobski. He came in to report to me that he'd found a skeleton.

"You made my day, Private Pob," I said.

I went on a skeleton hunt, hiking out of the compound toward Panmunjon for a mile. I don't have an extremely overactive imagination but when I took my first step off the pavement into the bush, I started feeling strange. I was alone in the woods, in a foreign country looking for a dead human being in some various degree of decay. My senses were sharp. I heard everything and I could smell all of Korea. I didn't know what to expect. I imagined the body looking like anything from hamburger to bleached white bones. I felt anxious. My blood pressure was up and my adrenalin was flowing.

I kept thinking, *what the hell is wrong with me?*

After wondering around blindly for an hour or so, all of that excitement and anxiety wore off. I decided to search in a more scientific fashion so I started walking in ever widening concentric semi-circles. An hour passed and I was on my fourth sweep. With the pumping blood and adrenalin completely gone, it was just routine and boring now and I was getting frustrated. The sun was sinking, the forest was grey, and the air was heavy. I felt dirty and the bugs were starting to swarm. I was just beginning to think that this was going to be a job for the Recon Platoon when I found him. Dead he was, old he was, and he was looking right back at me at eye level.

The skull was upright, shoulder high and peering out of an eroded part of a steep ravine about a foot down from the top of the bank. I climbed up on the bank directly above the skull and kicked at the loose earth. A small avalanche started and the skull rolled to the bottom of the gulley. I skidded back down the ravine and picked it up. It was packed with dirt and weighed at least five pounds.

I pulled out my knife and dug some of the dirt out of one of the eye sockets. After a moment I let the skull hang at arm's length. I felt flushed. I spun around! For a second, I thought that someone was standing behind me. "This is ridiculous," I said, "I'm actually scaring myself." I threw the skull on the ground. "Not only that, I'm talking to myself." I walked back to the pavement and jogged back to the compound, racing the darkness. I just made it to my bunker at sundown and put another pin on my briefing map for the battalion commander. It was labeled: SKELETAL REMAINS #3 "A" Company. The next day, I sent the 1st Squad Recon Platoon to police up the bones.

I locked the office and went to the Officer's Club and played in the nightly Ping-Pong tournament in which I placed second. I never could beat the doc. The doc was a great guy. He earned the Silver Star during Vietnam at the Sohn Tay Raid to free the American POWs. He never talked about it until he was asked to give a class on the raid. It was most interesting and full of facts, unlike a lot of war stories that floated around. The doc had my utmost respect.

Our best war storyteller was our second S-3 operations officer. He was hurt severely twice; once in a parachute accident, a crushed leg, and once in Vietnam as a company commander, a sucking chest wound. He was only in Vietnam for six months but he had hundreds of stories. I was talking to the

XO about some of the S-3's war stories and how he had so many of them. The XO responded, "A lot can happen to a man in six months." I was approaching the six-month mark of my DMZ tour and I was beginning to understand what the XO meant. I'd seen more than I ever wanted to and we were at "peace" here.

I was duly awarded the second place Ping-Pong prize which meant I got to buy the doc a drink. It was a good evening, the doc and I drank diet colas, the S-3 spun yarns over the pool table, Moose made people laugh and Miss Yi was in fine form.

The next part of the night was taken up by our ceremony. Every two weeks, on the average, a new officer was brought in (hailed) and an old familiar face was farewelled, and the brass plates were shifted around the walls of the club. At this time, my plate was hanging two places past the midway point. The farewelled officers had to buy drinks for the rest of the bunch. The range was generally opened on these nights and the new plate "on the range" was pelted with beer cans.

The doc and I played three more games of ping pong and after a short inspection of our plates to make sure they were in the correct place; we went to the hooch. The doc was my next-door neighbor and we stood in the hall for a minute, talking, when the chaplain came out and joined the conversation. We all decided that we weren't sleepy and we were going to try to get a card game going. Spades and Uno were the two most popular games.

We had trouble finding a fourth so we played Uno. The chaplain never lost. Ever! I got to the point where I hated to play the game. We eventually found a fourth and switched to spades. The chaplain was my partner against the doc and an infantry officer. The chaplain and I lost. Always! I couldn't figure it out, even though there was only one logical explanation: I was a terrible card player.

I felt like I was dealt one bad hand after another while I was in Korea. After a quiet night, except for my midnight run to the bridge looking for whirlpools and listening for drilling, I was awakened quite early by the sound of the alert siren. I heard men running and shouting. I flew out of bed, dressed in combat gear, and headed to my office to load the war plans on the vehicle. I grabbed my protective mask and M-16 on the way.

We usually had a practice alert every month but we'd already had our rehearsal for this month. The best guess was this was the real thing. However, there weren't any artillery shells landing and blowing up. To me, that would be the first indication since we lived within range of several hundred enemy artillery pieces. I didn't hear rifle fire and I didn't see any enemy tanks clattering onto the parade field. I figured that we were safe for the next couple of minutes anyway, at least long enough for me to get from my Quonset hut to my bunker, which was the only bunker on the compound. The general didn't want us to run underground when the shooting started. He wanted us up top, kickin' ass.

When I got to my bunker, the siren directly overhead was still wailing like a scalded banshee. My sergeants were already getting things rounded up when I walked in. "What's goin' on?" I asked.

"I don't know, Sir, lots of scuttlebutt, nothing confirmed. We do have a FLASH TOP SECRET message at brigade that we have to pick up. That means me or you."

"I'll go get it," I said, and walked back out of the bunker to the Headquarters building. I scrounged around for five minutes, looking for a jeep. The XO finally gave up his and I was off to the races. I felt like a coward. If the unit were to get hit while I was gone, I'd be the only Manchu soldier left alive, except those who were on pass in the villages. Me and the whoremongers would be all that was left of a once proud command.

The sun was just rising over the South Korean mountains when I crossed the bridge. Brigade Headquarters was thirty minutes away and I settled in for a cool morning ride. We passed a couple of Korean military compounds and I noticed that they were in full swing too. The reality of war was beginning to creep into my mind. If it were war, everyone I knew would be dead. It was very exciting but I didn't like it at all.

There was a line outside the message center and I stood at the tail end of it. Within seconds, another soldier walked up and I found myself between an aviator from the 7th Calvary and a sergeant from 2nd Medical Battalion. The sergeant asked, "Does anybody know what's going on?" Everyone just shook their heads "No."

After showing an identification card at the dispatch window, I signed for a shotgun envelope marked "TOP SECRET 1st Battalion 9th Infantry." I got back in the jeep and we started to roll.

"What's in the envelope, Sir?" asked the driver.

"I don't know."

"Are you going to open it?"

"It's Top Secret; if I did, I couldn't tell you what was in it."

"I still think I'd like you to open it."

"Not in the jeep." I felt the envelope with my finger tips. There were several pieces of paper in the envelope and I was afraid one might blow out on the road somewhere.

ROK Army activity was increasing rapidly. There were armed guards at every intersection and at every tank drop. Several truck loads of troops passed us heading into Munsan, the largest town in this area. When we arrived at the bridge there must have been a platoon of Korean troops at the south end. I probably saw a hundred soldiers monitoring activity within the thirty miles from brigade Headquarters to the river. I didn't know what was going on but it didn't look good.

I managed to force back my curiosity and didn't open the packet until I was in the battalion commander's Office with the XO.

"What is it?" asked the XO.

"I don't know. I haven't opened it yet." I said as I fumbled with the tie string. There were eight messages: Four unclassified, two confidential, one secret, and one top-secret flash message. I handed the top-secret message to the XO. I saw the words, RIOTS, CAUTION, ALERT, and SPECIAL OPS.

The XO gave a snort, "Tell the S-1 to assemble the commanders and staff," he said.

I did as he instructed and in ten minutes we were all assembled in the battalion commander's office.

"Dave, could you go get me one of those "rabbit" maps of South Korea?"

"Yes, Sir." I brought the one back with all the pins stuck in it and attached it to an easel that stood in the corner. The XO walked over to it with the top-secret message in his hand and began searching the map for a point in the southern portion of the Republic.

"Well, I won't keep you any longer," said the XO, "now that I know where this place is." He sat back down behind the desk.

"As you know the Korean president was assassinated last year and the military has been in charge of the government ever since. Riots in protest of military rule have broken out in a place called Kwangju in the southwest portion of the ROK. Point that out to them, Dave."

I hunted around for a second and then placed one of my flag pins on it.

The XO continued, "There were about a hundred thousand people involved in the riots."

Exclamations went up from all of us. "A hundred thousand!"

"The ROK military has increased its readiness and a special ops division has actually surrounded the city, letting nothing in or out. On top of all this, the students who are the leaders and organizers of the riots have stolen some weapons from a Korean Military Reserve Armory. Let's see," the XO flipped through some of the pages of the message, "approximately 400 automatic weapons and 15000 rounds of ammunition are missing. Other students have started smaller riots in Seoul and Taegu. Threats have been issued against Americans. As of now, all leaves and passes are cancelled." Huge groans came from the commanders. Stand down your companies and get your vehicles back in the motor pool. Sometime this afternoon, I'll make a conference call and we'll practice manning our defensive positions." There was a pause for a moment, the XO looked up, "That's all, go back to work."

We all stood up in unison, saluted, said, "Keep up the Fire," and scooted out.

I was putting away the classified documents and thermite grenades, for destroying the classified safe, when the bridge guards called requesting my immediate presence. There seemed to be a mob forming at the park near the south end. I rushed through the Headquarters and hollered to the XO that there might be trouble at the south end of the bridge and that I would be down there until it was straightened out. Faced with the problem of not having a vehicle, I drew my weapon from the arms room, a pistol this time, and jogged to the bridge.

The "mob" at the south end was a colorful bunch, all in Korean traditional dress with red and white headbands. They were singing, swaying, and chanting. It looked like a protest. We lined ourselves up and stood shoulder to shoulder across the road. There were five of us. We had two M-16s and three 45s. The mob was forty strong, maybe forty-two, I couldn't get a good count because they were milling around too much. Suddenly the chanting stopped and they began moving towards us. A young man was leading them, carrying a box of some kind. My first thought was a bomb.

"Call the north end and tell them if we start Kung Fu fighting these sons-a-bitches for them to haul ass down here." It was not the most military sounding order I had ever given. The group of Koreans were fifty feet away and closing.

"Draw weapons. Lock and load!" Everyone did as I said and that, really sounded like a military order.

"I'm going to step forward, if they do anything to me, shoot them." I looked at the sergeant. He nodded to me and I went out to greet them. I walked forward to the line painted on the ground and waited with my .45 that had five rounds in it. *Why only five rounds when there was at least forty of them?* We met, face to face, on the painted line on the ground. There was a signpost next to me that said in Korean, "Warning, go no further."

Up close, the people in the crowd looked small and pathetic. They had tears in their eyes and were crying. The young man carrying the box opened it and let me look in. An urn was inside the box. It looked like the type that holds ashes of the dear departed. This was a funeral procession and did I ever feel stupid. We locked and loaded on a funeral party.

I turned my back on this "hostile" crowd and said, "Clear your weapons. Private Kim, come here." After we cleared our weapons, the KATUSA interpreted for me. It took a couple of minutes of singsong Korean chatter before the KATUSA spoke to me.

"Sir, they wish to drop over bridge into river."

"Why?" I asked.

They talked a little more, then the KATUSA explained that the person in the urn was born in North Korea before the war. He wanted to have his ashes spread in North Korea after his death. The people in the crowd thought that everything on the other side of the warning line was in North Korea and if they could dump the ashes in the river, they would spread all over the country.

"Okay," I said. "One Korean National on the bridge, the KATUSA, and one bridge guard with him to escort him off and make sure they clear the area when they're through." The sergeant nodded again. "I'm going back to the office if you need me."

I turned my back on the whole mess and walked the length of the bridge. At the north end I stopped for a moment and explained the situation to the guards. On the way back to the compound, I began to think about the bridge. Instead of being called Freedom Bridge, it should be called Bridge of No Imagination. Frogmen were killed coming out of the river and then the bridge reported seeing frogmen within days after the shooting. The bridge reported seeing infiltrators on the north bank, of course that was after the ROKs and North Koreans had a shoot out up on the Z. Then after the Tunnel Neutralization Team appeared on the scene, the bridge reported drilling sounds and whirlpools. Then, the very day after the riots started, the bridge had a "riot" of its own; this funeral thing. The bridge, I thought, has no imagination. They have to wait for something to happen somewhere else before they can make it up. *I wish they would originate something of their own. No, I don't*, I quickly corrected myself.

On the way back to the compound, I thought that I would "sneak" in the back gate near the ammunition holding area and see if the guards were awake and alert. I stepped through the gap in the locked fence, taking note to fix the fence so people couldn't step through it. I looked around, peering through the Plexiglas on the shack to see two guards asleep. "Damn," I said under my breath.

I opened the door to the guard shack. The shack was warm and there were empty paper plates on the floor. The guards evidently just finished eating and dozed off. The door spring creaked a little but neither one of the guards stirred. I took a step inside and the floorboards also creaked but it also had no effect on the guards either. I reached down and scooped up two M-16s and stepped back out the door. I slung them over my shoulder and headed for the Charlie Company orderly room. I found the company commander and asked him to put an armed guard on the Ammunition Holding Area for a short while. "The guards assigned there seemed to have lost their weapons." The commander snapped his fingers and a couple of his clerks ran out to get their weapons.

I hiked back to my bunker stopping by the Headquarters building to tell the XO what happened and show him my two M-16s. He just shook his head. The two guards would probably be fined two or three hundred dollars, be restricted to the compound and be required to pull extra duty for forty-five days. Guards who fall asleep and lose their weapons are just another liability.

I walked in my bunker and was immediately hit with a fusillade of remarks from my sergeant. "Sir, the ammo dump guard shack is reporting two missing weapons..." his voice trailed off. He started smiling when he saw me carrying the M-16s.

"Call them back and tell them that I have the weapons and I want the soldiers who "lost" them to report to me immediately. I want their shift leader too." My sergeant picked up the phone and called the guardhouse. I stacked the arms in the corner and sat behind my desk.

"Jesus, am I tired," I said to no one in particular. "Did you know about the practice alert this afternoon?" I asked my sergeant.

"Yes, Sir, we'll draw weapons and go right up on the helipad and sit for a few minutes and then we'll stand down."

"What do I do?" I asked.

"I think they'll activate the operations center and you'll go there."

"Good, since I'm already here I won't have to do too damn much, will I?"

There was a pile of papers in my in-box. Nothing looked very important so I initialed them and put them in my out-box. Papers in my out-box were Sergeant Pettit's responsibility. He usually takes one or two and puts the rest back in my in-box and I'd look them over again. We'd keep this vicious circle going until only important papers were left. The rest got put in my circular file.

The last piece of paper that I shuffled was a directive from the division security officer. It instructed us to serial number our bayonets by company designation. That meant that each time I inventoried an arms room, I'd have to count the bayonets by serial number. That's an extra eight hundred more frigging things I'd have to count in the battalion and on top of that, we couldn't steal spares from other units.

"I'm done!" I went to the club for a grilled cheese sandwich and tomato soup. Once there, my fellow officers informed me that there was a T&A movie playing at the theater and we were all going to attend. The chaplain, of course, had to go with us to see that troop morale was boosted. I pretty much drank my soup and carried my sandwich down the hill to the theater forgetting to pay for my bill. That happened to poor Miss Yi three times during my tour. I always made it up to her in spades. It got to be a standing joke between us.

Seven of us officers sat together in the movie. It was a tough job to find seven seats in a row in our theater. A great number of the seats were broken or completely missing. The screen was stained from soldiers throwing cokes at it and rats roamed relatively freely. Some of the soldiers brought homemade billy clubs or shillelaghs to bludgeon the rodents if they appeared during the feature. Every once in a while a soldier would jump up in a panic swinging wildly with a stick, banging seats, the walls, people's heads and sometimes they'd even hit the rat. During our T & A movie, a soldier batted a rat across the theatre and another guy batted it to the front and then another hit it back to the original soldier. The rat never touched the floor during the whole process. The movie was quickly forgotten and everyone concentrated on the "rat bat" in progress. We soon left to convene around the card table in the chaplain's room.

We raided our refrigerator and came up with a very old, half-eaten bag of corn chips and four diet colas. We started playing spades at 2130 (9:30 PM). I should have gone to sleep instead because I was really exhausted. I noticed my first grey hairs that evening. I had an even dozen, one for every day of the commander's leave. I attributed at least half of them to the bridge alone.

After a few hands, I relinquished my place to one of the on-lookers and went to bed. I just got settled in, when Captain Ryan, the brigade S-5, (he deals with public relations), knocked on my door. After answering the door, I went back and stared at the clock. 2340 (11:40).

"What are you doing here?" I asked in absolute dismay. "No, let me guess," I stopped him before he could say a word. "It has something to do with the riots."

"Yes," said the S-5. "How did you know?"

"What the hell else would get the S-5 up on the Z at nearly midnight?"

"We have reports that there will be a defection attempt tonight."

"Us or them?" I asked.

"What do you mean?" asked the S-5.

"Who's going to defect, someone from the south or someone from the north?" I asked slowly.

"Someone from the south, of course," he said as if I were simpleminded.

"What do you want from me?" I didn't really want to know but I felt obligated to ask.

"I want the camp to go on alert," he said.

"You want what?" I think I said that in a threatening manner. "Why on earth would we do that?"

"So you'll have a chance at catching the defector."

"Are you on drugs? Sir!" I added "Sir," after all he was a captain.

"What's wrong with that?"

"If you put the battalion on alert, you won't catch him, because they'll kill the prick if he comes anywhere close to the perimeter."

"I was told to get you guys to go on alert."

"Who told you?" I didn't give him time to answer. "No staff captain is going to tell my commander what to do, so take this pillow and lie down on the rug here. Here's a blanket, hit the light and let's get some sleep." I crawled into bed and left Captain Ryan standing in the middle of the floor with his mouth open in disbelief.

"The light switch is by the door." I said and paused. He still didn't move. "Are you going to turn out the light or what?" I said as I pulled the cover up to my chin. I was smiling to myself. *What an asshole, come down here from brigade and tell us how to run things. He's probably never seen the DMZ before.* I slept.

About two hours later, a jet plane flew over causing a sonic boom. We learned to like the sound, because it was the surveillance plane keeping track of the North Koreans. I remembered the first time I heard that boom that rattled the windows. I thought it was the bridge blowing up.

Captain Ryan woke up. "What the hell was that?"

"Go to sleep," I said.

"What was that?"

"The bridge blew up. Go to sleep."

"What?"

"Go to sleep."

We slept nearly two more hours before a soldier came to get me. In my sleep, I had forgotten that Captain Ryan was on the floor.

"Lieutenant O, it's the duty driver," he hollered from the hall.

"Just a minute."

"What's going on?" Captain Ryan woke up.

"I don't know. It's probably the bridge or Alpha Company since it's the driver."

"What's that mean?"

"Damn, Sir, just give me a minute to find out," I got out of bed. I had an erection poking at my underwear. How embarrassing. I put on a pair of fatigue pants that were hanging on the mosquito bar at the foot of my bed. I answered the door, smoothing my hair down with my hand.

"Sorry to bother you, Sir, but they have a prisoner at the bridge," said the driver.

"A prisoner!" shouted Captain Ryan. He started throwing blankets and pillows and fatigues and crap all over the room. He put his boots on before he put his pants on. He was hopping around trying to jerk his trousers on over his boots.

I stepped out in the hall and pulled the door shut behind me. "Do you know anything about the incident?" I asked the driver.

"No, Sir. The staff duty officer told me to come get you. I heard on the radio that they had a prisoner, but that's all."

"Okay, let me grab some more clothes." I went back inside and Captain Ryan was sitting on the floor trying to get his foot unstuck from his britches. I shut the door again so the private couldn't see the captain making a fool out of himself.

I grabbed my T-shirt, fatigue blouse, soft cap, boots, socks, and field jacket and carried them out to the phone in the hall. I called the north end of the bridge but they didn't know what was going on because all the action was taking place at the south end. I called the south end guard shack, dressing all the while. I heard a lot of background conversation. "What's going on down there, this is Lieutenant Osterhout."

"A man walked up and caused a commotion and tried to cross the bridge. We have him detained. The KATUSA says he wants to go north … "

"Okay," I said. "Was he armed?"

"No."

"Then just hold him there until I get there."

I went back to my room. I was ready to go, except for lacing my boots. Captain Ryan was still thrashing around with his pants down around his knees.

"Do you always dress like this, Sir?" I asked.

"Only when there's fighting and..." I walked out. What an idiot. *The only thing he's ever fought is his pants—and he's losing that battle.*

After five long minutes, the captain finally came out and joined me in the jeep and I instructed the driver to take us to the Headquarters.

"Shouldn't we go to the bridge?" asked the captain.

"In a minute."

"I don't like your attitude," he said, "I say we should get down to the bridge right now!" He punched his finger into the jeep seat to emphasize the word "now."

"What do you suggest?" I asked out of curiosity. Although I didn't really give a damn what he thought.

"We should go down there and get him," he said.

"Get him, what does that mean?"

"Capture him; bring him back here for interrogation."

"I don't think that would be a good idea," I said.

"Why not."

"Well, for one thing, he's already captured and for another, my XO would beat my ass if we helped him get across the bridge. Let's just keep him on the south side for now."

"You're wrong!" said the captain, "Driver, head to the bridge!" The driver looked at me and I shook my head no. We continued to the Headquarters.

"You're asking for it! Wait until I tell the brigade commander that you disobeyed my order." Captain Ryan was livid. I looked the captain in the eye and said, "Go ahead, tell the general if it makes you feel better."

The driver was a little shook. He'd just made corporal and he didn't want to lose his stripe. He'd always heard that the easiest way to make private first class was to come to Korea as a corporal and he was experiencing one of those possible situations.

We pulled up in front of the Headquarters.

"Wait here for us," I told the driver.

The staff duty officer and I greeted each other with the usual, "Here we go again," comments. After I got the low down and ascertained that brigade had been called and was sending a counterintelligence agent, I opened the S-1's safe and took out a .45 and a magazine with five rounds. I don't know why they always issued five rounds. Why not six or seven, but five always seemed so futile.

"Captain Ryan, do you want a weapon?" I asked him.

"What for?"

"Jesus Christ, because you said it yourself, we need to go capture him."

"Okay, give me one."

I threw him a .45 in a holster and a magazine with five rounds. "Five rounds is all we get," I said.

"One is all it takes," he retorted.

Stupid bastard, I re-retorted back in my mind.

We jumped in the vehicle and headed toward the bridge. I was wearing one of those aviator's shoulder holsters. I hadn't had a good night's sleep in a couple of weeks and it had a numbing effect. I was on some kind of natural high. Here I was, speeding along in the blackness, towards a fate unknown, in a foreign country, with my aviator's shoulder holster and an imbecile in the back seat. I laughed out loud. The driver looked at me and chuckled. I don't know if he was just good-natured or a mind reader but we both laughed again. Looking back on it, I realized that it was nervous energy.

"What's so funny?" asked Captain Ryan.

"Do you ever stop and think just how insane all this is?" I asked.

"No," he said. It figures, I chalked it up to his inability to think altogether.

There was a small crowd at the south end of the bridge when we got there. The prisoner, or I should say defector, was hog-tied eight ways to

Sunday to the bench in the guard shack. The defector was bloody and bruised. His clothes were torn and he was barefooted.

"Okay, sergeant," I said, "What happened?"

"Sir, there isn't a whole lot to it. We heard some sounds coming from down there," the sergeant pointed to a rice paddy off the west side of the road bank. "When we shined our lights down there, this guy started ranting and raving. The KATUSA said that he wanted to go to North Korea. We searched him and the immediate area. He's clean, no weapons, no map, no identification, no nothing."

"How'd he get beat up?" I asked.

"Found him that way, Sir. I think he was hung up in the barbed wire."

"Did the ROK MP call anybody?"

"Yes, Sir."

"What about the Korean Intelligence guys from the hut?"

"Yes, Sir, them too."

The south end of the bridge, like the north end, had a ROK MP permanently stationed there. In addition, the south end had a Korean intelligence officer permanently assigned to it.

"Keep everybody out of the guard shack, except one man to guard the defector and I want another man right outside the door. Get the KATUSA to ask him where the others are."

The sergeant instructed the KATUSA who stepped inside the shack and rattled off the question. The defector didn't respond. The KATUSA slapped him across the face, causing the defector to slump against his bonds for a moment. I shuddered to think what would happen to me if the bleeding hearts found out that we were down here slapping around the prisoner.

"Tell the KATUSA that we can't hit him," I said to the sergeant. He turned to go into the shack, but I grabbed him by the arm and waited. The sergeant just stood waiting for me to say something when we heard another "pop" from the guard hut. The KATUSA had slapped him again. "Okay, tell him now." I heard the sergeant speaking Pidgin English to the KATUSA. They came out and the KATUSA was smiling.

"He say, that he alone," the KATUSA said.

"Thank you, Private Kim," I said. "Make a perimeter and keep everybody out, and I mean everybody. I'm going to make some phone calls."

I went into the shack and called the staff duty officer. Captain Ryan stuck to my heels like a little dog, taking notes all the time. The XO answered the phone at the Headquarters. He told me to sit on the situation until the counter intelligence men came to get the detainee.

"And don't give him up to anybody but our guys," said the XO.

"Don't worry, Sir," I said. "Nobody's getting him."

I went out to the center of the bridge. Captain Ryan was still shadowing me.

"What are you going to do out here?" he asked.

"Would you believe a North Korean spy if he told you he was operating alone?"

"No."

"Then did you believe this guy when he said that he was by himself?"

"I guess not."

"Just keep taking notes so you can report our mistakes to the brigade commander?" I said in a fairly smart assed tone.

"Look, lieutenant," he said, "I'm a captain and you better do what I say or ..."

"Or what?" I said. "The most important thing that we're doing right now is trying to deal with this situation but you run around totally oblivious to what's going on. If you had any sense at all, you'd understand that we're in a good bit of danger here."

"Here," he said pointing to where we were standing.

"No, not right here on the bridge, I mean this situation. Have you given it any thought?"

"No, not really."

"Why not? You're the ranking officer. I guess I'll have to report to the brigade commander that the ranking officer admitted that he didn't think through the situation and was incapable of making decisions." I raised my eyebrows at him.

"Well," he said, "what do we have to think about?"

"The primary concern is watching out for any of his buddies. Did your sources tell you whether or not the defector would be operating alone?"

"No, just some of the villagers of Bong Gil Chon said that they knew of someone who might make a break for it."

"Do you think this guy is the one?"

"How should I know?" he said.

"Did you get a name and description?"

"Yeah, he was Korean."

"Don't tell me they all look alike to you."

"As a matter of fact..."

"Jesus, captain, how did you ever get an S-5 public affairs job if you are prejudiced against the Koreans?"

"I got assigned the S-5 job because they wouldn't let me command—"

"Never mind that. Problem two, assuming that he's alone, we're going to have to hold him until the Counter Intelligence agent gets here."

Captain Ryan laughed a little, "He's tied up like an animal. He's not going anywhere."

"The ROKs will want to take him. Have you ever fought a Korean?"

"They're half my size, it shouldn't be too hard"

"Sir," I said. "I've seen a pair of pants kick your ass. Why don't you go to the north end of the bridge and send a man down here. Watch things up there for me. Don't let any ROKs come across the bridge. It's important."

"Yes, Sir." Captain Ryan just called me "Sir." I went back to the south end and got inside the "circled wagons." Altogether we had nine men, including me, in the immediate vicinity of the prisoner. We all stood staring at the ROK MP and Korean Intelligence Officer in their guard shack.

Waiting in the middle of the night like I had so many other nights, a truck pulled up at the north end. Maybe Captain Ryan could handle it. I heard another vehicle in the distance coming in my direction on the main highway from the south. I hoped that it was the US Counter Intelligence contact but more than likely it was the ROKs coming in force. The first man out of the truck was a Korean. *Crap.*

"Tighten this up!" I yelled to my band of merry men. "Bring it in!" I got everybody in front of the guard shack. I turned around to confront the Koreans. Altogether, four ROK soldiers got out of the truck. The ranking man was a first lieutenant. I was glad we were the same rank. If he was a colonel or general, I'd have had a hard time standing my ground.

The ROK first lieutenant walked up to me and began to speak in very slow and deliberate English.

"You—have," he pulled out a pack of Korean cigarettes and lit one, "a— Korean—defector."

I think it was a question. "Yes," I said.

The Korean smiled, "We—have—come—to—take—him."

I started to say, "Over my dead body," but I thought he might take me seriously. Instead I said, "When I get orders from my battalion commander, I will release him to you." I really thought that was a diplomatic answer. It gave him a legitimate way to get our prisoner without putting up a fight and it would buy me some time.

"I—am—First ROK Division," he said as he puffed on his cigarette. "I— take—orders—only—from—General Chong," he smiled. "He—say—'Bring me a defector.' That's—what—I—do—now."

He made a motion with his hand and another four soldiers got out of the truck. That made the odds nine to eight, still in my favor.

"What is your name?" I asked.

"Lieutenant Li."

"Look, Lieutenant Li, isn't there some way we can work this out? I take orders only from my commander. He told me to keep the defector here. That's what I do now."

"We—have—problem." Lieutenant Li smiled and waved his hand again. Four more soldiers got out of the truck.

"Shit, how many more does he have in there?" I said over my shoulder to the bridge sergeant. "Get the bridge platoon on the phone and have them march down here in formation with weapons, then call the staff duty officer and tell him we may have a problem." The sergeant made his way through our stalwart line of defense and into the guard shack. I could hear his muffled voice on the phone.

"Lieutenant Li, let's talk a minute." We stepped several feet away from where the battle lines were being drawn. "What do you suppose is going to happen in the next ten minutes?" I asked him as I offered him a piece of gum that I found in my pocket.

He took the gum. I've never known a Korean to refuse anything that you offered. They always took but rarely gave.

"What name you?" he asked.

"Lieutenant O," I said knowing that Osterhout would be impossible.

"Lieutenant O, we—must—take—defector. We—will—fight. You—will—die. You—must—give—him—to—us."

"Are we really going to kill each other or just kick some major ass?" It was a rhetorical question. "I can't give him to you, I have orders too. It's not that important who gets him first. We'll all get a chance to interrogate him."

"We—must—have—him—now!" He spit the gum out. "We—will—fight."

"Lock and load!" I screamed. The troops slammed the magazines home and jacked rounds into the chambers. The ROK troops were already locked and cocked. There we stood. Face to face. I stood firm, with my .45 in my hand with five rounds. Why didn't I have a zillion rounds? Seven men stood behind me, one was in the shack with the prisoner. The ROKs had twelve. I just knew that the men behind me could see my knees shaking. I told my friends later that I heard the theme from "Gunsmoke" when I was facing them down, making light of the situation.

"Sir?" one of the men behind me said.

"What?" I snapped, not taking my eyes off the Koreans.

"I'm gonna choke."

"You'll be fine," I said. *We're all going to die anyway.* I didn't say the latter but I sure thought it.

"Listen," another soldier said. The Korean lieutenant even turned his head to look down the bridge. It was the Freedom Bridge Security Platoon, falling out for formation. There must have been thirty of them. I could hear the shouts and rattles of an armed muster. The Korean lieutenant's confidence had fallen. The cavalry was coming.

We just waited and listened. "Forwaaard! Haarch!" Crunch, crunch, crunch. The platoon was on the bridge only five hundred meters away. "Double time! Haarch!" Boom, boom, boom. Four hundred meters and closing fast.

The RO's finally backed off and got back in their truck. "Quick Time! Haarch! Platoon! Halt!" The platoon sergeant came over to me and saluted. "This better be damn good, Sir." he said.

"Don't worry, sergeant." I said. "You just saved our lives. If you don't believe me ask some of these men when they get back to the barracks."

We could see the lights of another vehicle approaching from the south. It was a jeep and it drove right up to the guard shack. A chief warrant officer stepped out and saluted me which is unusual for a warrant officer to salute a lieutenant.

"I'm Chief Goodman and I've come for the defector."

"He's in the shack and he's all yours!" My men made a hole for the Chief.

"How'd he get cut up?" the Chief asked.

"He just came that way. We think he got hung up on the barbed wire."

"Where are his shoes?" the Chief asked the guard in the shack.

"Fuck if I know," the guard answered in a strained voice, still high from the adrenaline.

The Chief loaded his human cargo in the back of the jeep. He had a guard and a driver. That was all.

"Let us know what you find out," I said.

"Sure," he said as he drove off. The ROK truck followed, as did my hope of ever receiving any information.

"Sergeant Katko!" I bellowed.

"Yes, Sir."

"Take the platoon to the billets and put them back to bed."

"Yes, Sir. About! Face! Forward! Haarch!" Thump, thump, thump. I watched the formation as it moved in unison down the bridge and faded into darkness.

I turned to the bridge sergeant of the guard, "Sergeant, you did good tonight. Let's get the bridge operations back to normal."

"Yes, Sir!"

"Make sure everybody clears their weapons in the barrel. You check each one personally."

"Right, Sir."

There was a truck parked at the north end of the bridge that was drawing my attention so I started walking in that direction. I had almost forgotten about Captain Ryan. Half way across the bridge I heard shouting coming from that area and I started to walk a little faster. I could see two men yelling at each other. They were standing in front of the truck and were just silhouettes in the headlights. I could make out Captain Ryan, the one with a pistol in his hand.

"What's going on?" I yelled still a hundred meters away.

"They want to go through!" yelled Captain Ryan.

"Let 'em pass!" I motioned for them to come on.

BAM!

A shot rang out. Everybody hit the deck.

I pulled my weapon and fell prone on the bridge railroad ties.

"What's goin' on up there?" I shouted.

"I shot him!" said Captain Ryan.

I went rushing forward. "Who did you shoot?" I holstered my weapon. There was a man in the darkness down the bank.

"I don't know," said Captain Ryan.

"You don't know!" I exclaimed.

Several guards were around us now.

"It was the guy I was just talking to," said Captain Ryan. "I don't know his name."

"An American?" I asked.

"Yes."

"Oh, God." I went running down the hill into the darkness.

I found the man. He'd been hit in the leg but I couldn't tell how bad it was in the dark.

"I need two guys down here!" I yelled. "We're going to get you up the hill, okay!" I said to the injured man.

"Does it hurt badly?" I asked him just making conversation for my sake more than anything.

"Not real bad. I've been hurt worse..."

"But you just can't remember when," I finished the sentence for him.

Two soldiers started carrying him up.

"Call the aid station, the staff duty officer and the south end, in that order, let everyone know it was an accident."

It took a minute to get the man up the hill and into the light. He wasn't hurt very badly. The bullet went through the muscle of his left thigh. It was clean.

The wounded man was the "vehicle commander" of the truck. We got the bleeding stopped fairly well. All the while, Captain Ryan was still standing relatively in the same position.

"Sergeant, help Captain Ryan clear his weapon without killing somebody."

"Yes, Sir. captain, would you hand me your pistol please, keeping the muzzle pointed down," said the sergeant.

"What? Oh yeah," the captain was dazed.

"Why did you shoot him?" I asked the captain.

"I didn't mean to. It just went off."

"Why were you pointing the weapon at him?"

"I didn't know I was."

"Well, captain, I want you to take out your little notebook and write down the fact that you just shot an enlisted man for no apparent reason and give that to the brigade commander." The ambulance arrived and the doc looked the wounded man over but didn't get very excited about the wound. The XO showed up on the scene also. He was as mad as I've ever seen him.

The next day, I should say, a little later when the sun came up, I was feeling refreshed, even though I didn't sleep more than two hours. The first thing I did when I was in the office was stick another pin in the commander's briefing map, labeled: Defector, South Korean. Then I stuck another one near the same spot that said: CPT Ryan, Friendly Fire, 1 WIA, Then I sat down and wrote a six page report on the events from the time Captain Ryan knocked on my door to the time that the wounded man was loaded on to the ambulance. It was noon by the time I finished.

CHAPTER 12

Commander's Leave

Part VI

I was alone in the bunker that day. My staff sergeant was at a meeting at Camp Casey, the division Headquarters and my buck sergeant was at the rifle range, zeroing his weapon. Everyone had to zero their weapons before the general inspection.

I was going to spend the day straightening out my files. My classified safe was a mess. I had so many, "go to war" plans that I wasn't sure which one to use if the balloon were to go up. I put every plan into an enormous three ring binder. Then I went through it page by page and made sure the pages were marked with the proper classification. I must have stamped the word "SECRET" in red on a thousand pieces of paper. It was a real time consuming pain in the ass process but I knew that the plans would be checked during the inspector general's visit.

It was getting late in the afternoon and I was beginning to wonder why my buck sergeant hadn't returned from the rifle range. I called the Headquarters' company commander to find out if the men were still in the field.

"No," he said. "They are at the infirmary. The Gama Goat they were riding in turned over."

"Why wasn't I told about this?"

"Sorry, I thought Sergeant Eggenburg would have called you by now."

"Was anybody hurt?" I asked.

The company commander's voice trailed off in the phone as Sergeant Eggenburg walked in the bunker.

"He's here," and I hung up. "What the hell happened?" I asked.

"It's a long story," said Sergeant Eggenburg.

"Sit down and tell it to me. You look like shit."

"I know," he said. "I feel like it too."

He sat down behind his desk, propped his feet up and lit a cigarette. "We were at the zero range, it was getting close to chow time, and there were thirty of us. Our choice was to walk back to camp or hop a ride on the Gamma Goat aid vehicle. We rushed the Goat and somehow we got half of us on board."

"It's only designed to hold eight people in the back, two in the front, right?"

"We got fifteen in the back, the medic and driver weren't part of the zero bunch, so they were up front."

"Seventeen altogether?"

"Yes, Sir," he laughed a little, "I had a guy sitting on my lap and another one's butt in my face."

He continued, "We got everyone in and started rolling down the road around the Alpha Company compound. The Goat started fishtailing and two guys fell out the back. When the driver hit the brakes to stop for them we just went into a slow roll. Two more guys jumped out before it went upside down. Smoke started coming from the engine and we thought that it was on fire so we panicked and trampled everyone in the way getting out. Herman had a broke leg and Casey had a broke arm. There were a couple of other cuts and bruises but the worst casualty was the Goat. The whole damn thing is warped, burnt up and won't run."

"Who was in charge?" I asked.

"For a while, I thought that it was going to be me but Sergeant Clavell outranks me by six months."

Sergeant Clavell was sent to division Headquarters away from the DMZ. His judgment was considered to be too poor for a front line battalion. It was the old 'screw-up-move-up' syndrome.

Sergeant Eggenburg just smiled with his swollen lips and blinked his blackened eye and said; "See you in the morning, Sir."

"Right, stay out of trouble."

I resumed my flipping pages and automatic stamping of the word "SECRET" on classified documents. There was a knock on my inside door and I looked through the peephole. It was Gung Ho Joe.

"What's the password?" I asked.

"They're in the wire?"

"No, not it," I said.

"The bridge has blown up?"

"I wish, but wrong again," I said. "You have one more chance. If you don't get it right, you will be considered armed and unidentified and I'll have to smack your forehead with this SECRET stamp until you are dead."

"How about you go with me, south of the river and get laid."

I opened the door, "That's it. How'd you know?"

"Lucky guess. Really, I've got to go to the message center and pick up a FLASH message. Want to go?"

"I'll have to clear it with the XO, but sure, when do we leave?"

"Five minutes."

"Let me put this classified crap away and call the XO. I really shouldn't go, Sergeant Pettit is down range already."

"It'll be alright. What could go wrong?"

"Surely you jest," I said.

I banged around locking things up and making calls for a few minutes, then I grabbed my field jacket and was ready. Even though it was warm outside, a field jacket was not an unreasonable precaution for a twilight ride in an open jeep.

We were held up at the bridge while a column of north bound vehicles came across. A black propeller driven plane started approaching from the Han River Estuary, the seaside of the bridge.

"Joe, have you ever seen a plane up here?"

"No."

"Boy, he sure is low."

"He's right on the deck. He may hit the damn bridge if he doesn't pull up!"

It roared over. Joe ducked and we watched it disappear down the river valley.

"Why did you duck, it was at least a hundred feet off the ground?" I teased.

Joe shot me the finger.

About halfway to Camp Howze, Joe turned to me and said, "I wonder if that was a North Korean plane?"

"I was just thinking the same thing. Did you see any tail numbers on it?" I asked.

"No, I didn't really look."

"I know, you were too busy ducking." Joe shot me the finger again. "I saw two Hanguk letters and four numbers but that's all. I didn't see a flag or insignia on it."

"Surely someone has reported it."

"I bet you a Manchu pizza that we're the first ones to report it to brigade." Joe agreed to the bet.

ROK soldiers were still at every intersection. I suspected that this FLASH message also had something to do with the riots in the cities. As we wheeled through Bong Gil Chon I saw the watermelon chested girl standing in a store front.

"Look, Joe, you see that girl? She has got the biggest tits I've ever seen in my life."

"Yeah, that's Cannonball. You didn't fuck her did you?"

I shot Joe the finger this time.

Joe went to the message center and I went to the S-2's shop. The major I was talking to hadn't heard about the airplane flying up the river in the Buffer Zone but he said that he would check it out. He also told me that things were getting pretty rough in Kwangju. The Korean Special Operations Division surrounded the city and attacked the rioters, killing three hundred and some odd civilians. The special operations division lost two men. Most of the stolen weapons were recovered but there were still a few hold outs. Another SCUNK boat hauling North Korean infiltrators was discovered beached at Mok Po on the southwestern seaboard. Three of the infiltrators were killed by militia and two more were killed by Special Operations soldiers as they tried to get into the city. Nobody knows how many were in the infiltration party. Their apparent mission was to organize the riots into a full-scale insurrection. Two more infiltrators were killed near the DMZ in the Chorwon Valley. The North Koreans were trying really hard to get in on the riots.

Joe and I met up at the jeep. "What ya' got there?" I asked Joe. He was carrying a familiar shotgun envelope.

"I've got an interesting FLASH message that you may have some interest in."

"Oh, yeah," I said. "Does it have something to do with the special operations division attacking into Kwangju and killing over three hundred people, a spy boat and a DMZ infiltration incident?" I paused, "And you owe me a pizza."

Joe shot me the finger, again.

We drove back to the river. Smoke was rising several kilometers to the east and it looked like it was coming from north of the river. I rushed back to my office to make some calls and find out what was burning. I called our Bravo Company first to see if they had any of their men in the field. They were notorious for catching the woods on fire. It wasn't any of them. I called brigade, not expecting to get any information and I didn't. I called Sergeant Han into my office and asked him if he would please call the ROK units and find out what was burning and where. He left to do his work.

I put more pins and labels on my map, stepping back to admire it like someone viewing a painting. I heard Gung Ho Joe come back into the bunker.

"Hey, Partner!" he yelled. "The XO wants you to read all these messages carefully. We have a staff meeting at 2100 (9 PM) and you're supposed to brief him on anything important."

"How many are there?"

"About forty."

"Crap," I said.

Joe piled them on my desk, laughing at me. "I'll see you at the meeting." I shot Joe the finger.

I started searching through the papers. There were only two messages that caught my eye. One was about two spies being captured at the rail station in

Kwangju. A fifty million won reward was given to the two women who turned them in. That was a lifetime worth of money. The second unusual thing was a planned announcement by the Korean government that war was expected to break out with North Korea tomorrow. This tidbit of information was supposed to have originated in Japan because there are several anti-South Korean organizations in Japan. North Koreans sometimes fly to Japan, then catch a hop to South Korea. It's a lot more logical than crawling across the DMZ in the face of minefields and machine gun fire.

However, this announcement of impending attack was just a ploy by the government to get the rioters to oppose a common enemy, North Korea, and not the South Korean military government. The military government had quite a few indicators to expose to the public: spies, infiltrators, and SCUNK boats. Spun correctly, the media would make it look like North Korea was already attacking.

I stuck a pin in the map where the spies were caught in Kwangju and labeled it SPIES (2). Sergeant Han knocked on the door and I made a minor effort to cover the secret messages. "Come in."

"Sir, I have news of fire."

"Go ahead and tell me."

"Plane crashy and burn. It catchy on fire."

I repeated, "The plane crashed and burned?"

"Yes, Sir, not really crashy. It shoot down."

"By whom?"

"ROK DMGee guard."

"Do you know anything more? Why was it shot down? Was it a South Korean plane? Why was it flying over the DMZ? Do you know the coordinates?"

"Yes, Sir." I paused waiting for him to say something else but he never did.

"Tell me all you know."

"North Korean spy, stole plane. Tried to fly North Korea and shot down. South Korean DMGee guards have orders: shoot down plane over DMGee. Not know pilot was spy. ROKs don't know what plane … just shot plane. SOP make shoot plane.

"Show me on the map where it crashed and burned," I said.

"Right here." He pointed to a place about five kilometers away from Freedom Bridge.

"One more thing, was the pilot found alive?"

"He was live."

"How bout now?"

Sergeant Han grinned.

"Right," I said. "That will be all."

After Sergeant Han left, I tried to figure out why the pilot decided to follow the Imjin River into North Korea instead of following the coastline and then cutting into the mainland when he was sure that he was far enough north. Maybe his mission was the river, the bridges, and the fortifications. Maybe he infiltrated, like the frogmen did, down the river into Seoul and that's the only route that he knew to get back. Too many maybes. I got ready to go to the meeting.

The meeting lasted one hour. We discussed the seriousness of the riot situation and discussed the facts. We added the total of dead that had been reported since the disturbance began and came up with a grand total of 384. However the South Korean government was only reporting 140 dead to the news media.

I got back to my office a little after 2200 (10 PM), and literally threw my hands up in surrender. I quit and went to the club. It usually closed about 2230 (10:30 PM) so I had just enough time to get a bite to eat, that is, if a problem didn't crop up between here and there. It was about a five minute walk and I had to cover a quarter of a mile.

I didn't get a hundred meters before I ran into a problem. I briefly heard something in the river, way down the hill by the pump house. It sounded like a boat motor of some kind. I thought, *If there's a boat on the water, somebody is going to get killed tonight.*

I found my Korean security guard and walked with him to the perimeter fence. I didn't want him to see me standing there by myself and shoot me. He and I both thought we heard noises and saw lights. Every patrol that I ever debriefed that heard something or saw something, described it as "noises and lights." I'm pretty sure it was workers at the pump house getting ready to flood the rice paddies with river water. I told all of the Korean security guards to be exceptionally alert. I'd go personally and check it out tomorrow.

I glanced at my watch, 2224, (10:24 PM). I had six minutes before the club closed. The grill was long since shut down. I had a choice of hurrying and getting there before the door was locked and maybe getting a "tuna pishy" sandwich or taking my time and eating beef jerky and crackers in my room. By the time I got to the club, it was closed anyway, so I went on to my room and ate a chunk of jerky and two large pilot bread crackers.

I was exhausted. I stripped to my shorts and lay down on top of my bunk. The wool army blanket was scratchy but somehow felt good. As I lay there in bed, I realized for some stupid reason, that my underwear was the only non Olive Drab green piece of clothing that I ever wore. I'm GI down to my drawers. I kicked off my shorts and lay on the bunk naked. I curled up in the fetal position and slept but woke about an hour later. I was cold as ice. *Maybe I'm getting sick.* I crawled under the covers and tried to sleep again but I couldn't. The electricity had gone off so I lit a candle that was fastened to the bottom of a C-ration can and placed it next to my bed. I read the Bible until I was tired again and slept once more.

While I slept, four miles away, eight men were huddled together in a stagnant rice paddy, fighting for their lives. A routine patrol was dispatched from friendly front lines at 2200 (10 PM). Check Point 1 was called in okay but they never made it to Check Point 2.

After insertion, the patrol feinted one direction to Check Point 1 and then came towards the main road that led to Panmunjom. The young sergeant patrol leader detected movement sixty-five meters across the road. The patrol set up a hasty ambush, lying prone, half submerged in stagnant rice paddy water. It smelled rotten and was thick with algae. Not a single American had a round in the chamber and it would make a lot of noise chambering one so they waited until the last possible moment to give away their position with the clatter of charging handles. Hearts were pounding and it was hard for them to breathe.

"Get ready," whispered the patrol leader.

"Now!"

In unison the Americans raised above the dike with a rattle of weapons and began firing wildly and frantically into shadows. The unidentified insurgents they had seen seconds earlier disappeared into the night at the first sound of the metallic clack of a bolt flying home. In five seconds every patrol member was changing magazines: 180 rounds flew down range.

There was yelling: "What did you see?" "Got him!" "What did we shoot at?" "Nothing, Goddamn it!" "Fuck us, we're in the shit now!" "Shut up, shut the fuck up." "Call it in, now!"

The patrol leader raised his head above the dike and saw nothing. He eased back down behind the dike into the water. He rolled over on his back and pushed his helmet up on his head. The radio operator was trying to call in a report but he was struggling. The patrol leader tried to figure out what to do next and someone was saying, "Holy Mary, Mother of God..."

The patrol leader didn't have long to think. Another set of unidentified insurgents appeared to the rear. The patrol leader was looking directly at them.

"Oh my God, look over there!" They heard a rustle of brush as an enemy squad was coming on line. "Get over the dike!"

The Americans scrambled and splashed up one side of the dike and down the other, back into the mud. Two helmets rolled off and disappeared under the water. Enemy rifles cracked, dirt flew, and rooster tails of water spiraled into the air. The muzzle blasts from the enemy AK-47s looked like fireflies in the woods.

"Okay! Okay!" The patrol leader was gasping for air. Everybody else was yelling.

"We're in a crossfire!"

"We gotta get out of here!"

"I don't believe this shit is happening!"

"Are we gonna fuckin' run or what?"

"Hell, no!" shouted the patrol leader. "Let me think."

Green tracer bullets zipped overhead sporadically. It was only a second or two but the patrol leader finally said, "Let's fuckin' run!"

The patrol jumped up from the muddy dike and fired a magazine on rock and roll. The sound was deafening, like a fighter plane on a low bombing run.

"Let's go!" and they all began to run down the rice paddy, crouching, using the paddy dike for cover, dropping empty magazines in the mire on the way.

There is no feeling in the world like fleeing in panic. They ran for thirty seconds, which meant about seventy-five meters sloshing through knee deep water and carrying a full load of combat gear. The radio was crackling with traffic but the patrol didn't have time to answer any of the calls. No sooner had they stopped and leaned against another dike to collectively catch their breath when the fireflies flickered again and the crack and thump of the AK-47s sounded in their ears. The enemy patrol had no intention of breaking contact. There were at least two groups of enemy soldiers, a main body and maybe a rear or flank security of some kind. The American patrol was caught between them.

The patrol leader answered the enemy fire with a burst of ten rounds on automatic. The rest of the patrol fired at will into the darkness. They were firing at a range of about three hundred meters which decreased the probability of an aimed, night time hit to a phenomenally small fraction. But the men fired anyway, burning up precious ammunition. The assistant patrol leader realized this and took an inventory of the remaining ammo. He had four magazines left out of the original seven. They just used up forty percent of their ammo and they had only been fighting three minutes.

"Get that radio going and call in our position. Tell them we want artillery illumination." The radio operator couldn't remember any of the call signs and couldn't find his cheat sheet. He never memorized the artillery call sign because artillery hadn't been fired into the DMZ in over ten years. Who needed it, right?

"C'mon, get somebody on the horn and get some illume out here. I want to see what we're shooting at before we run out of ammo."

By this time, the radio operator had lost all his composer and was screaming into the handset. "Any station this net. Come in. Over! Any station this net, please come in. Over." Every unit that heard him tried to answer at once, complicating the situation.

The enemy opened up on them from both directions. Twenty rifles flashed fire at the Americans. The bullets took bites out of the ground, churned the water, and ripped through the air. When the enemy volley ended, the Americans fired back. Some raised up to aim, others just held their weapons above the dike and fired blindly into the woods. They shot twenty or thirty rounds and were convinced that they had the enemy on the run.

The patrol leader was down to his last three magazines; sixty percent of his ammunition was gone. Total elapsed time since the initial shot: four minutes eighteen seconds. The radio operator finally locked into a call sign and started normal radio exchanges. The call sign that he was talking to was Guard Post Collier, the closest American unit.

"What is you location? Over." It was imperative that the guard post knew the patrol's location. However, the patrol leader had no idea what grid coordinate to send back. Then he remembered that he was supposed to send up a flare if enemy contact was made. The flare went up and the guard post identified it. Then the guard post called for artillery illumination.

It took the artillery battery commander forty-five minutes to get permission to make the shot. The guard post sent coordinates and the artillery fired illumination into the DMZ for the first time in over a decade. The illumination lit up the sky for one square kilometer. One of the parachute flares drifted into North Korea. For the posterity of it, the patrol fired a few more rounds during the illumination although they didn't actually see the enemy. The flares ruined their night vision, so they had to keep calling for continuous artillery flares to be able to see anything. The artillery guys loved it but the patrol was tired, scared, and filthy.

At 0500, after the last cannon round was fired. The predawn glow took over where the flares left off. At sunrise, a very weary and somber group of men, walked to the road and boarded a truck, bound for Warrior Base, a cup of coffee and a grueling debriefing.

I slept through the first critical minutes of their firefight but woke up when the artillery rounds started flying overhead. Camp Greaves lies right between an artillery battery and an impact area called Sand Island. We were accustomed to hearing arty rounds flying overhead but not in the middle of the night.

The boom and 'whiz' of the rounds was very faint but it was loud enough to wake me up. I walked outside and listened to the guns. I searched the horizon for the flash from the gun barrels but I couldn't see it. The 'whiz' of an artillery round sounds like a rocket flying overhead. Sometimes, especially when you first wake up, it's hard to tell which way they're going. It just gets louder and louder and then trails off.

I listened to the big bullets flying overhead for a few minutes. The regularity of the rounds impressed me. Then it hit me like a ton of bricks; the rounds were being fired north, into the DMZ. *Into North Korea? Oh, no!* I ran to the phone. I was still nude, what a fool. I called the staff duty officer and he told me that he was listening to all the radio traffic and there was one hell of a mess up on the Z. I dressed and went directly to the Headquarters at a double time.

I sat in front of the radio like everybody else, watching it like a television, listening intently, and hanging on to each word. I was scared, excited, and envious of the men who were actually experiencing this.

"Has the XO been called?" I asked after a few minutes.

"No, I've been too caught up with the radio traffic," responded the duty officer

"I wonder why we haven't been alerted yet?"

"Maybe they can't believe what's happening."

"Can you? Has anybody been killed yet?"

"Not that I can tell."

We called the XO and he decided not to do anything until the brigade called and gave us official orders. However, he was dressed and down with us in five minutes. He was breathing hard when he showed up so he must have run, although he gave the appearance of being nonchalant. Even a man with steel nerves couldn't really be nonchalant about this could he?

When we heard that the patrol was coming in, I requested a jeep to go up and listen to the debriefing at the Alpha Company compound where our summer help was bivouacked. The professional debriefers from Division were already there when I arrived.

One of the debriefers was a female lieutenant who I had met before. She had sky blue eyes and long straight dishwater blonde hair tied up in a bun. Her major personality flaw was that she had a heart made out of a dirt clod. She was a real ball buster. I wanted to witness her emasculating the members of this patrol. What I secretly wanted to see was the patrol leader get pissed off and knock her out. Not really, it was just a pleasant thought.

The debriefing was boring and technical. I felt sorry for those guys who'd been up all night and had to try to answer the questions intelligently. At 0800, it was all over and we headed to the breakfast table to discuss the incident. The chief debriefer, the G-2 himself, headed back to the division Headquarters to report his findings to the general and his staff.

The poor patrol leader and assistant patrol leader had to go out with another patrol around noon to retrace the steps and look for bodies, brass, flare canisters, and lost equipment.

I was chatting with the nut cutting female lieutenant even though I didn't really like her much. I hadn't seen a round eyed (blue and blonde on top of that) woman in two months. She wasn't paying much attention to my small talk because she was too busy insinuating that we (us, up on the Z) were all incompetent. I told her that she had penis envy. She got really pissed off and I figured that I might even get a reprimand of some kind and screw up what little support I got from Division but I wasn't going to lose any sleep over it. Sleep, that's what I really wanted. I hadn't had a good night's sleep in two weeks or a year and a half, I couldn't tell the difference at this point. But there was no sleep for me.

Especially now, I needed to check out the motorboat noises I heard down by the pump house. I got rigged up in full battle rattle and checked out an M-16 from the arms room and a magazine with five rounds. I went back to my office, opened my classified safe, and pulled out two magazines with twenty-eight rounds each. I felt much better with them. I checked in at the Headquarters to let them know that I was headed to the pump house.

I set out on my trek. As I went through the front gate, the Korean security guard saluted me. He was holding a chicken drumstick in his left hand. No doubt, it was an illegal appropriation from the mess hall. I made a mental note to check it out later. My brain was becoming a garbage can of mental notes.

I slid a twenty-eight round magazine into my M-16 as soon as I stepped on to the dirt trail leading to the pump house by the river. At one point, the trail had high banks on either side from which it was impossible to escape if there were an ambush.

It was a warm afternoon and my flak jacket was unusually uncomfortable. The high collar had black waxy face paint on it that rubbed off on my neck. I jacked a round into the chamber and checked the safety. I walked very slowly and very quietly, hearing only sounds that seemed normal: magpies squawking, a dog barking, and the leaves in the breeze. I smelled wild onions or was it the mess hall? I could hear voices from the compound and immediately thought that I should have also told the perimeter guards that I was going to be outside the fence. I turned around and started going back to tell the guards because I didn't like taking the slightest chance.

I was passing back through the high-banked area when the barking dog I'd heard earlier appeared right in front of me. My thumb instinctively switched the indicator on my M-16 to "automatic."

The dog bared his teeth and hunched his back with all the hairs standing up. It was twenty meters away but I felt like it was right in my face. I don't know why, but I squatted down, holding my weapon by the pistol grip, never taking my finger off the trigger. The dog moved closer. He was ugly. He had one brown eye and one blue-white cloudy eye and half of one ear was missing. He was bob-tailed and extremely muscular. I picked up a rock and tossed it at him. The rock hit him on his flank, back near his haunches. He snapped at the rock and actually bit himself. I'd seen enough. I was going to shoot the bastard. I raised my rifle to my shoulder and took aim. The dog was only twenty feet away now. He must have known what was going to happen because he attacked before I was ready. I jerked the trigger and it rattled like a jackhammer. The dog just slammed to the ground flat and never moved a muscle. Not a single twitch. I counted later and found that I fired seven rounds, which meant I pulled the trigger for seven-tenths of a second.

I hit the dog two or three times. Both his back legs were shot through and broken. There was a gaping exit wound in his left flank. I flipped the limp dog around a bit looking for an entry wound. After a thorough examination I determined that a bullet went right down his throat, rattled around a bit and came out his side.

I heard shouts in Korean and English coming from inside the perimeter fence. If I wasn't careful the battalion would alert on me and I'd end up like the dog. I slung my rifle barrel down over my shoulder, leaving both hands swinging freely in case somebody asked me to put them up. I wanted to be able to oblige them. I walked all the way back around into the main gate un-accosted, went straight into the Headquarters and asked, "What's going on?"

"Somebody's shooting right on the outside of the compound." The XO appeared worried.

"I know. It was me. I had to shoot a dog."

"You had to shoot a what!"

"A dog."

"That could have been considered a provocative act.," said the XO.

"Who am I going to provoke, the animal kingdom? The nearest hostile forces couldn't possibly have heard the rounds being fired."

"Yeah," he chuckled a little, "I guess you're right. Now you better have a damn good reason why you shot some farmer's dog."

"He attacked me," I said. "Maybe he was rabid."

"Why do you think that?"

"Well, he attacked me," I repeated. "Another reason is when I threw a rock at him to scare him off, he turned around and bit himself in the ass."

"Was he foaming at the mouth or anything like that?" asked the XO.

"Sir, I lost my observation skills when he tried to eat me. Why don't we send some medics down there to take some blood samples or whatever needs to be done to confirm it was a rabid dog...or if it really was just an ugly ass puppy and I owe a farmer an apology."

"Won't the patrol love it, getting sent after a rabid dog?"

"It's not like he's going to bite them. He's deader than a smelt," I said.

"You go tell the doc. If he starts bitchin' tell him to call me."

"Yes, Sir."

I went back to my bunker and called the recon platoon leader and the aid station. Within an hour I had a seven-man patrol (five infantry, two medics) ready to go. They had orders to "shoot to kill" strangely behaving animals.

Two hours and nine gunshots later, the patrol reported back with the dog wrapped in a garbage bag. I knew I should have made my instructions a little more specific. They killed two magpies, a pheasant, and a really sad looking box turtle. I didn't say a word to them because they thought they'd done good. Anyway, I knew they could always throw the "shoot to kill strangely behaving animals" order back in my face.

After a debriefing, the patrol left in a state of excitement. That was the first time that any of those guys got to shoot their weapons during a real mission. I'll admit that killing birds wasn't something to brag about but they thought it was really important, therefore it was. It would make a good story to tell their grandchildren or girlfriends, or whoever would believe it. The doc sent the dog to the 121 EVAC Hospital in Seoul but we never got any information about what made the animal behave erratically.

I rescheduled a small recon fire team to go back down to the pump house and look for a boat with a motor or any other small engine that could have made the noise I heard last night. I also instructed them to take a KATUSA and find out who owned the dog and tell them that it had been killed. It was midafternoon before I got all the patrols debriefed. They didn't find a motor or a boat but they found the owner of the dog. The KATUSA told me that the owner wasn't very pleased. I sent my report of the day's events to brigade.

I was beat and ready to curl up in the dying cockroach position. I wanted to go rest but my old "friend," Captain Ryan, the brigade S-5 called and told me that I'd have to pay for the Korean's dog. One of the S-5's functions is reimbursing Korean Nationals for losses that are caused by US military operations. If we ran over a tree, we had to pay. If we ran off a rice paddy dike and squashed some rice sprouts, we had to pay. If we shot a Korean's dog, we'd have to pay. Captain Ryan now had a chance to get me back for embarrassing him at the bridge. I was surprised that he hadn't been fired or demoted for shooting the truck driver. It hadn't been that long ago so maybe charges were still pending or maybe he was just somebody's nephew.

At 1500 (3 PM), the battalion got another FLASH message about the riots. Captain Ryan delivered it to me in person. It said that the students surrendered after a short battle with the National Police and the Special Operations soldiers. Only eighteen students, two national police, and one soldier were killed. The policemen died when the students made a last ditch effort to run the blockade around the city by driving a school bus through the police picket line. I put another pin on the map and then went to brief the XO and took my time because Captain Ryan was waiting for me to finish. When I finally got back to Captain Ryan, he was reading a paperback book called, "Gorgon, the Great."

"Sir, did you want to talk to me or did you come up here to read comic books?"

"It's not a comic book, lieutenant; it's a science fiction novel."

"Whatever," I said. "Does the Korean want me to pay for the dog?"

"I sincerely hope so," said Captain Ryan with a grin.

"Have you been to see him?" I asked.

"No, we're going together."

"Well, let's go."

I grabbed some gear, flak vest, helmet, pistol belt, and smoke grenade. I didn't need the smoke, but I figured that I'd make Captain Ryan feel insignificant. It was silly but it worked. He asked me three times why I had the smoke. I just told him that it was standard operating procedure. He just *harumpfed* and let it go. I had a .45 that I checked out of the arm's room. I offered Captain Ryan a pistol but he wasn't allowed to handle firearms any more

We went around to the pump house to talk with the old Papa-san. We didn't do much talking because neither Captain Ryan nor I could communicate with the old man. I knew about twenty Korean words, the word for hurt (or pain), thank you, I'm sorry, hello, beef, and believe it or not, dog, only because the word for beef and dog varied by just one letter and I wanted to make sure that I ordered beef and not dog in restaurants.

I said the word "dog" in Korean to the old man and he became excited. Then in my best Korean I said, "How muchi."

The old Papa-san thought for a moment and said something that I didn't understand. He held up two fingers.

"What do you think he means?" I asked hoping it was two dollars.

"How should I know?" said Captain Ryan. "I don't speak Korean, you do."

"Right," I said. I pulled out two one-dollar bills but he wouldn't take them. I didn't have any more ones in my wallet but I did have a five. I offered it to him. He took it and chattered away to his wife inside the small hut.

"I must have gotten taken," I said.

"I hope so," said Captain Ryan. "I wanted you to pay a couple of hundred dollars."

"I could have bought his daughter for that much money."

Korean money is not any good on the international market. They like to get as many American green backs as possible. A Korean with greenbacks had hard currency to trade to international dealers for dope or to trade back to soldiers for black market goods out of the commissaries and PXs. Captain Ryan and I started walking back to the compound. I was happy to get away with only paying the Korean five bucks. I figured that Captain Ryan would try to get me in trouble by accusing me of giving the Korean illegal money. As soon as I thought it, Captain Ryan said, "Lieutenant, you do know that it's against regulations to give indigenous personnel American money?"

"Yes, I know that. Do you know that?"

"Of course I know that. I'm going to report you to the brigade commander."

"Well okay, if you want to play that way. You were the ranking officer who drove up here with the specific purpose of making me pay the Korean and you were the ranking officer present at the transaction so I think I'll file the report. Your career ought to be hanging on by a thread after the shooting at the bridge. This should just about get you mustered out, I don't care whose son you are."

"I'm going to get your ass one of these days and how did you know my father was a congressman?" I grinned from ear to ear.

Back at the bunker, I just kept smiling at him and went on about my business. Captain Ryan got in his jeep without saying a word and drove back to the rear. I was sure wishing that they would get rid of him because he could be dangerous. One of these days he might actually trump up something that would stick.

The sun was setting quickly. I closed shop and was going to the house early. I stood in the doorway to the bunker listening to the night sounds of the DMZ. I could hear artillery firing from two different directions. The friendly artillery was firing flares into Sand Island, practicing due to recent events in the DMZ, and the North Korean artillery was firing into a place called the Horseshoe. The only day the South didn't fire artillery was Sunday. However, the North did. The North Koreans started out very early and we could hear it all through church services.

I went up to the club to undress Miss Yi with my eyes. She must have known what I was doing because she giggled every time I looked at her. I ate a deluxe cheeseburger with French fries and watched MASH on TV. I played the doc in Ping-Pong and was beaten royally. Then I played the S-3 a game of pool and lost just as badly. I played Moose a game of Space Invaders, our new electronic game. It was supposed to take quarters but Gung Ho Joe rigged it to give us free games. Moose slaughtered me unmercifully.

By the time the club closed, I was a three game loser and a zombie from lack of sleep. I had averaged less than four hours sleep a night for what...ten, eleven...twelve nights. I went to my Quonset hut and caught the doc before he got into the fart sack. I asked him for some aspirin.

"Do you want something stronger than aspirin?" he asked me.

"No, I just want a headache remedy."

He gave me three gigantic buffered tablets. I took one of them and went to bed to read. I closed the Bible and turned out the light at 2215 (10:15 PM). I slept like a dog curled up by a glowing fireplace, like a child after a warm glass of milk, like death itself.

The alarm went off at 0645. I turned it off and wondered what happened. I had a good night's sleep, eight and a half hours. I felt like a new man.

I went to the latrine with toothbrush and towel in hand. The chaplain was there in his usual good humor. "Did you hear?" he asked.

"Oh Lord, about what?"

"The battalion commander came back last night at eleven o'clock."

"Thank God he's back," I said half under my breath.

"Yeah, I'm glad he's back too."

No wonder I slept so well. The Curse of the Commander's Leave had finally ended as did one of the worst chapters (I should say worst six chapters) of my career.

CHAPTER 13

River Crossing

The staff briefed the battalion commander at 0730 that morning. Of the primary and special staff, my briefing was the most interesting. Over the two weeks that the commander was on leave, (thank the Lord, he came back three days early), we had experienced riots, infiltrators, SCUNK boats, defectors, frogmen, a building fire, a dozen unrelated shooting incidents, a friendly fire injury and a mad dog. Death toll: 405, plus the dog, and Captain Ryan's career.

By that afternoon the commander had things smoothed out and progressing toward the annual general inspection. There was only one obstacle left to overcome, it was called the Indian Head Olympics. Every unit in the Division was required to participate in the Olympics. The 2nd Infantry Division patch had an Indian head wearing a feather headdress on it. That's how the games got their name.

Our battalion had won the Olympics for the last two years. We were going to try to win again but the IG inspection took precedent over the games. We did not have time to concentrate on practice. On the other hand, a battalion at Camp Casey, 4th Battalion 23rd Infantry (the Tomahawks), didn't have such a pressing mission being forty miles from the U.S. sector of the DMZ and took every afternoon off from military training to rehearse and practice for the Olympics.

Even after performing our mission related duties flawlessly and preparing for the IG's inspection, we made a good showing at the Olympics. Sergeant Zok, our heavyweight boxer, beat several chumps damn near to death, winning first place. Our Assistant S-4 lieutenant won the arm wrestling contest "hands down" to coin a pun he would say. He wasn't that big or that strong but he had a technique that was unbeatable. It's hard to believe that one could outsmart an opponent at arm wrestling but this guy could do it. The animals from Charlie Company won a group contest that must have been tailor-made for them. It consisted of a confrontation between six of the biggest, meanest guys from one Company and the counterparts from another Company. They were put into a ring together and had to shove each other out. The Company with a man left in the circle was the winner. Charlie Company won that contest. They actually had plays where the biggest guy would grab three opponents and hold them while the rest of the team threw the others out. It was fairly apparent that our battalion was good at doing anything that required brute strength and awkwardness. One of our redeeming qualities was a KATUSA who could shoot the balls off a gnat at fifty paces with a forty-five. He won the pistol competition.

There was another event in which we showed well. In it, participants pushed a gigantic, ten-foot diameter ball around on the parade field trying to miraculously shove it through a goal. Our battalion didn't win; we came in second. In my estimation, the only reason we didn't win was because the ball was smarter than most of our troops. Our soldiers devised a play to guide the ball into the goal but it never worked. The play involved the biggest, fattest guy running full tilt boogie at the ball and trying to belly-buck it into moving forward. Most of the time, the biggest, fattest guy just ran forward, smashed into the ball, and belly-bucked himself backwards, falling on the ground.

Our commander appeared to be very proud when we brought home the overall second place trophy. I think he secretly regretted not directing the battalion to practice more. We would have been winners but we would have been less than combat ready for the DMZ.

After the Olympics, we discovered an excess of money in the unit fund. It had something to do with money that was allocated for us to entertain Republic of Korea dignitaries that visited Camp Greaves. In our opinions, any dignitary that visited us was entitled to a cup of coffee and a free meal at the mess hall and that's how we ended up with $1400.00 in our coffers. The battalion commander wanted to use it to do something for our soldiers. The Charlie Company commander wanted to buy beer and give the guys a chance to let their hair down. A beer bust would allow every man in the battalion to have about six beers apiece. The battalion commander knew some guys would be on duty and couldn't drink any beer at all and others would drink twice their share. The battalion commander reluctantly agreed to the beer bust but he said there would be no cancellation of training the next day.

The battalion commander was a man of his word. After a wild 600-man beer bust, hung over or not, the battalion road marched out for a three-day bivouac. Each company was assigned to a different area. I was sent out right behind them to evaluate their intelligence training.

Bravo Company was my first stop. I walked out to find them, taking a short cut that was seven miles long. The company had to hike fifteen miles so I was lucky. I didn't have a map but I figured I could find them. It's pretty hard to miss an infantry company digging in. I found one of their outposts by the road and asked directions on how to get to the company command post (CP). Once found, I told the company commander that I was going to wander around and observe the training.

I found the 1st Platoon lines and walked the perimeter with the 1st Platoon commander, Lieutenant Raines. Everything looked okay but I wasn't a combat arms officer and the machine guns could have been in the wrong place and I wouldn't have known it. All I knew was that they were supposed to have interlocking and grazing fire. I knew very little else about machine gun tactics. My expertise lay with DMZ patrolling. It was a unique kind of patrolling that had its own special rules and I knew all the rules very well.

Walking around the perimeter, the 1st Platoon commander and I discussed the next day's training. When I was satisfied with the way he was going to conduct it, I moved to the 2nd Platoon location. They were a little further around the Company lines. My buddy, Frank, led this platoon. His real name was Francis.

The 2nd Platoon was in an open area. I could see several of the fighting positions from the 2nd Platoon CP. The men were digging steadily. Most of the holes were knee deep, except one, I pointed to it. "That guy must be half way to China by now," I said.

"You mean half way to America. We're on the Chinese side of the world," Frank corrected me. I could see constant motion in the fighting position. It was steady up and down movement. The pace was more than one stroke per second.

"Is that guy digging that fast?" I asked.

"He's a hard worker," said Frank.

"I've got to see this," I said. "I've never seen a soldier move so fast. He must be eyeball deep. All I could see was the top of his head bobbing up and down."

As I got closer, I realized that it wasn't his head bobbing up and down it was his ass. He had a girl in there that he was screwing.

I turned to Frank, "What's going on here?"

221

"Field whores," he said. "They follow us around and when the time is right, they hustle the guys."

"How much do they cost? I mean is there a service charge or what?" I asked halfheartedly.

"A C-ration pack of coffee," Frank said.

"You've got to be shitting me. You mean for two tablespoons of instant coffee, I can get a piece of ass from one of these girls?"

"Right."

"Do you think we ought to break it up?"

"No, I sorta turn my back on it. I have an unwritten agreement with my men. I'll allow them to meet some field whores so they like to come to the bush. If they don't have a pass, they can go to the field and get laid cheaper than they can in the village. The other stipulation is that they must do all their business in a foxhole. It has to be deep enough so I can't see what's going on. That way, when we stop marching, the men jump right in and dig their fighting positions. The first one with a hole deep enough usually gets the first piece of ass. That's a good thing to happen when at least fifteen other guys are going to screw the same girl during the night. They call these girls double breasted fur-lined foxholes." When Francis finished speaking, the guy's ass quit bobbing up and down and two heads poked up. "We better leave, she's about to switch foxholes and we can't blatantly let it continue." Frank and I walked back to another portion of the perimeter.

The 3rd Platoon also had a small following of field whores along with young boys selling ice cold Coca Colas to the troops. A cold cola cost more than a field whore. *Only in Korea*, I thought.

I didn't get a close look at any of the women in the field until I bumped into a small band of girls as I was hiking back to the battalion Headquarters. They could speak very little English but they wanted to know where the company camp was located. I told them that I didn't know. I lied because I felt sorry for the soldiers that got this bunch. I hoped it would be after nightfall when they found each other because these women were ugly. Not just unattractive, but "chew your arm off rather than wake her up coyote ugly." They were plump, rotten-toothed with unkempt lice ridden hair and smelled like kimchee. They were definitely two baggers, put a bag over her head and one over your head in case hers fell off. I'm not sure they were even worth a

222

spoonful of instant coffee. The soldiers for whom these women were destined should just make their cup of coffee and enjoy drinking it. But, I guess they looked normal for women who get screwed in the bottom of a muddy foxhole twenty times a night. I was pleased with Bravo Company training but a little perplexed about some of their incentives.

As soon as I returned, I found out that I had to be a Korean National pay officer. I did this extra duty four times during my tour. Since I was a primary staff officer, I really wasn't required to do it but it was a good policy to keep from alienating the other lieutenants. The next morning, four of us pay officers met in front of the Headquarters building to catch a ride with the mail truck to Camp Edwards. We showed up with our brief cases and side arms with five rounds.

The truck was late, as usual, and we got down to Camp Edwards at 0800. There were two dozen other pay officers there before us, collecting their money. The finance officer in charge was a major. He took particular care in briefing me since it was my first time to pay. I was personally liable for the money that I was about to receive. I followed the major into a small cage to pick up my dough. The major said, "You'll be getting one of the larger payrolls and I'll have to apologize but they didn't have any 10,000 Won bills." I heard what he said but the consequences of what he said weren't apparent until he handed me a small grocery bag full of 1000 Won bills.

"I don't think I can get all that in my briefcase," I said. I had a small but expensive Samsonite briefcase.

"No, you can't." He pulled out four more small bags full of money. "There's over 50,000 bills in these bags. You should count them."

"You have got to be kidding, sir?"

"You signed for them, not me."

"It'll take me hours to count to 50,000."

"Sorry"

"Well, damn, Sir, I can't even carry five bags full of this crap."

"Here, take this mail bag."

With the help of my comrade pay officers, I finally got all the bills counted. I looked like old St. Nick dragging the mailbag over my shoulder filled with sixty-three million won and nothing more than a 1000 won bill.

Paying these Korean workers was one of the most miserable additional duties I ever did. I started at Camp Grant and paid about a dozen guys there. Then I went to a water pumping station and paid people there. Then I went (via helicopter) to two radar sites and another small compound that I think contained an underground ammo dump but I wasn't sure.

When I finished, it was after twilight and I was tired. I'd paid about three hundred people at a dozen different compounds. I didn't have time to eat breakfast, lunch, or supper. My fingers were numb from counting over 50,000 bills, twice. I just thanked the Lord that I didn't run out of money before I got through paying everyone. There would have been a mutiny, riot, or good old fashion lynching, but I would have taken some of them with me. I did have my five rounds of forty-five-caliber ammunition.

When I got back to Camp Greaves, the club was closed for insect fumigating. I went to my Quonset hut and heated a six-ounce can of chili in a sink full of hot water in the latrine. Someone else's can of ravioli was already heating up in the other sink. The label had been soaked off the ravioli. I soaked the label off mine and traded cans just to haze the guy's mind.

We had a good twelve hours of work to do each day but the last four hours before sleep was sometimes hard to occupy. I tried to fill the time by writing letters. The new postal clerk told me that I got more mail than anyone in the battalion. The clerk was called "Thunder" because he could, or I should say, "could not help from," cutting incredibly loud farts. His assistant was nearly driven crazy. It's hard to escape the effects of a fart when you're enclosed in a eight by ten foot mailroom with no windows.

I filled the following weeks with Annual General Inspection preparation and sending the Recon Platoon on many vital missions; route recons, bridge classifications and minefield surveys.

One day in early June, I had to send the Recon Platoon on one of the blackest missions of all. I sent them out to recover the bodies of some dead American soldiers. Thankfully they weren't from our unit. I mean, it's a shame that they died, but I'm glad that all the paperwork, investigations, ruined careers, and heartache didn't involve us.

Our sister battalion, a mechanized unit, was practicing river crossings at a place called Crab Island. The water was usually so low that you could wade across it. However, the late spring monsoons had caused the river to swell to an enormous size. After careful deliberation, the company commander decided that it was safe enough to continue the river crossing exercise. The word was passed down the line and the first M-113 armored personnel carrier (APC) hit the water at a crawl and started floating across the river. The tread action was just barely strong enough to keep the vehicle headed in the right direction.

Safely on the far side, the first APC radioed back that the crossing was a piece of cake, however everyone in the vehicle had their doubts that they going make it. The second APC lurched into the water and also propelled itself to safety on the southern bank of the Imjin River. The third APC entered the water and began maneuvering to the far side. In midstream, the treads stopped turning and the heavy armored vehicle slowly started to sink.

The vehicle commander was the first man out and into the water. The driver escaped next as the vehicle disappeared under the surface.   A   third man came up, his hand raised above his head, but he went down again. A fourth and a fifth man came up and started swimming to the bank. One of them went down but the other made it. Three more men followed, swimming frantically towards safety. All three were found alive a half-mile down river from the crossing site.

Six men survived but there were ten in the vehicle. Two died in the vehicle and were recovered when the APC was raised from the water. The other two men were presumed drowned and at the mercy of the river.

I alerted my bridge guards to be on the lookout for bodies in the water. Our Recon Platoon scrambled to run a recovery operation along the north bank. As the 1st Battalion 9th Infantry was out searching for bodies, the brass from division was investigating the incident. They found that someone left a drain unplugged which caused the vehicle to fill up, resulting in the deaths of four soldiers. Drowning in a murky, Korean river was a bad way to go.

While the Bridge Platoon was wrestling a body ashore with a grappling hook and the Recon Platoon was pulling the other body from the high water mark in the branches of a tree, the general was busy firing everybody in the world. The poor vehicle commander was going to be court marshaled, the platoon leader was relieved from duty and sent to guard a museum and the company commander was sent to division to be a property custodian and the battalion commander got an official reprimand and a transfer to division Headquarters (screw up, move up) to be a dining facility inspector. All of their careers were over.

Meanwhile, my unit, 1st Battalion 9th Infantry, got a "job well done" for retrieving the bodies. The body at the bridge was recovered too quickly for me to see it but I saw the Recon Platoon bag their body and carry him up the steep bank of the river bed to the waiting ambulance. People, when they are dead and in a bag, seem small.

Things didn't settle down for weeks. Every other day, the bridge guards reported seeing bodies floating down the river. No one believed them, however, I gave them the benefit of the doubt because it was my job to be suspicious. Then one day the ROKs pulled a dead fisherman out of the Han River Estuary. After seeing another body fished out of the river, I also became gun shy and every time I saw a floating log or bush, I thought I saw a body. It faded, like most of the bad experiences. The reason the bad experiences fade is because there was always another bad experience right around the corner to take its place.

The floating bodies were long suppressed in my memory when we were at the officer's meeting in the club. It was a mandatory meeting for the professional development of our careers. We professionally developed all that we were going to that night and the bell was rung twice. Everyone had a drink in each hand. The XO was about as shit-faced as I had ever seen him and the boys had succeeded in getting Miss Yi to start crying and provoking old Miss Kim into screaming and spitting. It was just like party night but there were no women to go to bed with, just two Korean waitresses, one to make cry and one to make spit.

About 2100 (9 PM), I got a most unusual and frightening call from the Headquarters Company. When he was making his rounds through the billeting area, he saw, or thought he saw, some parachutes coming down. Parachutes! Paratroopers strike fear in any tactician's heart. The North Koreans had 5000 paratroopers that they could drop on us at any given moment.

"Open the Arms Room," I said and went careening down the hill as fast as my legs could carry me. I met the Headquarters Company orderly and asked him where he saw the parachutes coming down.

"They ain't coming down," he said.

"What do you mean?" I asked.

"Look up there, Sir. You can still see them!"

I stared blankly into the night sky, until I focused on three ghostly apparitions hovering silently above the compound. They looked like parachutes but they weren't. They were propaganda balloons. They were as big as parachutes and made from a clear plastic that looked like silk in the darkness.

"Close the arms room," I told the orderly. "Those are propaganda balloons. I think we'll capture one."

"Capture one?" asked the orderly.

"Yeah," I said.

"How?" he asked.

"Well, we'll just wait and let 'em come to us." One of the balloons was sinking slowly while the other two were drifting towards the south. A small crowd of soldiers was gathering around me as we waited. I started lecturing them on propaganda balloons. No one had ever captured an intact balloon before, but we were about to do the deed. The balloon was fifteen meters off the ground and looked like it was slowly going to crash on the tin roof of the Headquarters' orderly room. I got my merry band of followers to surround the orderly room so they could catch the balloon when it came sliding off the roof.

We were all cheering and shouting when automatic weapons fire sounded from the south bank of the river. Everyone crouched into the ready position and waited for orders. I was crouched in my ready position also. Then I realized that I was supposed to give the orders.

"You and you," I said as I pointed. "Come with me, the rest of you guys stay here!" My two companions and I ran up the hill to the perimeter fence. We lay down in the grass and watched the riverbanks closely.

"Do you see anything?" I asked, but no one answered. Shots rang out again and red tracer bullets rocketed into the air towards the balloons.

"It's the ROKs," said one of the soldiers.

"They're shooting at the balloons," I said.

"Hey everybody!" I yelled. "Come up here and take a look at this!" A mob of twenty-five or so soldiers ran up to the fence line and knelt beside us.

"The ROKs are trying to shoot the balloons down," I said. We watched intently.

A burst of automatic fire broke the silence. Red-hot tracers screamed across the sky again and pierced one of the balloons. The balloon flamed instantly and fell blazing into the rice paddies. The fireball was so intense that we thought we could feel it on our faces three hundred meters away. Evidently the ROKs enjoyed it too because a steady stream of gunfire broke out in an attempt to shoot down the second balloon. In moments, it caught fire but didn't burn as fiercely as the first. It crashed into a rice paddy dike that was covered with straw and it burned for several minutes.

I turned my attention back to the third balloon coming down on our compound. We surrounded the building once more. The balloon was carrying a basket filled with propaganda leaflets and was sitting high center on the crest of the roof. I figured that as the balloon deflated it would slide down the metal roof and fall off the edge. It was working just like I figured until it got caught in some electrical wires and I had to free it. I was a little afraid that an electrical spark may cause it to ignite. My twenty-five fearless infantry comrades had all backed off so far they needed binoculars to see what I was doing.

I was apprehensive, pulling the fifteen-foot tall, twelve-foot wide balloon through the intricacies of the compound electrical system but I managed to get it to the center of our dirt parade field. I asked the Headquarters Company orderly to call the Officers Club and ask the battalion commander to come down to the parade field. I waited five minutes for the soldier to come back and he told me that the battalion commander wasn't coming anywhere, "bring the damn thing to him."

I had my "orders." I maneuvered the balloon through a quarter of a mile of telephone and electric wires. The balloon was carrying about a hundred pounds of leaflets, tightly packed in the basket and ready to be triggered with a small altimeter mechanism. The release gizmo was designed to open the bottom of the basket and drop the leaflets en masse at a high altitude and have them scatter in the wind across as much area as possible. For some reason the release mechanism didn't function properly and the balloon lost altitude and came to rest on the orderly room.

I had the balloon corralled pretty well. One soldier was going with me to the Officers Club while the others went on about their business. There was a steep bank that we had to climb. The dirt was loose and muddy and we began to slip. I was unbalanced for a moment and had to retreat down the slope a few steps. When I did, the altimeter triggered and the leaflets dropped to the ground still in the plastic bag that lined the basket. As the balloon released its cargo, it became a hundred pounds lighter and so did I. With two giant steps, I leaped up the steep bank, my feet barely touching the ground.

"Grab the leaflets," I hollered over my shoulder, "and follow me."

With moonwalk-like twenty-foot bounds, I went bouncing off to the Officer's Club having the most fun I'd had in ages. I could jump at least six feet in the air and travel twenty feet or so across the ground but my arms were getting tired from holding on.

I sent the soldier ahead to assemble the officers on the veranda. I could hear very loud music coming from the club. No wonder they didn't hear the gun fire from the ROKs. I waited for the music to be turned off and the officers to assemble before I made my grand entrance. I stood just out of view around the corner. When the assembled officers quieted down, I took one exaggerated comical leap and sailed around the corner, floating like Peter Pan. I hit the ground again and sprang into the air, floating into the group of officers. They caught me and shoved me around in mid-air for a few seconds, spinning me in circles. Everyone began to buzz about the balloon and of course each one wanted to take his turn flying with it. I passed it around and it was great fun.

After a few more drinks, it was suggested that we tie old Miss Kim to the balloon and see which one would win. If she happened to weigh one pound less than the magic number she would've floated off to Kansas. "What the hell—Korea—Kansas, same-same but different." Everybody was as drunk as I'd ever seen them and weren't making any sense.

Finally, the doc pulled out a knife and attacked the balloon. It gasped its last and collapsed limply on the guardrail of the veranda. The S-4, two platoon leaders, and the battalion commander were smoking cigars. I forgot to mention to them that the balloon was filled with highly flammable hydrogen gas. Drunks are always lucky, like in car accidents, the intoxicated person invariably comes out without a scratch, and the sober one ends up a paraplegic. The same held true with us. Fortunately since everyone was drunk, they were all blessed.

The deflation of the balloon climaxed the evening and we all went home to our bunks. I had to go to Camp Casey Division Headquarters for a G-2 meeting the next day. I was going to take the propaganda balloon with me for display. I got permission to spend the night down range as long as I returned for work call at 0730 the following morning.

The bus pulled out at sunrise. I had a small AWOL bag and a large box stuffed full of the balloon and some of the leaflets. I'd get to Camp Casey at 0930, the meeting was at 1100. *We should be through by noon, and I'll be in the ville by 1300*, I thought.

The G-2 meeting was held in the general's conference room. I was amazed at how well the division staff lived, but if the general and his staff can't have good things, then who can?

It got to be my turn to speak (my name was even penciled in on the agenda) and I laid out my balloon, passed around samples of the four separate kinds of propaganda leaflets and described the capture of the balloon in detail. I threw in the story of the two balloons that were shot down and "flamed in." I left out the part where all of the officers were drunk and attacked the third balloon with a knife.

After my presentation, Mike, my friend, and I went to the local bathhouse. Mike had more than a platonic relationship going with the manager at the Camp Hovey steam and cream. She didn't give massages, she was legitimate.

There was a hotdog stand right outside the steam and cream. When I finished, I found Mike out there, sucking down his second dog. I never bought a hot dog from a stand because I was afraid that it might be real dog, so I never ate one. Mike had to return to his unit but I headed down to the ville. I'd changed clothes in the bathhouse and gave my uniform to Mike to store until the morning.

I liked being down range in the cold light of day, especially when I didn't have a heavy sexual drive between my legs. Tokko-ri was my favorite of the villes of the few that I had been to. Besides losing my Korean cherry there, I knew the roads better.

I went to my favorite restaurant and ordered up a huge bowl of ramen with egg. The old Papa-san and Mama-san there liked me because I played peek-a-boo with their grandchildren. I also liked them because they treated me like I was special. I was the "D M GEE Guy." However, I also tipped 100% which probably had something to do with it. What the hell, they won't get rich slinging chop to soldiers. They'll be there from now until the twelfth of never.

I said goodbye to the proprietors and walked down the street, shopping. Throughout the year I ended up buying a beautiful mink blanket, a black bedspread, two tailored three-piece suits, a handmade pair of dress boots and a set of paintings of the four seasons. I bought some other clothes but they were purchased out of necessity. My Korean economy underwear fell apart after the second washing. Of course, Mr. Yi my houseman, washed them in a trash can, stirring and beating them with an axe handle. They were clean afterwards, mainly because there were holes where the dirty spots used to be.

I wandered fairly aimlessly around the streets, going in bar after bar just to see what was happening. Sometimes I played pool with the businesswomen working in the clubs. Every now and then I bought a drink of ginseng or other exotic liquor. Once, I tried some kind of homemade Mokali, a rice wine with a kick. Saki is a good comparison. It's the Oriental white lightning.

I fiddled around the ville for three or four hours and watched the soldiers start to come down range on pass. It wasn't long before Mike came through the gate with a big grin on his face. We made the round of bars (my second time) until we settled into the Papa-san Club. That was where I picked up my first businesswoman. It had been remodeled since I'd been back from the Z. There were a million flashing lights and the name had been changed to the Bonanza Club. It had the same effect that you would get if you turned a MacDonald's into a disco. Mike arranged to meet his real girlfriend there and they went off together. I preferred the streets so I left.

I was walking back to the center of the village when I heard a female voice, "Excuse me!"

I turned around to find a very attractive woman behind me. She looked too white to be a pure oriental.

"Yes?" I said.

"Could I walky with you? This man bother me."

I thought for a moment, trying to decide what was the right move when she came up to me and grabbed my arm. We walked for a few steps until this soldier came up behind us and started speaking harshly to the woman. I stayed out of it and it ended quickly with the soldier walking away.

"Thank you," she said.

"I didn't do anything," I returned.

"Yes, you did."

We walked arm in arm for several blocks talking all the while. She was twenty-three years old and married to a soldier who had rotated home and left her holding the bag. The bag was a one-and-a-half year old kid. The soldier that accosted her thought she was a businesswoman and wanted a short time with her. I felt sorry for her but I couldn't show it or she would more than likely try to take advantage of me. I'm not sure she wasn't already using me somehow. She asked me if I had ever been to TDC (Tongduchon) the big village outside Camp Casey. I told her that I had but it was too big for me. She suggested that we take a cab over there and play some pool. I figured that this was the rip off; she needed to get to TDC and wanted me to pay the three dollars for cab fare. I talked with her for a minute or two trying to convince her that I didn't want to go to TDC. She finally said, "I'll pay for taxi!"

Those words convinced me that I wanted to go. Any Korean businesswoman is not going to offer to pay three dollars for anything. That's why they call them businesswomen: money comes in but it doesn't go out. All they give up is their bodies and they have an unending supply of that.

We hailed a cab and drove the narrow, winding road to TDC. Once there, we went into a club and headed upstairs to a pool hall and played several games of eight ball and drank Cokes. It was all her treat too. There had to be a catch somewhere.

We got into a cab and started driving back when it began to rain. She made the cabdriver stop and we walked the rest of the way back to Tokko-ri in the rain. To her, walking in the rain was a romantic thing to do but to a soldier, who spends half his time wet and dirty, it was just plain stupid. It wasn't exactly the way to win my heart. I would've enjoyed a home cooked meal much more. Well, maybe not a Korean home cooked meal. I may have preferred a walk in the rain after all.

It was 2300 (11 PM) when we got back to downtown Tokko-ri. I wanted to try to find Mike before curfew and told her that I was going on my own for a while. She asked me to meet her under this particular street lamp at 2330 (11:30 PM).

I went to several clubs searching for Mike but he was buried in the bowels of the alleys in some hooch, where no one could find him. I returned to the lamppost at the designated time to wait for Jenny (Gin He). The soldiers were being run out of the bars and the courtesy patrol was ushering everyone home. I'd just decided to wait two more minutes when she came racing around the corner to meet me. She ran up to me and threw her arms around me and put her head on my chest. She smiled and said, "I hoped you would be here." We kissed very deeply, embracing beneath the lamppost. There was a light drizzle in the waning hours before curfew that chilled my bones but tonight, it didn't dampen my heart.

She told me that she wanted me to come home with her but she had a roommate, therefore, I couldn't do it. I told her that I wasn't real disappointed. I liked her too much to have sex the first night. *Who the hell said that?* I thought. She wrote her address on a piece of paper and asked me to write her from the DMZ. I promised that I would. This was almost like a real relationship.

I went back to Mike's room on the compound. The door was locked because he was down range for the night. I took up a "rest" position on the last commode in the latrine. The last commode afforded a corner I could lean into. It took me thirty minutes to realize that sleep was impossible in that position. I found an open room that was used for junk. It had a couple of bicycles chained together and a few cardboard boxes full of paraphernalia. I took the tops off the boxes and made a pallet and fell asleep on the floor.

I heard noises at 0500 and figured that it was some of the officers getting in from the ville. I was right; it was Mike and two others. One of them was still so loaded that the other two had to help him walk. They began wrestling in the hall until they knocked several holes in the walls. It was great fun to watch but I was glad I was only visiting. The brawl ended in a rather short time and they went to their rooms to sleep. I had to leave right then or I couldn't make the 0730 work call.

I threw my uniform on and went to the gate to find an early taxi. The driver offered to take me to Munsan but no further. Munsan was a fairly large town so I could catch the bus from there. I paid the driver twenty dollars to get me there alive and in less than one hour.

He did it. I caught the first bus from Munsan that went to the propaganda villages, Unification Village and Tae Song Dong in the DMZ.

Miss Kim, the most attractive of the three barbershop ladies, was on the bus also.

"Aren't you a little early?" I asked her.

"Me washy hair before open shop," she said.

The Koreans that worked on the compound had access to a shower facility of one kind or another, so they preferred to wash themselves in an American shower instead of a Korean creek or if they were lucky, an outdoor water faucet.

Back at my compound I went through a relatively normal day, which meant that I operated at borderline insanity. Jenny was prevalent in the back of my mind through most of it. As retreat sounded over the loud speaker, I pulled out a piece of paper and dashed off a letter to Jenny. I printed it in first grade block letters hoping she would be able to read it without getting someone to help her. I gave my houseman a couple of bucks to copy the Korean address on to the envelope and mail it on the Korean economy.

Several days later, I received a Korean letter. I ripped it open in excitement having no idea what to expect. It was three pages long and written in English script and read like a poem. She spent hours composing it, I was sure. She used words like "melancholy," and "sublime." It was beautifully written. I wrote back immediately in script this time and in comparable English grammar instead of GI slang. I paid the houseman to mail it again. He made a joke about having a Korean girlfriend. I laughed even though I wasn't sure why it was funny.

I was in my office when the Headquarters Company commander came in and told me that he had captured a spy and had him in the orderly room. As we went back to the Headquarters building I asked, "Do you have an armed guard on him?"

"No need," said the commander.

"Maybe I should draw a weapon." I said.

"No need." We entered the building and the Headquarters commander said, "I captured him on the bus and believe it or not, the spy asked about you."

"You're shitting me!" I said.

"No, I'm not, here he is."

Jenny stepped through the doorway and smiled a nervous smile. I grinned from ear to ear. I went to the phone, called my office, and told my sergeant that I was taking some time off. Jenny and I took off across the compound to my Quonset hut.

She sat on my bed and I sat on the desk chair. She told me that she was scared to come up because she didn't know what the DMZ would be like.

"It's not so bad," I said, trying to keep a straight face. It really sucked like a Hoover, but not right at this minute.

"How did you get across the bridge?" I asked out of professional curiosity.

"I have ID card."

I'd forgotten that she was married to a soldier and had a dependent card.

"They didn't ask you any questions?"

"Yes, guard man, ask me who I see. I show him this letter." She held out the envelope that I'd sent to her with my name on it.

"Oh my God," I said under my breath.

"I do something wrong?" she asked.

"No," I said, knowing I would be the butt of a joke for months.

I moved over to the bed and put my arm around her. I didn't want to be obvious about what I wanted but I couldn't help it. I told her that making out in a fatigue uniform and combat boots wasn't my idea of romance. Of course making love with another man's throwaway wife wasn't exactly romance either.

"I'm going to take a shower," I said. I started to undress. The more I undressed the more she undressed me with her eyes. I felt what I thought a stripper must feel. When I turned my back to take off my underwear, I could feel her stare still on me. I grabbed the towel off the mosquito bar at the foot of the bed and wrapped it around me. I told her that I'd be back in a few minutes. "Hurry," she said.

The whole time I was in the shower I had an erection. I was afraid that someone else might come in but it was quite early for anyone to show up. As soon as I thought that, the outside door of the Quonset hut slammed. *Must be the chaplain.* He's one of the few people who have the flexibility of getting off work early. I was wrong, it was Mr. Yi, the houseman who was the most logical person to be in the billets at that time.

I listened intently and heard another door open. My door! Jenny gave a little shout and Mr. Yi started apologizing. The door shut quickly and he immediately came down to the latrine to see if the person taking the shower was me.

"Your girlfriend from Seoul?" he asked.

She was from Tokko-ri, but I just said, "Yes." Mr. Yi laughed a mischievous laugh thinking that he had it all figured out. I entered my room, with just a towel wrapped around me. Jenny's eyes widened and she ran over to me.

"Some Korean man came here."

"Yes, I know, that was Mr. Yi, the houseman."

"I don't like him."

"You don't like Korean men period."

"How you know?" she asked.

"Most Korean women who have been with American men no longer like Korean men." I said, hoping it was true. It was a generality that I inferred from the few cases that I knew about. Korean men are the center of attention in the family and the woman serves him. American men tend to spoil their Korean women in hopes of increased sexual favors. The Korean women don't mind, because they'd have to put out no matter to which man they belonged so why not get all of the goodies that they can get along the way?

I sat on the edge of the bunk; the towel was loosely draped around me. Jenny squatted on the floor between my legs with a hand on each of my knees. My erection began to grow again making a tent out of the towel. Jenny giggled and placed her hand on it through the towel. "Are you embarrassed?" she asked as I lay back on the bunk. She opened the towel. Her face was so close to my penis that I could feel her breath on it.

"I make you feel good," she said. "But there is trick."

"What are you saying?" I asked, sitting up on my elbows thinking that the "trick" was me and she wanted money.

"You stand up," she instructed. I did. She was still on her knees.

"Now is trick," she said. "I make you cum and don't touch your..." She pointed to my penis.

"Penis," I said, embarrassed, mostly because I didn't usually say the word penis. She blushed a little.

"Okay," I said. "I'm game, but I don't think it's going to happen."

"Shut eyes, no looky," she ordered.

I stood there with my eyes shut, hands behind my back, waiting for something to happen. I thought what she might conduct a slow form of torture but I didn't think she could get me off without touching my manhood. I heard her change position and could feel her breath on my thighs. I thought she was going to give me a blowjob but she didn't, after all, she did say that she wouldn't touch my penis.

She cupped my testicles with her hand and started scratching the back of them with her long nails. She reached her other hand between my legs, parted my cheeks, and slid her finger up my ass. I went up on my toes and made some kind of strange sound that would be impossible to repeat. She began massaging my prostrate. She was a little woman with tiny hands, but her finger felt like a broom handle. She began blowing her breath on the head of my cock. It was torture alright but I wasn't really sure I wanted her to stop. I don't know exactly how long it was, but it wasn't long before I started doing some kind of hokey pokey dance, shaking it all about, screamed like a two year old getting spanked in the five and dime and almost blacked out. When I opened my eyes, she was wiping her face with the back of her hands and there were droplets of semen on the floor between us and out behind her about eight feet. I thought, *Alright, good distance.*

That ranked right up there with one of the best and most unusual sexual experiences I'd ever had. Except for a dry hump in high school, this was the only time that I had ever had an orgasm without having my penis actually touched.

She began to disrobe. "Don't looky," she said, in false modesty. I pretended to turn my back. She was short and very buxom. Her skin was white and her nipples were pink. She was really attractive. After seeing her, my throbbing penis never sank below half-mast before it began to grow again.

I guess what happened next could be described as conventional sex. She wore me out but I could tell that she was at her limit also. I deduced that I won the duel because she got a "free" one on me before I started on her. It was well after dark and we were hungry. As I walked her to the bus station, we stopped off at the Korean snack bar and had a hamburger and a Coke.

After that night, I didn't hear from Jenny for two weeks. A letter finally came that asked me to meet her in Sanyuri outside of Camp Pelham at my convenience. It took me three days from the time I received her letter to develop an excuse to go south of the river. I had some directions to her new hooch but I ended up asking two different storeowners anyway.

I found her building complex. She was in the center of it near the water fountain. A beautiful blonde haired baby girl stood in a tub, naked, and Jenny squatted beside her, washing the baby's bottom. It was a wonderful sight but this family didn't fit into the Korean setting. The lovely white skinned mother was auburn haired and the baby was blonde. Neither would be accepted in the Korean culture, they were breeds, two generations of war babies.

"Jenny," I yelled over a four-foot high fence.

"Oh," she glanced at me almost nonchalantly.

I walked into the little fenced in area. "I got your message and came as soon as I could. I'm sorry that it took three days."

"If Mama-san ask you, you my husband."

"What?" I said a little baffled.

"I had to tell Mama-san that I had American husband or she would not rent to me."

"Okay," I said. "You have a pretty baby."

"Comsamnida, her name, Rebecca."

"Rebecca of Sunny Brook Farm," I jested. Jenny had no idea what I was talking about.

"You hungry?" Jenny asked me.

"A little."

"I have supper ready. Come in to house."

It was furnished with a stove, a mat, a chest of drawers, and a shelf. That was all.

"How much you pay for the new hooch?" I asked.

"Forty dollar."

"Where do you get your money?"

238

"You think I'm businesswoman?"

"No," I said emphatically.

"I have money!" She was beginning to get mad.

"Okay." Let's play this game. "Where do you get your money?"

"You think me whore!" she shouted.

"No, I don't, but I know you don't work."

"I have husband."

"Stateside? Right?"

"No," she said.

"No? Well, where the hell is he?"

"Camp Hovey."

"What! You have a husband, here in country and you come up to the DMZ to be with me!"

"Yes."

"I don't believe this! You told me he left you and went stateside! What rank is he, a private?"

"E-4," she said.

"I can't believe that you let me do this!"

"It's okay," she tried to console me.

"No, it's not. I'm an officer. I can't screw around with an enlisted man's wife. I thought you had been abandoned"

"It's okay, he sleepy with other women."

"I don't believe this! " I said again. "Why did you move over here to Sanyuri?" I asked.

"To be closer to you," she said.

That did it. I was in her kill zone as far as I was going to get.

"I can't see you anymore." I reached in my wallet and gave her two twenties. "Take it! I feel responsible for you moving, so I'll give you a month's rent. I've got to get out of here. Goodbye, Jenny." I knew this was too good to be true and I started walking away. She called to me but I didn't turn around. Her baby started crying.

I went straight into the first club and sat down at the bar. I had my uniform on so I couldn't stay but I just wanted to disappear for a minute. My remorse passed quicker than I thought it should and I caught the DMZ Express back up to Munsan. I walked around there for a while until I was bored stiff. Then I hopped another bus to Yongtori outside of Camp Edwards, the medical and supply compound.

I bought a few clothes, went to another club, and changed. I put my bag behind the bar at the club and paid the Mama-san to watch it. I went to the heart of the village. There were about five clubs worth going to and I went to all of them. I met a woman named Sin in one of them. I went to her hooch and we started to converse. She was at least half American.

We talked about sex for a minute. She wanted me to short time her with a rubber and I wanted to get masturbated. Half the time when I used a rubber, I would get over zealous and break it or it would work itself off. So I might as well not even have used it at all. It was safer to get a hand job. We got all the way to the point where we were both naked and we still couldn't agree on a price or a specific act. It was about as exciting as haggling with a pawn broker over a used lawn mower. I got dressed and left.

I went to a country/western club. Two of the women were wearing cowboy hats. I sat at the bar and ordered a Coke for a buck fifty. I felt like I was back in Alaska with prices like that.

Several women came over to me and wanted to know if I would buy them a "drinky." I didn't feel like it. I finished my first Coke and was on my second when a very pretty young school girl came up to me and wanted me to give her a donation of some kind. She evidently didn't speak any English but she had a can with a slit on the top and a symbol that looked like the March of Dimes or something like that.

She was in her school dress and her hair was in pigtails. I started to give her an American dollar but she shook her head "no" and said "Korean." I didn't have any Korean money on me but I asked the bartender to change my buck. I gave the 600 Won to the young girl. She thanked me and left the bar. Another woman, about twenty-four years old sat down beside me and said, "Thank you," in English better than I could speak.

"Thanks for what?" I asked.

"That girl was my friend's daughter. She's collecting for an orphanage. Your dollar will buy a child three days worth of food."

"What do they eat?" I asked in jest.

"Mostly rice and kimchee but your dollar goes toward meat and milk."

"You seem to know a lot about such things."

"My mother and father help run an orphanage outside of Seoul."

"Very commendable," I said. "Where did you learn your English?"

"All Korean schools teach English as a manda—mandatory subject." That was the first word that she had trouble with but it came out perfectly on the second try. She continued, "I was exceptionally proficient and got accepted to the University of Massachusetts. I spent four years there."

"You are an exceptional lady," I said. "Could I buy you a drink?"

"No, but perhaps I could interest you in a bowl of ramen at the restaurant across the street."

"I'm flattered," I said. "I've never been asked to dinner in this country. It's a first."

"For me too." She was attractive but not beautiful. She had long black hair and wore glasses.

"What do you do for a living?" I asked.

"I'm ashamed to say but I work as a prostitute."

"Why? You have a degree from the University of Massachusetts?"

"In Home Economics, not a very marketable field in Korea."

"Maybe so," I said. "But it's still a far cry from prostitution."

"After being westernized, I couldn't live at home when I got back. My father would treat my mother terribly. He wouldn't lift his finger to get a bowl of rice from the far side of the table. He'd call my mother in from another room to serve it to him. I couldn't live like that so I ran away from home. I took a bus out of Seoul. I only had 500 Won and when it ran out, I had to get off the bus. I looked around and saw Americans here. I asked one what he was doing here and he told me that he was stationed at Camp Edwards as an MP. I asked him if he knew where a woman could get a job and he brought me to this club. He evidently knew the Mama-san really well. I started out tending bar and gradually started servicing the soldiers as I learned the ropes. Someday, I'll save enough money to pay Mama-san back and leave this town."

"And do what?"

"Open a store of my own, near an American military complex, so I can make some real money. Koreans don't pay much for anything but Americans will."

"What kind of things do you want to sell in your store?"

"Clothes mostly. Maybe suitcases and mink blankets or Korean flags, anything that American soldiers would buy."

"If you ever get out of this prostitute racket, I'm sure you'll be a good legitimate businesswoman." I smiled at the pun, because whores are called businesswomen.

She looked up at me over her teacup and said, "I'm a damn fine illegitimate businesswoman too!"

My prick tingled when she said that. "I say, are you propositioning me?"

"I suppose you can say that."

We finished eating quickly and she paid for the supper. Her name was Lee and she liked to be called Lee instead of Miss Lee. We went to her place. It was small and fairly typical but it had some memorabilia in it that looked more like home because of her four years at the university. She was so American that it was frightening. We sat down on the bed together and she read aloud to me from a book of poems. The poem was a sappy story about star-crossed lovers. Normally I would have just said, "gag me," but I was totally at ease when she finished reading.

"I want to make love to you," she said.

I think I just nodded.

"Due to my unfortunate circumstance, I am forced to ask you for a donation."

Her voice pitched at the end as if it were a question.

"It'll be my pleasure," I said. "What size of donation do you require?" I asked. I was having a more intelligent conversation with this woman than I had with anyone else in Korea including most of my soldiers.

"The market value of my services is twenty dollars from dusk to dawn."

I thought to myself, *that works out to about two dollars an hour.*

"Acceptable," I said.

"Then we are in agreement?"

"Yes."

She began to tell me a story of her roommates at the University of Massachusetts. They took Lee to all the campus parties, showed her how to smoke cigarettes and marijuana, and taught her how to give head and satisfy a man. But most of all, they taught her how to use a man to her own advantage.

Now that she was a little older, her passive Korean upbringing and her turbulent four-year stint in New England blended together to make a total woman. Lee and I began to kiss. Her breath smelled like wine, a great relief from the kimchee breath of most Korean women. She took her glasses off and pitched them on the floor.

We disrobed and sized each other up. I lay down on the bed and Lee began to fellate me with exquisite precision. With expert skills, she brought me to the brink of orgasm and then she wrapped her long hair around my phallus and stroked it gently. She slid a rubber on me before I even knew what happened and mounted me from the top. She began to pitch and groan, becoming frantic, nearly to the point of frenzy. She was grinding into me so hard and fast that I thought my pubic hairs might catch on fire from the friction.

"Oh, Babe," she screamed. "I'm cumming!" We climaxed simultaneously but I only acknowledged it with a grunt and then she collapsed over on me. Her hair fell all about my face and her breath exploded into my ear. Her pointed nipples tickled the hairs on my chest. A shudder originated at her vagina and raced through her body. It happened again and then she shivered continuously for several minutes. It was the second most intense post orgasm reaction to which I had ever been witness. A cheerleader I dated in college would sometimes blackout if the orgasm were intense enough.

"Lee, are you alright?"

"Yes, I needed that."

"So did I," I said. "But I'm not sure if I'm finished."

"You need more?" she asked.

I rolled over and climbed on top of her and began pumping into her with long thrusts. I pulled her legs way up so I could get deeper penetration. She arched and clutched at me and panted rasping breaths. She climaxed continuously for a minute or so and then went limp. I still held her legs up and ground my pelvis into hers. Slowly, she began to shudder and her whole body vibrated. Her post orgasm quiver was just enough to make me ejaculate again. For an instant, I'd forgotten that I was in Korea and that Lee was Korean. When I "came to" from my post coitus collapse, I didn't really remember where I was.

"What village is this?" I asked.

Lee thought I was kidding or making some kind of a joke. Then she said, "I live in Yongtori."

I stayed a while and listened to Lee read to me from books and magazines, even a PX catalog. She finally tired and fell asleep. I got up, dressed and took a twenty-dollar bill out of my wallet and placed it on the pillow beside her head. I was tying my boots when she stirred. She blinked herself awake and said, "Do not forget the business part of this businesswoman."

"I haven't," I said. "Look beside you and sleep well. Goodnight, Lee."

She clutched the bill in her hand. "Goodnight, Master David," she said.

Those words, "Master David," stuck with me for a long time. I always wondered why in the hell she called me "Master David." I went back in a week or so to ask her about it and to repeat the performance but she was gone. I never saw her again. I hoped that she saved enough to buy her way out of the business. Maybe I would run into her by chance at a curio shop outside some American compound somewhere.

CHAPTER 14

Bungle in the Jungle

Weeks dragged on and summer crept up on us after the monsoons. The rains left us with little damage: leaky roofs, two washed out piss tubes and a quagmire for a parade field. The only drownings were the ones that our sister battalion incurred during the river crossing operation. There were a few Koreans that were swept away and never seen or heard from again but they didn't count. It was a terrible attitude to take but I'd been here for my six months and a soldier's attitude and ideas change in that period of time.

Things were normal through the first part of summer, at least until June 25th. It was the thirtieth anniversary of the start of the Korean War. We went on a special alert that lasted only twelve hours but of course it was from 1800 (6 PM) to 0600 The North Koreans stuck it to us again without ever firing a shot.

Absolutely nothing happened. Propaganda was normal, shooting incidents were minimal and weather factors were against a full scale attack. However, the weather was against an attack thirty years ago also. The North Koreans should never have attached in June back in 1950 but the initial assault was just after the monsoon season, rivers were high, rice paddies were full of water and every dirt road in Korea was a slip and slide.

The heavy rains caused mines to be washed down from the high ground to the valleys. Wooden box mines, originally designed in China, tended to float quite a way from their original emplacements. We found one sitting in the middle of the road, armed and ready to explode. We called Explosive Ordinance Disposal (EOD) and they took care of it. I was with them when they did it. Usually they show a great display of professionalism but this time they didn't. Instead of setting charges and blasting caps, the EOD sergeant loaded thirty rounds into an M-16 and blasted it until it exploded. It was fun but frightening because we weren't very far away. Shrapnel and shit flew all over everywhere but the EOD guys just laughed as it all rained down on us.

The summer came on strong and every day was another steam bath. The mid-nineties was about as hot as it ever got but the river and rice paddies provided enough humidity to turn Nevada into a jungle.

We celebrated the 4th of July by going on a twelve-mile road march in three hours. I had to run the last mile to make the time limit but I did it in two hours and fifty-eight minutes. I was an officer and set the example by packing my rucksack correctly, which made it weigh about fifty-five pounds. I weighed 168 pounds when I started the walk and 165 pounds when I finished. The pack also weighed a little less because I drank the half-gallon of water that I carried. I hated these marches. They didn't do anything for my morale and did even less for my legs, feet, back and boogered up knee.

I went to my room to shower and change. Sitting on the edge of the bed with my pants pulled down around my ankles, I was staring at the small scar below my knee where the stake went through the flesh. Deep down, it still hurt, especially after road marches. I was rubbing my thighs, trying to get the rigor mortis out, when I noticed that my wounded leg looked smaller. I pulled a string out of my desk drawer and wrapped it around my left thigh, six inches above the kneecap. I marked the string with a pen and made the measurements of my right leg. My left leg was at least a full inch smaller than my right. I nearly panicked. I knew that I favored it but I didn't know that it was atrophied so badly.

"Damn, what next," I said to myself.

After I got cleaned up, I went to the aid station to see the doc about my shriveled leg. Our regular doc was on leave so we had a stand-in from the Division Medical Battalion. His name was Mr. Wilcox. Since I was an officer I got preference and didn't have to stand in line. The aid station was filled with VD cases and blisters from the road march.

The temporary doc pushed around on my leg a little and I told him the story about the patrol accident. "I'm going to send you down to Major Thiel, a physical therapist. She'll get your leg back in shape."

Good, I thought, *I get to escape from here again.* The doc wrote an appointment slip for the following week.

I looked forward to visiting Seoul, a real booming metropolis. I always wanted to go to a place called Walker Hill, a huge hotel/casino complex. Korean nationals were not allowed to gamble at the casino, but I certainly was.

While waiting for the appointment with Major Thiel to arrive, I spent several days clearing brush away from the perimeter fence with a squad of extra duty soldiers assigned to me. Since clearing brush was their punishment, I only had them after their primary training had concluded. We started brush clearing at 1800 (6 PM) after chow and worked until thirty minutes before dark. God knows I didn't want to be outside the perimeter fence after dark.

While on detail, we found a hole in the fence and a small marijuana patch near the hole. We cleared it, but the information about the "grass" went no further than me. If the top brass found out about it, we'd be going through locker searches until next Christmas.

Finally the day to go to Seoul arrived. I was leaving on the 0930 bus. I decided to run through PT (Physical Training) with the company that morning, eat breakfast, take a shower and head south without ever going to the office.

I showed up at the PT formation and noticed an officer, a captain, who I'd never seen before. He was an assistant to the assistant S-3 operations from division. That meant that he was here to inspect our physical training performance.

We started off with forty side straddle hops, forty high jumpers, forty sit-ups, twenty-five pushups and fifteen body twists, a gut wrenching exercise that will turn an iron stomach into a jelly belly. Army exercises are counted with a four-count cadence so, in actuality, the number of each exercise was doubled. It was about twice as many exercises as usual. Then we had the run. The division policy states that we must run three miles in thirty minutes. About half the company could do this easily and the other half struggles.

If I ran "screaming, go berserk crazy," I could run a mile in 6 minutes 30 seconds. Twice in my life, after Basic Training and after Officer Candidate School, when I was in Olympic contention shape, I could run a mile in less than 6 minutes

We took off running at a blazing speed. I wasn't wearing my watch but we were running much faster than the required ten-minute mile. At the one-mile mark, half the company was left behind. I considered quitting but quickly dropped it from my mind. The pain in my leg was horrendous. At the two-mile mark, we lost another one-quarter of the company but we still picked up the pace. It was a blistering speed for an organized run. At the two-and-a-half mile mark, the captain sent from division to evaluate us, fell out of the small formation and tossed his cookies into the minefield beside the road.

"Don't go off the road, Sir," I yelled over my shoulder, "there're mines!" I didn't know if I made any sense but I couldn't say another word, I was too out of breath. We ran on, sprinting the last half mile. Ten out of sixty of us finished the run in a group. We were all leaning on our knees trying to catch our breath.

"Why did we screaming go berserk crazy?" I asked.

"We were being inspected," said the sergeant in charge.

"How fast did we run that?" I asked nearly afraid of the answer.

"Twenty minutes and some seconds," said the sergeant.

"That's less than seven minutes a mile. I bet we ran the last mile in six-and-a-half."

"I wouldn't doubt it," confirmed someone else.

"I'm taking a shower," I said, "if I can get back to my hooch without a recovery vehicle coming to get me." I started hobbling off when the inspecting officer straggled in.

"You lost half the company," he said to the sergeant in charge.

"Yes, Sir..." The conversation trailed off as I got further away. It wasn't my problem. It was the company commander's headache.

I barely got showered and changed in time to catch my bus to Seoul. I thought I was dying. I nearly got cramps all the way to Seoul and had to stand up most of the trip. I just couldn't believe how bad of shape I was in. I tried to use my atrophied leg as an excuse.

Youngsan was a big compound and it took forty-five minutes to get from the main bus station to the hospital. I took a bus but it went in the opposite direction that I wanted to go. I got off and caught another bus going the exact reverse direction and it went the wrong way too. It defied logic, or maybe I was just plumb dumb from the excessive exercise. I gave up and hailed a PX taxi.

I met Major Thiel at the physical therapy room. She was as butch as I ever could have imagined. She probably knew that I thought she was butch because she really manhandled me in the examination. She almost sprained my leg seeing if I was hurt. She couldn't find anything wrong with my knee so she wrote out ten exercises for me to do every day with a ten-pound weight. I was supposed to do the exercises there the first time so she could observe. I was so candy-assed from the run that I couldn't do all the repetitions. Major Thiel laughed at me under her breath and sent me on my way. I'm sure she thought I was as much a pussy as I thought she was butch. I can't begin to explain how unmanly I felt.

I had three hours before the next bus back to the DMZ. I hit the officer's steam bath for a quick rub. I didn't enjoy it much. A hot bath is always better in winter and a massage, with sexual overtones is better on a rested and un-atrophied body. I stopped at the clinic one more time to pick up my x-ray package. Medevac helicopters began to land when I walked outside. The medics unloaded three stretchers and three walking wounded. All were soldiers wearing 2nd Infantry Division patches. When the helicopter pilots had a spare moment I went up to their hot choppers and asked them what the hell happened.

"Picked these guys up at Camp Liberty Bell They got blown up or something!" yelled the left seat co-pilot. Camp Liberty Bell was where my Alpha Company was billeted.

Those were my men. *I got to get back!* I flagged the first PX taxi I could find. "Get me to the DMZ, NOW!" I threw two twenties at him for a sixteen dollar ride. I figured a twenty-four dollar incentive bonus would get me there quicker. We went 'screaming, berserk crazy on the way back and made the distance in record time.

I arrived at the compound just in time to see the soldiers turning in their weapons and standing down. I ran as fast as my already overworked legs would carry me to the Headquarters building. There was a command and staff meeting in progress when I arrived. Sergeant Pettit was filling in for me when I got there. I slipped in and exchanged places with my sergeant.

"S-2!" said the battalion commander, addressing me.

"Yes, Sir?"

"There's been a serious incident involving mines near Camp Liberty Bell."

"Yes, Sir, I saw them unload the dead and wounded out of the choppers at the 121 EVAC Hospital."

"I don't want something like this to happen to us so..."

I interrupted, "You mean it wasn't our men that got..."

"No, Lieutenant Osterhout, they belonged to the DMZ Battalion." Our commander was visibly upset. *Thank God for small favors,* I thought.

"S-2, I want you to find out where every mine field is south of the MDL."

"Yes, Sir, I have it on a chart in the bunker—it's classified Secret."

"I want to see it," said the battalion commander.

"Yes, Sir." I left to get it.

When I came back in, I tacked the large map up on the briefing board as everyone huddled around. "All the company commanders have overlays of these maps," I said. The commanders glanced at each other as if they didn't know. "They keep them in the Company safes."

"Good," said the battalion commander as he was studying the map.

"I don't have one," said the Headquarters Company commander.

"I've got yours in my safe," I said.

The battalion commander pointed to a spot on the map and said, "It happened here and according to this map—hat's the date on this map?"

"Seventy-two," I said, "which is relatively current for Korea."

"There's a damn minefield on this map right where the incident happened. Right damn here on the map. S-2, does the DMZ Battalion have a copy of this map?"

"Yes, Sir, several copies. I gave their S-2 two copies and the Division G-2 gave them a copy according to DMZ SOP."

"They have copies of this map, then?"

"Yes, Sir," I said again. "I know for a fact that the S-2 has one. I gave it to him personally."

"So they have one of these maps?" he said again. I suppose he couldn't believe that a unit with one of these maps would let their soldiers walk into a minefield.

"Yes sir, they have three," I emphasized once again.

"Lieutenant Osterhout, I want you to go up on Z and find out exactly what happened and why. I really don't care how deep they get themselves into the shit bath. We just don't want to climb in the tub with them."

I was about to excuse myself when a voice rang out from the corridor, "Battalion attention!" It was the assistant division commander, a brigadier general. We all snapped to attention just like tin soldiers.

After all the amenities were over, the general expressed a desire to borrow me for a day or two. The battalion commander had no recourse but to let me go. My mission was to interrogate the survivors from the patrol and find out exactly what happened.

The general's mission and the battalion commander's were basically the same thing. The reason I was picked as an investigator by Division was the fact that I understood operating procedures north of the river better than any other lieutenant around. Better than anyone in the world, actually.

I was dismissed to get anything I needed for the night. I was supposed to stay at it until I felt like I had all the answers. I would report back to the general at Camp Casey as soon as I was finished.

I ran to my bunker and picked up a toothbrush and a disposable razor. I was ready. The general himself drove me to Warrior Base and escorted me into the Headquarters. I had a lot of power because I was the general's boy, at least for two days. It was nice getting the DMZ battalion commander to treat me like an equal but I wish the circumstances had been different.

The general introduced me as his personal investigator and emphasized that cooperation with me was imperative and non-negotiable. If they didn't cooperate, he would get some officers who would play team ball. The general left. I really didn't know where to start but I asked the DMZ battalion commander to assemble the remnants of the patrol in one of the briefing tents.

"They are already there. They've been there since this morning."

"They've been there since this morning?" I repeated.

"Several hours," said the commander. "They are having a meeting with their platoon leader and company commander."

That would make my job a lot tougher. They were probably getting coached on what to say. I entered the briefing tent and all fell silent. The company commander asked me who the hell I was. I told him that the general just dropped me off in his jeep and I was going to conduct the investigation. I asked the company commander and the platoon leader, to leave. The platoon leader's right index finger was stained a dirty yellow from cigarettes. He must have chain-smoked two packs since the incident. As soon as the company commander and lieutenant left, I stood behind the briefing podium and began to write the date and heading on a piece of paper.

"Let's begin," I said as I looked at their faces for the first time. They looked just like I thought they were supposed to look, like survivors of the holocaust, faces drawn, eyes sunken and their nerves on a razor's edge. A loud noise would have them hitting the deck.

"Who's the ranking man?" I asked. A sergeant raised his hand. "I want you to speak last," I said. I passed a sheet of paper around and requested that they print their names, ranks, date of rank and sign it. I started interrogating the least ranking man first. It took me until midnight before I interviewed the last man. Then they were released to take showers, (some still had to wash the blood off) and eat late chow.

I sat down at a table and tried to compile all my notes. I hadn't written the first paragraph when the company commander and platoon leader walked back in. "What's the verdict?" asked the company commander.

"I'm to report to the general first," I said.

"Yeah, but you can tell us." said the platoon leader who was about to instantly piss me off just by the tone of his voice.

"When you get to be general," I said. I assume the company commander took the hint because he ushered the platoon leader out of the briefing tent.

The sun was beginning to come up when I finished my report. I was feeling a little sick from exhaustion. Maybe a hardy DMZ breakfast would revitalize me.

The mess tent buzzed when I walked in. The DMZ battalion commander motioned me over to his table. I sat down apprehensively, as he shoveled some shit on a shingle into his mouth.

"How bad do we look?" he asked, never slowing from eating.

I said. "The line officers will probably come out of it okay but the staff may take a hit. Of course, I'm not the final judge."

"That's alright, I'm sure you were fair in your assessments."

I was supposed to report to the general first but giving the DMZ battalion commander a little preview fell into the category of healthy diplomacy. He was a powerful man north of the river, second only to my battalion commander.

At 1100 that morning I was in the general's office at Camp Casey. I didn't enjoy stabbing my counterpart, the S-2, in the back, but I was sent up there to find out who shot John and it appeared that the DMZ Battalion S-2 firmly had his finger on the trigger.

The patrol was a monthly dress rehearsal of a guard post evacuation. That morning was extremely foggy. The S-2 thought for an instant that he should postpone the drill but since he waited until the "no later than" day for the evacuation exercise, he would be out of compliance with the requirement to complete the exercise monthly if he postponed. He assigned the guard post personnel an evacuation route through a specific area. His downfall was that the route he picked clearly ran through a registered mine field. The minefield was recorded on the master minefield overlay, of which three copies were in his possession. He failed to look at any of them. When interviewed, the S-2 swore the patrol veered off route and went into a North Korean minefield. Even though the S-2 was one of my own kind (and Lord knows in the Army, we take care of our own kind), he had to suffer the blame. Other things would have been excusable, but not this.

It was a fourteen-man patrol, walking up a heavily vegetated hill. Because of the thick brush and fog, each man could only see the man in front of him and the one behind him. They were following no particular trail but were just walking in the direction their S-2 had plotted. The story unfolded:

Halfway up the hill two explosions shook the ground. The patrol froze in place, assuming the ready crouch. The FIFTH MAN back heard a 'whoop whoop' sound in the air. It was a man's leg spinning by him overhead, 'whistling' with velocity. The FIFTH MAN shouted, "Mines, freeze!"

The FIFTH MAN slowly moved his way through the thick vegetation to render aid to his comrades. The POINT MAN was rolling on the ground, holding the stump where his left leg used to be. The SECOND MAN sat leaning against a tree trying to figure out where his right foot could possibly have gone. It wasn't on the ground anywhere.

The FIFTH MAN yelled to the THIRD MAN to grab the soldier without his foot and help him back down the hill.

The THIRD MAN took one step and detonated a mine. The THIRD MAN's legs turned into spaghetti and he collapsed into the crater. His genitals were shredded. The FIFTH MAN made a decision to leave the POINT MAN and carry the SECOND MAN to safety. The FIFTH MAN struggled putting a tourniquet on the SECOND MAN's traumatic foot amputation and then hoisted him onto his shoulders. The FIFTH MAN was blessed that day; he walked right out, carrying his wounded buddy without killing himself. The FIFTH MAN then led the rest of the patrol down the hill to safety.

The FIFTH MAN slowly made his way back up the hill to pick up the POINT MAN. The FIFTH MAN made it to within seeing distance of the wounded POINT MAN. The POINT MAN was still rolling around on the ground, trying to stand on his stub. He fell down and rolled over on another mine. It ended his life; his left arm and jaw were blown off.

The FIFTH MAN didn't go recover what was left of the POINT MAN's body. He'd taken too many chances as it was. The FIFTH MAN grabbed the THIRD MAN with the shredded legs and carried him down the hill to rejoin the group and radio for a Medevac. The FIFTH MAN had a rip in his flesh where a small piece of shrapnel burned through him. He felt no pain. The FOURTH MAN was slightly wounded in the shoulder. There was a lot of blood but a few stitches would close him up. All in all, the price paid for the S-2's mistake was: one man dead, two severely wounded and two slightly wounded. Not a bad day's fuck up.

The FIFTH MAN was not the ranking man but thank goodness he was there. He was awarded the Soldier's Medal as an impact award for his actions.

The DMZ battalion S-2 was removed from office immediately. He was verbally reprimanded in the most abusive way I've ever heard and was given an Article 15 in lieu of a court marshal. He was given an Officer Evaluation Report that included the statement: "Prone to making stupid life-threatening mistakes," which made him look and feel like shit. Then, for the seven-month duration of his Korean tour, he was assigned to screen VD patients for the division medical battalion. He had no duties what so ever but to look at penises and see if they were dripping. If they were dripping he would send them down the line. If they weren't dripping he would glove up and "milk" them a little to see if any discharge would come out. A terrible fate starting at 0730 every morning.

An 8th Army survival assistance officer was assigned the duty of escorting the casket of the POINT MAN home. The POINT MAN's hometown was somewhere in the Tennessee backwoods. The POINT MAN was a popular boy in high school, a track star who made it to the State finals in the hundred-yard dash. He'd never been further away from home than Fort Benning, Georgia. Of course he had his faults too, as we all did. He'd been to sick call twice in the two months that he'd been in Korea, both times for post drunken nausea. He also had a counseling statement on file for disrespect to an NCO. It was torn up and thrown away along with the medical records. An official letter of commendation was framed and presented to the POINT MAN's mother, along with a casket labeled: "Remains, non viewable."

The SECOND MAN, who lost his foot, was nineteen years old, a body builder, tall and blonde. He had a chip on his shoulder now, so said the chaplain. I'm afraid that I would too.

The THIRD MAN whose legs were shattered and genitals were mangled was a city boy from Baltimore. I never found out much about him.

It was an awful tragedy. The guys in the unit wanted to hang drag the S-2 from the back of a deuce-and-a-half. I just thank the Lord that I didn't make the mistake. "Thank you, Lord."

CHAPTER 15

Pohang

July was a scorcher. The stagnant rice paddy water retained unbelievable amounts of heat and things grew in it that were not mentioned in polite society. It also smelled like the bottom of an outhouse since it was fertilized with human excretions.

On July 31st, I went to the Officer's Club and rang the bell, obligating myself to buy drinks for everyone. It was my birthday. I was twenty-seven years old and I told myself if future years never got any worse than this, I'd be alright. I said that honestly thinking that there couldn't be a year worse than this. I was wrong. My twenty-eighth year was worse.

The next month and a half was going to be action packed. Starting on August 1st and continuing to August 11th, the battalion had a field exercise. On August 12th to August 29th I had my R&R (Rest and Relaxation) and from September 1st to September 20th, the battalion had a joint field exercise with the ROK Marines at Pohang. Pohang Harbor on the large Korean map was the rabbit's tail, or in this case, asshole.

The day after my birthday, we got out to the field and set up the operations center at the base of a very high hill and then pitched our large sleeping tent right in the dead center of the main trail leading up the hill. The field exercise wasn't officially scheduled to start until the following morning so everyone would try to get at least one good night's sleep.

I slept very lightly. Every time I heard the slightest rustle in the bushes, I thought it was the "slicky boys" coming to steal our stuff. I awoke and fell back to sleep several times during the night. The last time I awoke before I officially got up, I heard someone enter the tent. I didn't think too much of it because several men got off their cots to go relieve themselves during the night. Then something wafted up my nose that I didn't recognize but it smelled like cooked vomit.

I raised up on an elbow and saw a South Korean soldier standing right in the middle of our tent. He had a bucket in each hand. One bucket was filled with squid tentacles and the other bucket had slimy, boiled fish heads in it. It's not often that one wakes up to a fish eyeballing you back, especially one that smelled so badly. The Korean exited, leaving behind a nearly visible odor.

I ended up pulling the night shift for the field exercise and was just about to go to bed every morning when the Korean walked through the tent carrying his fish heads and side dish, or should I say side bucket. There was always fish heads for breakfast but the other bucket had a variety of obnoxious consumables. Curiosity got the better of me and one morning I followed him. He climbed up the winding path to the top of the hill. There were two bunker systems on top of the mountain. One was occupied and one was barren.

I went to the empty bunker first and was looking at what I thought was some kind of closet when I heard a noise. Since we were on the south side of the river, there were no defined rules of engagement, but I felt like locking and loading anyway. I didn't though, I just yelled out, "Hello!"

Someone said "Hello" back. He was an American. We "hello'ed" each other until we found ourselves. My echo was none other than Gung Ho Joe.

"What are you doing up here?" I asked.

"Curiosity," he said. "Shall we go mingle with the natives?"

Joe and I went to the other bunker system about seventy-five meters up the hill. The occupied bunker was right on the peak. The view was tremendous, green rice paddies and lush foliage. It looked like an Asian postcard.

Joe and I went to the entrance of the bunker and knocked on the iron door. A Korean officer, a first lieutenant, opened the door. He was five foot two if he was an inch and weighed maybe a hundred and twenty pounds.

"Yes?" he asked with a curious glance.

Joe did most of the talking. He understood and spoke more Korean than me, although my vocabulary had expanded to twenty something words, up from six words several months ago. We were eventually invited in and had a VIP's tour of the facility. There were three large rooms and a couple of smaller ones with the bunkers spinning off from the center.

Koreans had strange sleeping arrangements. Twenty of them slept on one bed. All twenty pairs of slippers were lined up in a neat row beside the bunk. The alert gear was stowed in spaces above and below the bed. This bed was not what you would call conventional. It was really just a large wooden platform two feet off the ground.

The Korean lieutenant talked to us for a long time seeming to enjoy the company. He showed us pictures of his girlfriend and sister. His girlfriend was butt ugly but his sister was cute. Of course we said that both of them looked like number one. On a Korean scale of one to ten, one is the best. If you're a ten in Korean, give up.

We talked until it became time to eat. The Koreans sat down to chow and invited us to join in. Fish heads and squid arms didn't do a damn thing for me but Joe was Gung Ho. He sat down with them and I just watched. Actually I had to turn my head twice, once when I heard a Korean crunch a fish skull in his jaw and the other time when the Korean lieutenant sucked a fish eye out of its socket. Joe held his own but just barely. When he attempted to suck a fish eye out, it popped out and ended up stuck on the side of his face. He and I laughed until we cried. Joe also tried a squid tentacle, biting off the end like a sausage. He didn't make a sound or show disgust, but I did notice that he only took one bite.

We bid the Koreans goodbye and told them that we would visit again before the exercise was over. I got up that way one more time and brought them a second rate girlie magazine that some soldier brought out to the field and then abandoned. They appreciated it but they had to cut out the pictures and keep them in their wallets or helmet liners. The field grade officers frowned on such western decadence. They burned the other pages in a barrel.

This was one of the easiest and most trouble free field exercises that I'd ever experienced. We didn't move the operations center and we had a spring fed well in which we could take sponge baths. The chow was fairly decent too, with two C rations and one A ration (hot meal) every day. The A ration hot meal was cooked in the field kitchen and shipped to us in mermite cans. If the hot meal was breakfast it meant that we'd get green eggs but that's just part of the Army. Somehow the green can coating bled over into the eggs. It seemed to be the only food to which this phenomenon occurred. Thirty years ago, what was a little green lead paint in one's eggs anyway, just flavoring.

The low point of the exercise was briefing the general who just dropped in unexpectedly. The high point was going home. The day after arriving back at the compound I was scheduled to start my R&R in Hawaii for fourteen days.

We pulled into the compound, stored the equipment, and shuffled the paperwork. Then we hit the rack. The sunrise would bring the Freedom Bird for me. I'd never been to the Islands before but I really didn't care where I went as long as I didn't have to wear a helmet, flak vest and carry a rifle. If I wasn't required to wear those things it must be a little slice of heaven.

I couldn't sleep all night. I tried to imagine what it would be like, away from the Z and on a beach. I was meeting a woman in Honolulu. She was going to college there and rented a high-rise apartment on Waikiki for several months, so I didn't have to worry about a place to stay.

I almost didn't get to go. While I was dreaming of Waimea Bay, the North Koreans were hand grenading a nearby guard post. No one was hurt, but it disrupted everything for several hours and caused us to go on alert for half a day. We went on stand down minutes before I caught a bus to Seoul. I had to ride in my uniform, changing at the airport before I hopped on my plane.

Fifty-five minutes later, the Freedom Bird took off. My emotions were on a razor's edge and I didn't know if I was happy, sad, frightened or what, but I was very thankful that I got to escape. The few Americans on board the wide-bodied jumbo jet added to the international mix of Filipinos, Japanese, Chinese, Koreans, Vietnamese, and two guys with some sort of tribal robes on who looked like they just strolled out of early Africa. I closed my eyes and day dreamed about the Islands. We were out of Korean airspace, well over the Pacific, when I fell fast asleep.

The engines shifted pitch and I awoke as we started our decent into the Honolulu Airport, right on schedule. We flew over Pearl Harbor, the water looked so blue, waves to play in, sand, sun. I tried not to appear overly excited but I was.

I'd been in Hawaii once before on a two hour layover when I was deploying to the ROK. It was different this time. I remained in such a state of excitement that I forgot to eat or I just didn't get hungry. I was too busy doing "stuff" or even busier doing nothing. I swam in the ocean every day. The waves weren't extremely large but every now and then one would swell up that was eight feet high or so. However, the average was three to five feet.

I bought a large, hard Styrofoam and plastic floating device called a boogie board. It cost forty dollars but I got about four thousand dollars worth of use out of it. It allowed one to float around effortlessly waiting for that big wave to come along. Then when it did, the boogie board increased the results of body surfing ten fold.

However, during my R & R there were two disappointments. I wanted to see the pipeline waves at Waimea Bay. We drove to the north shore especially for that but the waves; the big ones that is, weren't in season. It was August and the biggest wave we saw at Waimea was a one footer. A true disappointment. The second disappointment was that I got a case of twenty-four hour diarrhea that nearly sucked my insides out. I made a quick trip to Schofield Barracks to see an Army medic. He seemed to think that it was brought on by a change of diet and lack of reasonable sleep. I managed to evade the most common affliction of the Islands: sunburn. A flak jacket would not wear well over a second-degree sunburn. I avoided it at all cost.

It was ten days of heaven. I nearly pitched a bitch when it came time to go back. I think I was almost clinically depressed. There was nothing I could do but return to the hot, humid, stinking, dangerous, damn Delta Mike Zulu.

I was heading back to the ROK a couple of days early so I would be sure to arrive at my unit at the proper time. I've always had a fear of being late. Arriving back at Kimpo Airport, I took a cab to downtown Seoul and rented a room at the Hyatt for two nights. I ate well and slept well making up for all the sleepless nights that I spent in Hawaii.

I thought back to the very long two weeks up on the Z during the curse of the commander's leave and compared those two weeks to the ten days I'd just spent in Hawaii. Hell and Heaven respectively.

Forty-eight hours goes by really fast when you sleep through thirty-one of them, eat during ten and I don't remember what I did during the excess seven hours. I may have even left my hotel room but I tend to think that I spent that entire seven hours in the bath, soaking the salt out of my skin and washing the grains of sand out of the crack of my ass. I found sand under my eyelids for three days after I returned. There's probably still some behind my eyeballs. I'll find them some day when they turn into pearls.

I was finally rested after two days of doing nothing but ordering the maids and bellhops around. I caught the express up to the Z and I tried to creep into the compound on little cat feet. It didn't work, the XO just happened to be at the gate and the battalion commander was standing in the doorway of the Headquarters building. I was tan and my hair was bleached a little more blonde and my face sparkled with that well laid look.

The battalion commander spoke to me. I didn't really hear what he said, but it was supposed to be funny because I laughed. When the battalion commander thinks he's funny, we do too. If we don't laugh or forget to, he'll egg us on in a good humored way by saying something like, "laugh damn it!"

The battalion pretty much had a vacation too. There were no hostile shooting incidents at all, nobody shot anybody! Well, I couldn't really say that. A private named Spradlin set his .45 automatic on the seat next to him as he drove the chow truck into the DMZ. An hour later, as he drove out of the DMZ, he reached for the weapon to clear it. The pistol discharged and he shot himself. The bullet passed through his right hamstring, through his nut sack, through his left hamstring and then stuck in the truck door. The doc said that the bullet only "nicked" him in the nuts. But I am here to tell you that there is no such thing as getting "nicked" in the nuts by a .45 caliber pistol shot at a range of twelve inches. The boy got shot in the balls.

Speaking of balls, every report I read concerning this shooting incident, guard post report, operations center report, shooting incident review, numerous spot reports and medical reports, all misspelled the private's name. He is now and forever known as, Spalding. Which is, of course, a famous ball.

In two days, the battalion was scheduled to be air lifted from a small airstrip just south of our compound to Pohang, 200 miles further south. There would be thirty plane sorties with only five planes. It would necessitate them turning around five times. The sixth trip would take them home to Osan or wherever C-130 airplanes come from in the ROK.

It took one complete day to load our field gear into the back of our vehicle and strap it down good enough to satisfy the Air Force. The day after packing, we sat around like poised tigers ready to spring into action. The next day we deployed to the airfield and camped for the night. The air base was very small and primitive by U.S. Air Force standards but the Army thought the slit trench "water closet" and creek fed showers were just fine, a luxury for a field exercise.

The perimeter fence around the airfield was so close that our soldiers had to bunk along side of the runway. There were 250 bodies in sleeping bags lined up on either side of the airstrip. If a plane had to make a forced landing and slide off the runway in either direction it would have killed dozens of men.

We ate cold rations that night, watched the sun fall below unfamiliar mountains, and racked out at dark. There's not much else to do in the middle of an airfield with no lights. We did start a game of football with a helmet liner but when a guy was tackled on the asphalt airstrip and incapacitated himself before the field exercise even began, we had to call the game off because of stupidity. I didn't participate, so I didn't feel quite as guilty as the others when the battalion commander chewed us out. The injured man was the sergeant major's boy and needed eleven stitches above his eye to close his wound. He was sent back to the rear to pull guard duty instead of participating in the joint field exercise.

I was sleeping like a grandchild when a roar of an engine woke me up. The sun was peeking over the mountains and a camouflaged C-130 sliced through the sky, turning for its final approach to the airfield.

"Drop your cocks and pull up yore socks!" a crusty old sergeant yelled. The pilot of the C-130 saw an army of ants race across the asphalt strip to the safety of the hangar. Seconds after the last man cleared the strip, the first C-130 touched down with a puff of smoke and a screech of rubber on the pavement.

The plane reversed thrust of whatever the hell airplanes do to stop so fast. They might just put on the brakes, I don't know, I'm ground pounder. The plane pivoted to the right and came to a stop at the beginning of the taxi lane. The first "chalk" of soldiers was ready to load in minutes. The drivers had their engines cranked and were backing the first two vehicles on to the plane's ramps.

We threw our scant bed things into our rucksacks and broke out our C-rations for breakfast. As we ate, the planes began to land and take off with regularity.

Our soldiers actually loaded all our equipment in the allocated time. The fly boys said that it was the fastest average time that they'd ever seen grunts obtain. We weren't fast enough to beat the darkness though. When the sun went down, we still had half a dozen chalks waiting to deploy. Loading five planes, flying 200 miles, unloading, turning around, flying back, and doing it all over again took a lot of time. I sat at that little airstrip all day and didn't get anything accomplished. I played cards with Lieutenant Anderson for four and a half hours and never lost a single game of anything. I should have been in Vegas. I was afraid I was wasting all of my good luck on a meaningless game of cards.

The remainder of the units that didn't fly on day one spent another uneventful night at the airfield. Our alarm clock was again the first C-130 of the day. It was a little late but we couldn't do anything until it arrived anyway. The last plane, my chalk, had wheels up at 11:45. The guys in my chalk ate their

C-rations during the flight. It was slightly turbulent and two men threw up; franks and beans and spiced beef respectively. The first guy managed to get to the piss tube in the back of the airplane before he barfed. The second man dumped his lunch in the bed of a vehicle trailer. We were lucky that it was confined to only those two men, although I did feel a little sick.

We swung out over the Sea of Japan, made a final approach to Pohang Harbor, and touched down on the Korean Marine Base Airfield. We deplaned and were escorted to our bivouac area. What a shitty place. Our site was in a grove of trees, which was nice, but the trees were planted to cover up an old landfill. Little bits of rubbish and paper were sticking through the surface of the entire bivouac site. There was broken glass, plastic and old rubber tires everywhere. It was a dump, literally. There were rats too! Big ones, fat ones! I guess good rat chow came sifting up through the landfill because the rats were actually grazing. The rats became excited when we moved the battalion in because American GI chow was a rat delicacy and we threw away a lot more of it than the Koreans.

Our camp consisted of five rows of about fifty pup tents. I got a tent to myself. The catch was that I had to carry both shelter halves so I wouldn't have to buddy up with someone carrying the other half. There was a small trailer-type PX near the bivouac site where we could get things like pogey bait (candy/snacks) and boot polish. After 1900 (7 PM), we could purchase moderate amounts of beer.

We picked up our garbage twice a day and burned it in a big concrete pit. The first time we burned the garbage in the pit, twenty or thirty rats escaped over the concrete walls and sought refuge in the bivouac area. This action prompted the Great Rat Killing: Pohang 1980.

We passed around axes, shovels and grubbing hoes as far as they would go. Then the remainder of us fixed bayonets on our M-16s and terrorized the land. Our kill ratio was excellent. Twenty-three rats dead, three captured and we only had one casualty. An overzealous soldier slapped his buddy in the shins with a shovel. It cracked his tibia and put him out of action for the rest of the exercise. So far we didn't have a good start, two soldiers were down, one from a football game and the other due to a "rat bat" gone wrong.

After the rat killing, I spent most of my time keeping guard rosters and pulling a shift in the operations center. The troops practiced rubber boat assaults and helicopter landings, exchanging ideas on both. This was in preparation of the Regiment size, joint amphibious assault that would take place in a few days. I'd never ridden in an amphibious vehicle before and was looking forward to it.

Unfortunately, a tropical depression was passing over the Philippines and heading our way. If the weather got rough, the amphibious exercise would be cancelled. One of my intelligence officer jobs was reporting the weather. I kept a close eye on the storm.

Gung Ho Joe, in the meantime, was trying to figure out a way to get electricity into the operations center tent so we wouldn't need to run a generator constantly. He wanted to tap into the Korean Marine's power source but he wasn't one hundred percent sure how to do it. I was in the middle of my graveyard shift at the operations center when Joe walked in wearing a pole climber's apparatus.

"What are you doing with your spikes on?" I asked.

"I'm gonna get you some electricity," he said. He waddled out, with his equipment clanking. He clanked off into the distance. When I couldn't hear him anymore, I went outside to find him but he was already half way up a pole. The top of the pole had some kind of transformers or something on top of it. Joe climbed up into the middle of it and positioned himself where his legs were the only parts of his body that were visible. I watched for a moment and a spark shot out from the transformers and a mushroom of white smoke billowed forth.

"Joe!" I shouted.

Joe slid down the pole like a fireman, released his safety strap, and headed towards me, clanking at a double time. More sparks started flying before Joe reached me. By the time he got to me and turned around, the whole transformer pole was ablaze like a sparkler. It burned, hissed, popped, and smoked for several minutes. Then one by one, the lights of the Marine Base started flickering and going out. In fifteen minutes, every light had faded into darkness. I could hear shouting all over the base.

Joe just turned toward me and said, "I wondered what that wire was for," and we both laughed. Joe took his gear off and sat with me in the operations center tent until a Korean repair crew came out to fix the transformers. Joe went out and simply asked them to run an electrical line over to our tent. And they did. Usually we would have gotten an argument but I'm sure the ROKs suspected what Joe did and didn't want a repeat performance.

Joe came back in the tent and slyly said, "I told you I'd get you some electricity," and he smiled as only Gung Ho Joe could. By morning the power was restored to the base. I found out later that some of the lights in the city of Pohang were also out. Joe probably caused upwards of 20,000 people to be without power. No one was the wiser. It was blamed on the outdated equipment and the high winds.

The winds really were beginning to be a problem. The weather reports were very sketchy because the forecast and outlooks were compiled by the US Air Force in Osan, which was near the other coast, a couple of hundred miles to the west. The reports predicted strong winds and rain, but that was all they indicated. I stuck my neck out in the briefing to the battalion commander and told him that we were going to get caught in the middle of a severe thunderstorm and we may need to postpone the amphibious exercise. The Korean Marine standard operating procedure called for cancellation of amphibious operations if the waves reached three meters, a little more than nine feet.

The operations officer (S-3) and I made a quick hike to the beach since we were only a half-mile away. The waves looked big to me, maybe four or five feet. Five feet doesn't seem high, but I remembered standing on solid beach in Hawaii and a five-foot wave crashing into my chest. I also remember that same five-foot wave knocking me down and dragging me up the beach on my ass right in front of two women I was trying to impress.

That night the rains came in sheets. The wind blew twenty knots gusting to forty all night long. Luckily, my two shelter halves were tied down really well and the trench around my tent was a foot deep. After the first two hours of rain, my trench quit working and one of my tent flaps broke free. After four hours, the back end of my tent was whipping around like a bird flapping and I was actually floating on my air mattress inside the tent. After six hours, there wasn't a dry piece of ground anywhere. All you could see was water covering the landfill. Most of the 250 tents were totally collapsed. The soldiers just huddled together under ponchos and cursed loudly. After eight hours the rain started to come down even harder. I was still floating around, relatively dry, but I was one of only a few who stayed dry most of the night. When the sun came up, the rain eased a little and we all ventured out to retrieve our equipment that was washed to and fro and left half submerged in our nasty landfill swamp.

The rain slackened to a drizzle but the sea-level land was saturated. Several of our large tents blew down during the night but the operations center tent survived. I was happy to learn that my "office" had endured.

The battalion dug out for most of the day and prepared for another siege, coming that night. It arrived just as expected, several more inches of rain and even higher winds. We were definitely losing the battle. There was no way that anything would keep us dry. We had to stay busy or it would really be miserable.

As darkness fell, we huddled around like cattle underneath the trees. Our ponchos whipped at each other in the wind. Except for the very highest spots in our landfill, the water was so deep that it came over the tops of our combat boots. All the shelter halves were collapsed and wrapped around our equipment, just to keep the stuff together in one place. There was no way that it was going to stay dry in a toad choker like this one.

At 0300, a message reached me, which indicated that the eye of the typhoon (Typhoon Orchid) would hit the Korean mainland in twelve hours. A typhoon is nothing more than a hurricane in another part of the world. It meant we could expect mega amounts of water and winds greater than seventy-five miles per hour. Our little landfill lake was already saline. The whole ocean would be on top of us in twelve hours.

The battalion commander called a command and staff meeting to decide what would be the best course of action to take. Obviously we had to get out of the weather and further away from the beach than a half a mile. The battalion commander went to speak to the Korean Marine general about the possibility of moving into a building even if it was just an airplane hangar. The general agreed to let us move into the Marine's billets and they would move out and double up with another battalion.

Within an hour and a half, every ROK Marine and all their possessions were out of the building. We moved in at dawn. The rooms were large, having four sleeping spaces with two bunk type beds that held ten people in each one. I got a top bunk on the right hand side of the room. I shared it with our fire support officer and an evaluator sent down from division. The evaluator totally wasted his time. We were supposed to be on the amphibious exercise that day but the weather caused a delay and maybe even a cancellation. As soon as the weather cleared, the evaluators left and they didn't spare any expletives when they told us what they thought about the whole Pohang exercise.

We holed up in the Marine billets for a day watching weather reports. It got black when the typhoon hit the coast. However, by the second day, after the typhoon had passed, the sun was shining and the winds were a moderate twenty miles per hour.

The decision was made to hold a thirty-six hour amphibious exercise instead of seventy-two hour one. We planned and briefed for a day and departed at dawn the following day to load in the amphibious vehicles.

We were sacked out on the beach waiting for the vehicles and watching the surf. I couldn't believe it. I was so pissed off. I went all the way to Waimea Bay looking for pipeline waves and here they were at Pohang Harbor, South Korea. The waves were officially five meters high, about fifteen feet. That was six feet over the maximum allowable safety margin. The safety SOP was waived, to coin a pun, because "we'd come so far" and needed to at least ride in the amphibious vehicles.

About mid morning, twenty-four amphibious vehicles roared on to the beach. They were bigger than I'd expected and they had faces painted on them similar to the Flying Tigers of World War II.

It was awe inspiring to see 500 men lined up, combat ready, on a sandy beach. I felt like I was in England, preparing for Normandy or, since I was a pessimist, I could imagine that I was at Dunkirk, waiting to escape.

I was slotted to ride in the command vehicle with the battalion commander and S-3 but somehow the seven-seat command vehicle filled up before I could get in. My sergeant didn't get in either. We went scavenging for a ride. These vehicles were lined up in one long line and the command vehicle was at one end. We went right down the line looking for seats. The next to last vehicle was empty and a Korean Marine encouraged us to ride in his boat.

My sergeant and I entered and it seemed to be very spacious, but we were the only soldiers in it. If it had been fully loaded, it may have been a different story. We strapped ourselves in and the ROK Marine laid out a small package of saltine crackers. I think it was to keep our stomachs from being upset but it could have been his lunch for all I knew. I ate a couple of the crackers as the big tracked vehicle's engine began to rev.

A Korean equivalent to "Wagons Ho" was ordered and the vehicles turned toward the ocean, plunging into the turbulent surf. There were two Marines in the vehicle, a driver and a spare Marine. The spare Marine was the one who gave us the crackers. The spare Marine had a cupola that opened through the roof on the right hand side of the vehicle. The spare Marine, who I assume was actually the vehicle commander, positioned himself in the cupola seat, looking out of the vehicle.

My sergeant and I sat quietly as we felt the tracks lose contact with the sand and the vehicle become buoyant. The vehicle began to buck violently as it negotiated the fifteen-foot waves. At times, the vehicle was completely submerged as water poured in the hatch. The look on the spare Marine's face told me that we were taking on more water than normal. A flashback of the deadly river crossing passed through my brain.

We bucked and pitched a few more times and the spare Marine ran to where we were in the back of the vehicle and pulled a long gaff off the back side wall. He skillfully got it through the hatch and frantically tried to pole the other crafts away from us. The Marine was standing in his seat and was protruding out of the vehicle from the waist up. Water still streamed in as we continued to go under the swells. The spare Marine was drenched.

We banged against other vehicles twice, hitting one on either side of us. We struck so hard that it knocked the spare Marine down on the seat, but he jumped right back up and continued to wrestle with his gaff. When we got out into open water where the sea was much more calm, the spare Marine relaxed his guard, sat in his seat and lit up a cigarette. He offered us one but we declined. He returned the gaff to its storage space. However, it was now only a few feet long because it had broken in half.

The spare Marine didn't speak any English but I communicated with him enough to make him understand that I thought he had a pair of coconuts to stand in the hatch in the face of fifteen-foot waves and gaff off the other boats.

He offered to let me a look out of the hatch. I climbed up in the cupola and peered out. The ten foot high vehicle only floated a couple of feet above the surface of the water. We were two-thirds sunk already and that was normal.

After the spare Marine rested from his ordeal, he went to the back of the vehicle and cranked up a bilge pump in an attempt to get the eight inches of water out of the passenger compartment.

We stayed in calm water, driving in circles for forty-five minutes. The Marines prided themselves on being able to hit the beach at the precise moment that they say they will. They said they'd hit the beach at 1200 and we launched at 1105. After getting out into deep water, we had to cruise around for forty-five minutes before we assumed the attack position, which was just another long line of vehicles, this time in the water instead of on land.

The engine revved to a high pitch and the large amphibious vehicle surged forward. We sped along for a few minutes in smooth water and then I felt the roll of the waves around the boat. The vehicle began to chug and water poured in through the spare Marine's hatch worse than before. I was in a mild panic until the vehicle's treads dug into the sand and we were safely on the ground again.

The rear doors opened and we rushed out, "storming" the beach. What an experience. We were on a high sand dune that looked down upon all the other vehicles. Soldiers spilled on to the beach. Each soldier had a specific mission and mine was to link up with the command group and assist the battalion commander with the operations center. That's all well and good but I couldn't tell who was who. The word "uniform" means that everyone looks the same. Out of 500 people stretched out over a half mile, I couldn't spot my group because we all had on the same pickle suits, but that didn't stop me. One thing that has never been a problem for me is indecision. We charged forward.

My sergeant and I moved inland, taking the most direct route possible to where the operations center was supposed to be set up. Under my fine leadership, we got lost but we ran into some other soldiers who were assigned to the operations center also. As a controlled mob, we blundered around in the woods until we stumbled on to the Command vehicles. Some how we ended up exactly where we were supposed to be.

The line dogs had a tough time of it; climbing hill and dale while us operation center rats sat in one place and monitored the radios. We had a small guard force that secured the operations center and we had alert positions just in case we were "attacked." It would be a play attack of course; we were 250 miles from the DMZ. There were only thirty live rounds in the whole battalion and they were there by accident. An infantry lieutenant, out of force of habit, packed his thirty round magazine of M-16 ammo. I had to confiscate it before we got on the planes. There is an anti-sky-jack rule in the military that is designed to keep ammo, weapons, and explosives separated from the soldiers while on routine flights. During actual national emergencies, it didn't apply.

We ran the operation center like experts as Charlie Company attacked up the last hill to end the exercise. One of the Charlie Company soldiers broke his ankle on the rocks at the peak of the hill and the company first sergeant who later became the battalion sergeant major, carried the soldier piggyback nine kilometers down the hill to a place where an ambulance could pick him up. It takes something way down deep inside to carry a wounded comrade five and a half miles over rugged terrain. The first sergeant became grossly dehydrated and kept babbling something about a "French licker." It was a little scary to see a man so dehydrated, but he supplied us with a source of endless "French licker" jokes for months.

At ENDEX (end of the exercise), we returned to the Marine base via land vehicle and prepared for redeployment. Since we'd been in Pohang, we had a field laundry set up, a MASH unit move in next door and several, three-hole, wooden latrines built near the bivouac area.

We had to move out of the billets and back into the landfill since the typhoon threat was over. On my next to last night in Pohang, I woke up with the powerful hankering to take a dump. I slipped on my boots and headed through the blackness to the nearest new wooden latrine. It was cloudy and there were no lights near the landfill. The only thing I could see was the pale image of my own dirty white jockey shorts and the silhouette of the wooden three-hole latrine up against a few stars that were poking through the clouds.

I fumbled around, found the first hole, and occupied it, trying not to touch anything too much. It was darker than three feet up a bulls butt inside the wooden outhouse. I couldn't see the wall in front of me, but nonetheless, I was grunting away listening to the feces splash in the goop five feet below me. I was about half way finished when I became aware of some other splashing down below that I didn't cause. I first envisioned a monster or something growing in the shit but quickly put that out of my mind when my imagination couldn't comprehend an animal that could live in the bottom of an outhouse.

Still sitting on hole number one, I reached out and pushed the spring loaded door open, hoping some of the ambient light would filter in and allow me to see if I was alone. I wasn't alone. There was a Korean perched beside me. He was squatting with his feet on either side of hole number two. He was asshole to eyeball with my face! The Korean didn't even know how to take a shit in a civilized manner. He'd probably never seen a commode before. He just stood on the seat and squatted above the hole, like one would over a slit trench. I finished before he did and left him hovering above the seat like a shitting bird perched on a swing.

When I got back to my shelter halves and my air mattress, which by now had a slow leak in it, I couldn't get to sleep. I was actually excited about getting back up to the Z. I hadn't really been "home" in forty-three days ... ten-day field exercise on the hill with the spring, fourteen days on leave and nineteen days at Pohang Harbor. I'd been living out of suitcases and rucksacks for a month and a half. The comfort of a Quonset hut and bunker would be appreciated. I had to bang myself in the head a couple of times to get that thought out of my mind. Imagine, me, wanting to go back to the Z.

Just before dawn, I had to take another dump. My insides were just not getting along with the C-rations I was eating. This time I had a small flashlight. I checked the latrine to make sure I was alone. I sat down on hole number one again, funny how you develop habits so quickly.

After turning off the flashlight, it seemed even darker than before in the toilet. After my first release, I heard the plop-splash as it hit bottom. Before my next effort, I heard a grunt and it wasn't me. I popped my flashlight back on, wondering how it was possible that I missed another human in a three-hole outhouse, but there wasn't anyone there. Then I heard a louder grunt! Damn! I jumped up. The noise was coming from inside the outhouse trough. I took the flashlight and dared to look down into the hole. "Oh my God, I'm done." It was a pig at the bottom of the outhouse. It was looking up at me with a turd on his head. A vision that would haunt me for years to come.

I got zero sleep after the two experiences that I endured in the outhouse. Thank goodness, I was part of chalk number one and would fly home on the first C-130. I wouldn't be sorry to see this place left behind. The only good days I had were days when nothing particularly bad happened.

We landed at the small northern airstrip where it all started. The vehicles were late and we spent the night beside the asphalt just like before. Our vehicles arrived at 1100 and we convoyed back to the DMZ.

There were a few stay-behind officers and two hundred men who maintained guard and did contingency missions at Camp Greaves. The stay-behind officers were extremely glad to see us. The Officer's Club had been closed for the nineteen days that we were gone. The Officer's Club is a lifeline and it better damn sure be open when I get back. It was open, with Miss Yi and Miss Kim waiting to greet us. Miss Yi's legs looked finer than ever. She always wore a short dress and black stockings. What a fantasy! She even bought me a birthday present when no one else bothered. Of course it rained that day

272

and as I was carrying the present back to my hooch, the coloring from the gift-wrapping bled onto my uniform making a permanent stain. Korea, the Land of the Not Quite Right.

My birthday was a month and a half ago, the day before I left to go on the field exercise, R & R to Hawaii and Pohang. How time flies when you're having fun. I just spent twelve percent of my tour without laying my head on my own bunk even once.

I'd been from the armpit to the asshole of the "rabbit" and back again!

CHAPTER 16

Short Rounds

The battalion arrived back home north of the river on 23 September 80. We took a full day to get personal business squared away and the equipment cleaned up and become combat ready again.

One of our worst fears was that barracks thieves would have gotten into our belongings while we were gone. The soldiers' lockers were banded and locked and the empty billets were protected by three strands of concertina barbed wire. We had twenty-four hour walking guards but who kept the guards honest? Don't ask, just inventory your things, and hope that they are all there. My stuff was accounted for, but a three hundred dollar camera from one building was missing and a personal collection of pornographic movies was gone. The battalion mourned.

After inventory, check cashing, and clean up, we fell into our routine. The grey specter of the DMZ mission hung over our heads. In sixty days, we'd be back up on the line, running patrols. *God, I hated it.* I would be one of only a few officers out of thirty who had seen the mission conducted. Everyone else was ready to kick ass and take names but we knew differently. You didn't kick ass on the mission. "Mission" may not have been the right term; it was more like a "sub-mission." Gradually, day-by-day, it beat your ass into submission.

The recon platoon had two basic responsibilities during the mission: man the scout towers on the guard posts and conduct the daylight recon patrols. The recon platoon had a leader who was the most unique officer I'd ever seen. He was fairly tall, six feet or a little more, with blonde hair and broad shoulders. He was a West Point graduate; a Russian linguist, a concert violinist, a collegiate boxer, a 10,000-meter runner, a pilot, a scuba diver, an Airborne Ranger and he called Miss Yi and Miss Kim, Ma'am. He was a polite son of a bitch, but he was a hard-core platoon leader.

In preparation for the DMZ mission, he conditioned his platoon to such a fine pitch that all of them could run nineteen miles. I struggled with five. He'd always invite me to run with them but my leg just wouldn't hold up. Three miles for me was comfortable, which was the minimum required for our battalion. Hell, our forty-one year old battalion commander could rip off four miles in less than thirty-two minutes with no problem. Of course he was tired but he could do it again the next day and the next and the next, just like a machine.

The whole Army was like a machine. Once it got in motion, there was no stopping it. If you weren't for it, you were against it and you would become crushed in the system.

Sergeant Papadopoulis was one such casualty. He had a wife back home in Jersey or some place on the east coast. His wife was pregnant but not by him and he wanted to go home and straighten things out with his old lady, which may have involved murder. His troops knew the whole story and teased him unmercifully by calling him Sergeant Papa, which in this case, he wasn't. He had just returned from an overnight pass that he'd spent in the VD capital of the world where he immersed himself in a sea of sex. Very few men ever remained faithful. Some of the older men considered having sex on the side as one of the benefits that Korea offered. My recruiter showed me pictures of all the Korean businesswomen that he'd been to bed with, attempting to entice me to join.

The chaplain tried to get a compassionate reassignment for Sergeant Papadopoulis, but he had nearly two months left on his tour. The reassignment officer suggested that the sergeant hang on for thirty days and get credit for an early tour completion. Sergeant Papadopoulis couldn't wait. He left the unit, not to go home, but to go to Seoul and drown his troubles in Mokoli (rice white lightning). He was AWOL and he held a key squad leader position. The battalion wanted him back, first to assume his duties, second, to punish him for his action and third, to try to keep him here for thirty days until the early release came through.

None of it seemed to work out. Police confronted Papadopoulis in a bar. The sergeant didn't want to leave and took a swing at one of the cops with a bottle. The bottle hit the cop in the left eye causing permanent damage to his eyesight. The worst problem was that the police were Korean National Police and not US MPs. The Korean Nationals put him in jail and charged him with "Aggravated Assault on a Public Official during the Discharge of Duty." Sergeant Papadopoulis was sentenced to six years in Suwon Prison, no parole, no pardon and no embassy or American military interference. The man went straight to jail and didn't get a chance to even think about passing GO.

I'll never understand why people act the way they do. Sergeant

Papadopoulis only had thirty days until freedom. Now it will be 2190 days before he sees home again. We never heard from Mrs. Papadopoulis, so we don't know how that went. However, we all secretly hoped that she died in childbirth, or worse yet, married another soldier.

Another terrible tragedy occurred on the firing range. Everyone had to live fire before they could participate in the DMZ mission. We were trying really hard to rush as many soldiers as possible through the firing phases because we only had the range scheduled for a hectic three days. I was the safety officer, there was a range officer, and there was a platoon leader of whichever platoon was firing at that moment. That was a minimum of three officers at the range at any time. We were all lieutenants and you know what they say about lieutenants. "Rank among lieutenants is like virtue among whores." The range officer, by "virtue" of his position was considered to be in charge, even though I was a first lieutenant and he was a second lieutenant.

We were just moving a new group of soldiers from the ready line to the firing line when the range officer came out of the tower to talk with the platoon leader and me. We had thirty men working for us as spotters, graders, ammunition loaders, road guards, and radio operators. We three officers started walking down the firing line as the new shooters adjusted the sandbags used for support. Foxholes were spread out about every three meters. While walking the line we heard a "click" and a "snap." Our eyes riveted on a soldier in the second foxhole in front of us. He'd just locked a magazine into his M-16 and jacked a round into the chamber.

"What the hell you doing?" yelled the range officer.

There was no time to think. The man with the rifle turned around and fired, sending a bullet ripping through our lane grader's chest, killing him instantly. I heard more shots being fired and some screaming but I didn't see a damn thing. I had dived face first off the firing line into a muddy ditch. Someone jumped on top of me with a knee to the kidney.

When the firing stopped, I sprang straight up. My .45 was in my hand. I was looking directly at the crazed soldier and the three bodies around him. He was grinning and reloading. I started to frantically run up the hill. "Stop, Goddamnit. Stop!" He slammed a magazine home and chambered another round. As he raised his rifle to his shoulder, a hail of bullets sliced through him. I pulled off two shots myself but didn't realize what I'd done until I saw his mutilated body drop to the ground.

I ran to him. He was dead, but somehow still twitching. Three bodies lay near him and another man was shot through the neck and died within seconds at the bottom of his foxhole.

"Call the Medevac up," ordered the range officer. The ambulance vehicle assigned to our range was already racing forward. The range officer's .45 was smoking and so was the platoon leader's. We'd all fired at the crazy soldier. Another soldier from down the line had loaded his M-16 and fired into the man also. I fired twice, the platoon leader fired twice, the range officer fired once, and the soldier with the M-16 fired three times. The crazed man was hit four times so it's really unknown who killed him. I got sick thinking about it. The first time I fired a weapon in anger and it was at one of my own men and he was dead.

I just thought I was sick until we collected the dead bodies. We put ponchos over the four bodies and left them where they lay. The man in the foxhole was a different story. He was crumpled in the bottom of a three-foot diameter concrete foxhole. The human body holds six quarts of blood and every last drop of it had leaked out of the man's neck and formed a puddle in the bottom of the hole. It would have been hubcap deep if it had been on the street. Thank God when I said, "Let's get him out of there," a private jumped in the hole, picked up the blood drenched body, and handed him out to us. I don't think I could have done it. The truck with the firing range water trailer hooked to it, drove up to the firing line, and flushed the pool of blood out of the stained foxhole. The earth ran red, literally. The guy working the hose threw up. Watching vomit run down hill in a river of bloody water was about all I could take also. I had to walk away.

The shock of that incident stayed with me for a long time. I was afraid, for a while, that we might be charged with manslaughter or some obscure Army code violation. The interrogation was brutal but all of us emerged unscathed. It turned out that the crazed shooter was a man like Sergeant Papadopoulis, who had more troubles than his shoulders were broad. He just couldn't carry them all.

The soldiers who shot at the man, including myself, became somewhat of folk legends around the division area. The senior commanders tried to make sure that our fame was very short-lived and I was glad. I thought some other crazed soldier may call me out someday like a gun fighter.

We got through live firing, but the next day was really tough. Everyone kept looking around at each other thinking that someone might cut loose on them at any moment. I had eight rounds in my .45 instead of the usual five. The blood stained foxhole remained covered all day.

Before anyone knew it, Halloween was upon us and the winter was closing in. To celebrate November Eve, we decided to have a costume party and we were all going to come dressed as soldiers. Har! Har! We came dressed as Soldiers, got drunk like Sailors and acted as stupid as Marines. We broke tables, chairs, two windows, three ping pong paddles and our electronic Space Invaders game now shoots crooked.

I didn't even drink, but it was the second day of November before I felt normal again. It only took until the third day to revert back to feeling like hell. The battalion commander called me in to his office at 0730. I stood before him at the rigid position of attention. "Sit down, David." He sounded so fatherly that I knew something was wrong. I just sat down and prayed silently that my family was alright. I soon found out that I should have prayed for my own mental well being.

"David, I leave three weeks from now and I don't want to leave my successor in a jam. I'd like for you to extend for thirty days to finish the mission with the new commander." He fell silent and I must have looked as if life itself had been sucked out of me. The commander could read it on my face. "I'd never ask any of my officers to extend unless it was absolutely critical. I'll leave it entirely up to you."

"Can I have a couple of days to think it over?" I asked.

"Sure, but I'll need to know in two weeks."

I tried to get a telephone line out to Washington, D.C. My branch manager worked there and she had complete control over my assignments. She (Major Hemphill) had been really good to me so far. Somehow she got what I wanted and what the Army needed, to be the same thing. There was a huge time difference between Korea and D.C. I had to call at midnight to reach D.C. in the middle of the afternoon the previous day.

It took me three days before I finally got through to her. She scheduled my advanced career course to start on March 1st. If I extended for thirty days on the Z, I'd miss the beginning of my course by several days.

I met with the battalion commander again and solemnly confessed that I would willingly give him two weeks. That would give me ten days leave, travel and buffer time before I had to report to Fort Huachuca, Arizona, one of my favorite places. The battalion commander was pleased that a puke intelligence officer like me was willing to extend at all. He didn't say that of course but all infantrymen thought it. Anyway, I was inked in for an extra two weeks. The other two officers who were scheduled to leave during the DMZ mission also extended. They extended for the duration of the mission because they were infantry officers and had nothing else to look forward to but another crappy infantry assignment. One foxhole is pretty much like the next. However, I was scheduled to go to southern Arizona: California beaches, Mexico, Las Vegas and the Grand Canyon all within a day's driving distance.

Army Officer Intelligence School is a real experience. During my seventeen week Intelligence Officer Basic Course, I spent three days in the field, not nights, just three days. I did spend until 2100 (9 PM) cleaning weapons one of those days. Work call was eight or eight-thirty and we got off at 1630 (4:30 PM) on the dot every day. Tough life, Intelligence School.

The three of us who extended bought drinks for everyone at the club that night. I don't know what we were celebrating but every time we saw an officer who had just come in to the unit, we started telling him that next year at this time he would be celebrating his extension also. That usually sobered them up pretty quickly.

As the evenings got cooler, my wounded knee experienced more pain. I went to the doc again only to have him pound around on it a little bit and tell me to work it out every day. "The cold weather was making it stiff," or so he said. I didn't know any better so I ran four miles a day come rain or shine and did enough exercises to kill even the strongest plow horse.

The battalion change of command approached quickly and unbelievably, the DMZ mission was over shadowed by it. The 7th Cavalry recently had a change of command that was screwed up royally. Several ceremonial mistakes were made that must have embarrassed the general because he had some words with the outgoing commander and said that the screwed up change of command would follow him to his next unit and then he added, "You won't ever work for me again." And another lieutenant colonel bites the dust.

Our battalion change of command wasn't beautiful but it wasn't screwed up either. The general was happy, the full colonel was happy, the two lieutenant colonels were happy and to hell with everybody else. If they weren't in our chain of command and if they didn't like it, they could kiss our royal reds, because they couldn't do anything about it.

The brigade change of command was scheduled to take place the following week. I had to be part of it so I got to escape to Camp Howze, south of the river, three times, twice on the weekends. Not that weekends were any different because we worked everyday anyway, but on Sundays I usually took breakfast at the club, one of the few diversions I enjoyed. The brigade change of command was the first crisis for our new battalion commander who was also redheaded. Two redheaded commanders in a row. I really think it was a conspiracy.

The new battalion commander was a good commander. He was pretty easy going, especially in the face of the DMZ mission. Our old battalion commander had some of his men die in the DMZ and the new battalion commander had not, thus his sense of urgency was less than that of his predecessor. The new battalion commander actually gave us a day off on Thanksgiving. A day off was something that had never happened before and I'd been there for ten months. Most of us didn't know what to do with ourselves until the orphans came to spend the day. The children sang some Korean songs to us and played some games that I didn't understand. One game was similar to Red Rover but there wasn't supposed to be a winner. It was a game that you played for the hell of it.

I played with them for a while. I had no idea what I was doing, so I ran around like a chicken with my head cut off and made all the kids laugh. The chaplain was the only other officer who would act like a fool with me. The chaplain and I just ran around and fifty kids chased after us. I wondered what would happen if they caught us and I didn't have to wait long. We were dog piled by all of them.

After Thanksgiving, the pressure became unbearable. We were all business, working sixteen-hour days and still not having enough time to get everything done. One of the jobs that our scouts had to do was make a route recon to the bridge that crossed the Imjim River at Changpari. The route to Changpari was our alternate escape route and we had to have a route classification performed on it every few months. The heavy monsoon rains often washed out the roads. Sometimes the minefields were rearranged or the ROKs would establish new guard posts and check points and all of them needed to be documented.

While our scouts were in the city of Changpari, three artillery shells landed very near the Changpari Bridge a few miles out of town. Unfortunately, two people were killed and two more were wounded. We were on the scene ten minutes after the artillery shells landed, just in time to see the ROK ambulances speed away with the bodies. One shell landed close to the road and the other shells hit the soft mud out in the rice paddies. The shell crater near the road was a perfect textbook aid for teaching crater analysis. Crater analysis is a system of evaluating a crater to determine the direction from which the shell came and the caliber of shell. The recon platoon leader got two teams of his men performing a crater analysis while he sent two more teams to look for shell fragments in the soft rice paddy mud. If we could get the caliber and make of the shell and a best guess as a direction from which it came, we would have a good chance of pin pointing the artillery unit that fired the rounds.

If a North Korean unit fired them, we'd be obligated to retaliate somehow. If a friendly unit fired them, we'd be obligated to hang everyone involved. I hoped it was a friendly misfire; in the end it would be less dangerous.

The recon platoon leader and I stood on the road between the two work details, wearing our flak jackets and helmets, with our side arms strapped on. I had the military .45 caliber M1911 automatic standard issue pistol. The recon platoon leader had a .357 magnum with a six-inch barrel. He definitely had style. He told me that if he ever needed a personal defense weapon he wanted one that he knew was accurate.

We had two gun jeeps on the road at either end of our operation and two gun jeeps parked at each detail. Altogether there were six-gun jeeps and a command jeep. The teams finished their tabulations, brought us the nose fuse of one of the shells and some other pieces of shrapnel. We loaded up and gave a "yo," and the seven jeeps sped away in a cloud of dust.

We made our conclusions on the way back to our compound. The shells were 105 millimeter, High Explosive, American made which were used by Americans and South Koreans, and the direction that they came from was 207 degrees, south by southwest. In our learned opinions, some friendly cannon cockers did an "oops," killed two people and wounded two others.

When we got back to Camp Greaves, we went directly to the battalion commander's office and reported what transpired. To our amazement, the battalion commander was furious and here we thought that we'd done something good. He explained that it may have been an international incident and we had no place getting involved. It should have been left up to the United Nations Command. We were instructed to return the shell fragments to the site and not to mention the results to anyone. The battalion commander then stood up from behind his desk and moved to within inches of our faces.

"What did you guys find out?" he asked in a gruff whisper.

The platoon leader smiled, I smiled, the battalion commander smiled. The platoon leader spoke first, "Two Korean National KIA's (killed in action), two Korean National WIA's (wounded in action)."

I broke in, "Shell fragments indicate 105 millimeter high explosive."

Back to the platoon leader, "Coming from a direction of 207 degrees."

"Friendly fire," said the colonel. "Plot that on the map."

We moved to the battalion commander's briefing map and drew a line representing 207 degrees from the impact area. The line was twenty kilometers long, which would encompass the range of all 105 mm artillery shells.

"You guys take off and I'll get the S-3 to post his friendly units overlay to see who we come up with."

The recon platoon leader and I got back in our jeep with a KATUSA to help us translate in case we ran into any problems. Once we got back on the scene, there must have been a whole company of Korean soldiers milling around in a somewhat orderly fashion. We found a Korean captain and queried him as to what was going on. He wasn't very cooperative until he found out that we had arrived on the scene moments after the dead and injured had been evacuated. We told him that we knew which direction the shells came from and what caliber they were. After that, we had a good exchange of information. He told us that one of the people wounded was the wife of the Korean regimental commander.

She was on her way up to the Regimental Headquarters to bring her husband a special dinner when the shells landed. Her young son was with her. The boy was one of the KIAs. Some of this was lost in translation, but the ROK regimental commander's wife's finger, hand or arm, was blown off and was still in the area somewhere. She had a ring on her finger that was worth 2,000,000 Won (about $3200.00) and the soldiers were searching for the ring, finger, hand, or arm depending on who was translating.

The artillery shells did in fact come from a South Korean artillery battery.

The ROK colonel, whose wife was wounded and whose son was lost, made sure that the battery commander, firing officer and safety officers, all went to jail, which was expected. But the story took a weird turn several days later.

The Korean mess hall helpers, janitors, and housemen were forever going through the garbage trying to salvage some of our throwaways. The guy who worked in the hot dog stand called me on the phone from the gate guard shack. He was excited and didn't speak English very well so I didn't understand a damn thing he said. I just went down there.

Several Korean guards and the hot dog man were waiting for me when I arrived. They took me to the back of the hot dog stand and pointed into the trashcan. There was a hand, severed at the wrist, on top of a cardboard Coca Cola case. It was greatly disfigured from three days of exposure. There was no ring, only evidence that a ring had once been on the finger.

I picked the whole cardboard box out of the trash can with the hand resting on it, and placed a complement piece of cardboard over it and secured it tightly with a string from the hot dog stand. I thanked the Korean hot dog man and the guards many times and asked them not to say anything until tomorrow.

I carried the "box" back to my office. I've had some weird feelings in my life but carrying that box was one of the most unusual feelings that I'd ever had. This year I'd carried bags of bones, held a skull in my hand, shot a dog, shot a man, seen the biggest tits in the world, "rode" a propaganda balloon and threw rocks at enemy soldiers but none of that compared to walking across our compound carrying a woman's hand. I thought for just a second, that I felt the hand move between the box tops.

I called the battalion commander and asked him to come to my office. He said that it better be important because he was busy. I just smiled into the phone. "Yes, Sir, this is important." I asked my office personnel to leave the bunker. I didn't want anyone to know that there was someone in our battalion who was low enough to steal a woman's severed hand for the jewelry on her finger. Sick bastard whoever he was.

The battalion commander came in the bunker, "Okay, make it quick." I didn't say anything. I just opened the box and exposed a bloated hand and wrist.

"What the fuck?" A rather un-battalion commander like reaction, but highly understandable.

"It's the ROK colonel's wife's hand," I said.

"What are you saying?" The battalion commander looked like he might have a heart attack.

For some reason, I spoke very distinctly and clearly, "The artillery rounds that landed out of the impact area the other day at Changpari, traumatically severed a woman's arm. It was the ROK regimental commander's wife. The hand had an expensive ring on the finger and I have reason to believe, considering that we have the hand, that one of our soldiers has the ring."

The battalion commander looked a little dumbfounded.

"I found it," pointing to the hand, "in the trash can behind the hot dog stand at the back gate."

"Get Pedden (the recon platoon leader) in here in ten minutes. I'll be back at that time," and the battalion commander left.

I called recon. Lieutenant Pedden was teaching a class on Manchu field. I instructed a runner to bring him to the phone ASAP.

It took Patrick Pedden five minutes to get to the phone.

"What's up?" he answered.

"I need you in my office in five minutes for a meeting with the battalion commander," I paused.

"I'm teaching a class—"

I broke in, "Now!"

"Okay, do I need a weapon or anything?"

"No, just get up here before the battalion commander comes back in four minutes." As I said that, the battalion commander, the XO and the S-3 stepped in.

"Pat, they're here, so double time." I hung up.

The battalion commander and the two majors stood over the lady's hand, talking about some severed limbs that they'd seen in Vietnam. All three of our field grade officers wore purple hearts and combat infantry badges. Two of them had silver stars.

In two minutes, the recon platoon leader burst through the door and reported to the battalion commander.

"Tell me what you know about that," the battalion commander pointed to the hand on top of my desk.

Pat just hovered over it for a minute with a wide-eyed stare and then a squint. He looked up at me and then back at the battalion commander, "Is this the woman's hand?"

"Yes," I said.

"How'd you get it?" he asked.

"I found it in the hot dog stand garbage can." There was a pause.

"Oh, no," he said as he realized what had happened.

"Lieutenant," said the battalion commander, he called people by their ranks when he was angry, "get your Platoon in the billets and hold them there until we show up."

Pat left to round up his men. The battalion commander laid out a plan to shakedown the Recon Platoon. We called all the company commanders and borrowed ten lieutenants to run the shakedown.

Pat was inside the barracks with his men. Each one was sitting in the center of his bunk, listening to Lieutenant Pedden ramble on about the North Korean threat and other general bullshit. He was killing time until the shakedown started.

The battalion commander, XO, S-3, me, and ten other lieutenants met on the parade field and briefed the game plan. Two lieutenants would be posted at opposite corners of the building so they could see all four sides in case someone threw something out one of the windows. The battalion commander, XO, and S-3 would position themselves so they could see into all the compartments of the living spaces made by the wall-lockers. The rest of the lieutenants, including me, would actually do the searches through the bunks, lockers, and alert gear.

The battalion commander stepped in the barracks and Pat called the platoon to attention. The platoon looked stunned, it wasn't every day that the battalion commander came to visit. Then the XO stepped in, then the S-3 and then eight lieutenants poured in and then there was me. The platoon was aghast. I could actually see the trouser legs shaking on one of the men. We each picked two men and started searching their gear. A shakedown search took a long time because we had to turn every sock inside out, check every pocket and every hidden ledge inside the wall locker. We had to unpack every rucksack, strip every bed and check the rafters, windowsills and around the plumbing in the latrines. We searched for over three hours. The troops were not allowed to talk unless they were speaking to the officer inspecting their equipment and then it was only to answer questions.

When one of the officers yanked a pillow out of its case, a tinkling whisper of metal hit the floor and a twinkle of diamond slid under a bunk. Everything went deathly quiet.

After a five second pause, Lieutenant Pedden said, "I'm going to beat you to death," and lunged toward the soldier. It took five officers to subdue the lieutenant. Subdue is actually a bad word, he was anything but subdued, but we did manage to restrain him. The soldier who owned the pillow was read his rights by the battalion commander himself and taken under arrest to the Headquarters building.

The platoon was given an order to square away the billets for inspection in two hours. As we left, the men were scrambling around putting things back together. They were pissed off for having to go through a shakedown inspection but they were damn glad that they weren't the one for whom we were looking.

The soldier's name was Li, Sohn Jo, and a Korean. He was one of the KATUSAs attached to the battalion. Our military law couldn't touch a KATUSA for something like this but we could give him back to the ROK Army for punishment.

Our battalion commander made a call to the ROK regimental commander and personally extended his sympathy about the death of his son and injury to his wife. Then he said that we had the KATUSA in custody who stole the ring. The Korean regimental commander was on his way over and wanted to recover what was his. We prepared for his arrival.

The Korean colonel pulled up in front of the Headquarters building with two jeeps, the colonel, and a driver in the lead jeep with a driver and two armed soldiers in the second. The ROK colonel was escorted in to see our battalion commander. The drivers stayed in the vehicles and the two-armed Korean soldiers stood in the foyer.

I stood in the back of the room behind the large chair in which the ROK colonel sat. Our battalion commander expressed sorrow and presented the ROK colonel with the diamond ring. The ROK colonel looked at it in the light and then put it in his fatigue pocket.

He then said, in remarkably good English, "Please, may I have my wife's remains?"

My commander made a motion and I left to retrieve the woman's hand from my bunker. I got some white paper from a large briefing pad and wrapped the hand in it like a dead fish and Scotch taped it shut. *What am I doing*, I thought, *this is so bizarre.* I carried it back to the ROK colonel.

When I passed the package to him, I tried to be as reverent as possible but I was feeling a little green around the gills.

The ROK colonel thanked me and pulled a sheet of paper out of the same fatigue pocket that held the ring. "What's the name of the thief?"

"Li Sohn Jo," said my battalion commander.

The ROK officer wrote it in a blank spot on the piece of paper and then he handed it to me. I gave it to my battalion commander.

"These are orders," said the ROK colonel, "that release Li Sohn Jo from your unit and assign him to the 12th ROK Regiment. He belongs to me."

"Go get him," said my battalion commander. Li was under guard in the Headquarters' orderly room. The three-armed guards we had on him escorted him to our battalion commander's office. Li's eyes widened when they focused on the ROK colonel. He knew his ass was grass.

The ROK colonel's lip curled at the corner for an instant before he violently punched Li in the face, drawing blood from a nostril.

My battalion commander faced the ROK colonel and said, "Sir, I would appreciate it if you would discipline your men elsewhere." American officers could never strike a solider as punishment, or in Li's case, out of anger.

The two Korean sentries came in and escorted Li to the jeeps. The ROK colonel bowed to us all and gave us his thanks. I was glad that it was over. And another messy chapter in my tour came to a close.

CHAPTER 17

The General's Daughter

Four days before the actual takeover of the DMZ mission, we had several of our Squads attached to the DMZ Battalion. Two days out we attached a couple of platoons and one day out we attached a couple of companies. By noon on Friday, we had 100% of our men in position and we officially assumed the DMZ mission. The pressure was unbearable. This was the most critical time, the first days after the changeover, because 85% of the battalion was doing this for the very first time

We over-killed the briefing of the first patrol. The G-2 (a lieutenant colonel from division), Captain Wright from brigade, my battalion commander (lieutenant colonel), my S-3, (major) the company commander (captain) the platoon leader (1st lieutenant), and me (1st lieutenant) all gave the briefing and conducted the inspection.

After the guys got all their flares, grenades, ammunition and other equipment packed away, we made them pull it all out and show us, just to let us know that they had it. It gave us peace of mind knowing that they had everything. Peace of Mind was spelled C. Y. A. (cover your ass).

The patrol went out and came back without a major incident. However, the point man managed to lose one round of M-16 ammunition. How he did that I don't know but I think he must have had a short magazine to begin with but it was just enough to label the first patrol a screw up. You can lose gloves, batteries, and spare socks but not ammunition. The children of the propaganda village, Tae Song Dong, tended to find these things, take them home and kill themselves with them.

The first two ambush patrols went out, losing a bayonet, a red flare, and a compass. The next six recon patrols went out looking for a bayonet, a red flare, and a compass, instead of the enemy. The red flare was found in a guy's locker during an inspection the next day and the bayonet was found on the ground by the DMZ gate and a Korean soldier somewhere, I'm sure, has a new compass.

The first days of the mission were a little sketchy. We got through them okay but we were setting all kinds of new precedents. We (our new battalion commander that is) would tell the brigade commander how we were going to run things and the brigade commander would just say "okay." The former brigade commander would actually have nervous attacks if anything new were suggested. "Old Nervous in the Service" was what we used to call him. Others at the Headquarters Company knew him as "Shaky Jake."

We cancelled a patrol one night, five minutes before it was scheduled to go out. Under our old brigade commander that would have been a very serious mistake. His view was that there was no reason for a patrol to be cancelled except piss poor prior planning. If we cancelled a patrol it was because we weren't prepared. Therefore, the battalion command was considered screwed up and needed to reassess its priorities. That meant the brigade commander was going to fire somebody. This was the school of thought that governed my first DMZ experience. I still adhered to that school of thought. The new attitude was: "A patrol needs to be cancelled? Well, okay, see what you can do about it."

The reason we cancelled this patrol was because we couldn't get the radios to work. We tried seven different radios and no less than a dozen lithium batteries. We chalked it up to acute atmospheric conditions or gremlins and sent the patrol home.

I felt that canceling the patrol was just wrong. That was the only time I ever yelled at a major. My S-3 and I screamed at each other for about five minutes. I lost. And slowly I was beginning my training in the new school of DMZ missions.

On the third day of the mission, Sunday, I needed a break. I think I went to sleep Saturday night but I'd forgotten to sleep Friday night. Sleep had been OBE (overcome by events). I hadn't had my uniform off for more than three hours since Friday and that was during my only shower and what little sleep I had gotten.

At noon Sunday, things were running fairly smoothly so I informed my office staff that I was going to go to the movie at 1400 (2 PM) and then I'd return to the office.

The Muppet Movie was the feature. The guys on the DMZ were crazy about the Muppets. They were always imitating Kermit's voice. Several officers, who could break away, and I sat together. Joining us were five soldiers with camouflage on, each had their weapons with them. They were scheduled for the early ambush patrol.

We settled into our seats with bags of half popped popcorn and canned root beers. Those were the only two refreshments that the snack bar provided on that day. Our theater was so broken down that we couldn't find enough seats in a row without at least one being broken or totally missing so our seating arrangement was pentagonal instead of in a row.

As usual, the film was spun on the reel upside down and backwards. After all, we were in the "Land of the Not Quite Right." We waited for thirty minutes for the Korean projectionist to figure out how to rewind it correctly. Two of our group went to sleep before the movie started; their bags of popcorn lay spilled by their chairs. Finally Kermit started to sing to us and we began making wise cracks at the screen. I was actually having fun.

At 1500 (3 PM) on the dot, the alert siren blasted us out of our frivolity. The sabers rattled as we stampeded through the exits. Our imaginations ran wild. I figured that something was really wrong because practice alerts were always held at night. The compound was swarming with excited soldiers. I was one of them. I swarmed on down to my bunker to find out what was going on, signing out my weapon on the way.

Our vehicles rolled out and we threw our equipment in them according to the load plan. The scout's gun jeeps were racing up and down in front of the compound. The gunners were standing in the back of the jeeps with ammunition belts strapped across their shoulders. Within thirty minutes, all of our vehicles, except a gamma goat and a jeep that wouldn't start, were lined up and ready to streak into battle, or away from it, depending on our orders. We waited anxiously for word from the top. It came by way of a phone call. The general himself called and he was furious.

It seems that the person responsible for pushing the panic button was Private Joe Shit, The Ragman. He was a member of the division Headquarters and his sole responsibility was to activate the alert at 0300. Zero three hundred is 3 AM, not 3 PM, that's 1500. But Joe Shit must have missed the Army time class in basic training.

After we found out that it was a mistake practice alert, we were happy that it wasn't the real call to battle, but pissed off because we missed the Muppet Movie. Big deal, you say? It damn sure was. I'm not sure why it was such a big deal, but I'll remember it always.

Monday morning found a brisk wind, snow on the ground and a river freezing on the edges. I had to climb about thirty stairs to get from my

Quonset hut on the edge of the river cliffs up to the top of the hill. I got halfway up the stairs when I felt a twinge in my knee. I went a few more steps and collapsed completely. My knee hurt, but I almost beat myself to death on the concrete stairs before I stopped rolling and sliding. I glanced up and saw a Korean Security Guard at the top of the hill. He was just watching me flop around. It must have been pretty funny, but he didn't dare laugh. I was trying to hold my leg, my head, and my ass all at the same time and I was one hand short.

When I didn't get up immediately, the Korean ran down the hill to help me. Before it was over, his M-16 slid off his shoulder and accidentally banged me on the bridge of my nose.

I hobbled into the Headquarters building to brief the battalion commander. The S-3 gave a talk about the ambush patrols and then I talked about the recon patrols and guard post operations. Then the battalion commander gave his blessing. Sometimes he sent us back to the drawing board but not today.

During the S-3's presentation, I had to move to the back of the room and squat down, cradling my knee to my chest. I grimaced, trying to think of more pleasant things than the pain and the fact that I'd been carrying it with me for ten months.

After the morning briefing, some routine office work, and a debriefing of an early patrol, I limped up to the aid station. The thin layer of snow was mostly melted or blown into drifts and the bald earth shown through. The ground was frozen and felt extremely hard. Every little mound of dirt was a potential ankle sprainer. Our parade field had frozen tire tracks on it and it felt like walking across angle iron. The physician's assistant (PA Warrant Officer) was the third one that I'd complained to about my leg. I didn't like this guy mostly because he didn't like me.

I got preferential treatment, as always, because I was an officer and zoomed right up in front of the VD cases. The doc greeted me and went right to work, bending my knee into impossible positions. The strange thing about it was that no matter what position he bent my leg into; it didn't hurt any worse than any other position. The doc kept asking me, "Does this hurt?" "Does this hurt?" I kept saying, "No, not really, no, not really."

After fifteen or twenty positions, the doc looked at me as if I were a malingerer and was trying to get out of work. It nearly pissed me off. I could tell he was puzzled and had no clue as to what was wrong. I hated for medical personnel to try to bullshit me. I'm not a medic but at least I know when and where I hurt and I had the feeling that the doc was about to feed me a line.

He did. "I'm pretty sure that it's a stress fracture. You need to stay off of it for a couple of days," he said. He probably figured that's what I wanted to hear so he said it.

"It's where I was hurt on patrol, doc." I said, trying to help stimulate his imagination a little. A stress fracture, what bullshit. "It's been hurting for ten months, would a stress fracture last that long without developing into something worse?" He just shrugged his shoulders. I went back to work and he started treating dripping gonorrhea infected penises again, which in my opinion was the primary and most appropriate function he should be performing.

For the next week, I walked from my Quonset hut to the bunker and back, spending as much time as possible on my butt. After three days, the pain went away, but after three more, it was back again, still a dull throb, but it was more intense.

Meanwhile we kept plugging along with the mission. We'd had a couple of exceptional sightings but nothing dangerous. We caught two Tae Song Dong residents without their passes and found a new minefield in the Z that had all of three mines in it. We still marked off an area big enough to sail a battleship through making an infiltrator's paradise. Two weeks before Christmas, we got the engineers to get rid of all three mines.

I spent a night on each guard post, just to mingle with the soldiers and get a feel for what they were going through. Sometimes I forgot what it was like out there when I was on the radio to them from the warmth of the operations center. I'd ask them a question and expect an answer, forgetting about how hard it was to compile information in twenty degree weather, taking notes on a piece of paper the size of a playing card and using a pencil about an inch and a half long that was sharpened with a bayonet. I had to be patient and expect slow responses but they always got the job done.

That night a report from the ambush patrol indicated that men with uniforms (non US) were walking around on the south side of the Military Demarcation Line. We tried for two hours to get the patrol to update us and send descriptions. We finally decided that maybe our men in the ambush patrol were too close to the unidentified soldiers to talk on the radio. Of course, in the back of our minds was the possibility that our patrol might have been wiped out by the unidentified force. We debated for an hour whether we should send out another patrol to find the first one but the battalion commander nixed the idea. We waited some more.

A call came from the south gate of the DMZ saying that the patrol had cleared their station. Apparently nothing had happened because the south gate said everything appeared routine. The battalion commander was getting really mad. "Both radios better be totally destroyed," he said, "or I'm going to have someone's ass in my briefcase." I believed him.

The battalion commander meant what he said. The staff sergeant in charge of the patrol had decided that the brass at battalion Headquarters (that was me) was just harassing the ambush patrol so he ordered the radiomen not to respond to my inquiries. The battalion commander, "for intentionally not responding in a hostile and dangerous environment," gave the staff sergeant a field grade article 15 which meant he lost a stripe. The two E-5 buck sergeants got company punishment. The two E-3 radio operators were given a "cussin" by the sergeant major, the likes of which I've never heard. It involved a discussion of the private's mothers, the ugliness of their physical persons and the lack of size of their penises. A sergeant major cussin' was very, very bad, but beat the hell out of getting an Article 15, getting a stripe taken away and getting your career ruined.

The ambush patrol not reporting in was a major screw up. Unfortunately it wasn't our last. A couple of days before Christmas, the four star general's (Army commander's) wife decided to pay the boys on the guard posts a visit and bring them some cookies. The idea was great but she forgot to tell us that she was headed up our direction. She also made the mistake of bringing along her good-looking twenty-one year old daughter, who was "home" for the holidays.

The general's wife was driving her Buick La Sabre when my bridge guards stopped her at the south end. They explained that civilian vehicles were not allowed to cross the bridge. The general's wife was smart enough to know that the rule was probably one that her husband had approved so she didn't argue with them. She never told the guards who she was. The women did flash their dependent ID cards, but the O-10 in the Rank slot, which indicates a four star general's dependent, was more than the E-3 guards could comprehend. They probably, psychologically, skipped over it and passed her off as a senior NCO's wife.

The bridge guards made the general's wife and her daughter hitch a ride in the back of a deuce-and-a-half. There was a squad of soldiers in the back, huddled under their parka's trying to stay warm from the long trip from Seoul. The soldiers loosened up quite a bit when the daughter smiled at them. One soldier offered the daughter his parka, an act of chivalry rarely seen in a field troop. The Mrs. General was also offered a parka more or less as an after thought. Mrs. General took it, which pissed off the soldier to no end.

The daughter was acting coy. When your dad has been a general ever since your were eleven years old, it's hard to tell if people are friendly because you're you, or because you're daddy's little girl. She sat quietly, wishing she was back at the University of Pennsylvania. She didn't like soldiers very much but she thought she'd tag along and make a token gesture with her Mom. Anyway, Mom wouldn't have it any other way. The men helped the ladies out of the back of the truck and sent them up to my bunker to be outfitted in flak jackets and helmets as per SOP.

Hark, there was a rap at my door, "Come in," I yelled in my best command voice. Young Miss General walked in wearing her white rabbit fur waistcoat, designer jeans, and knee boots with the pants stuffed inside. She had short fashionable hair and big eyes. My two sergeants snapped to attention. It was an unusual reaction. This was a first for me; I'd never had a woman visitor in the bunker before.

Mrs. General walked in next, carrying a box of twelve dozen cookies. I didn't recognize her as she pulled up in front of my desk and said, "Lieutenant Osterhout?"

"Yes," I said.

"I'm supposed to see you about getting the necessary equipment so my daughter and I may go to the guard post."

"Why do you want to go there?" I asked.

"To give the boys some cookies," she pointed to the large box.

"I'll see that they get them," I said.

"I'd rather do it myself," she said.

"Why?"

"Because I want to see for myself what it's like up there. I've heard that it's awful."

"Yes, ma'am, it's not a place for you. I'm not even sure if I can allow you to go up there. Even if it's permissible I don't know if I will let you go. It'll disrupt operations."

"Whatever do you mean," said the daughter in a coquettish manner.

Immediately I didn't like this bitch because she knew that she was hot stuff. My sergeants still stood at attention with their mouths gaping open confirming her hotness.

"Ma'am, who are you?" I finally asked.

"I'm Mrs. Williams," she said as she stuck her hand out to shake mine.

I shook her hand. "I need to see your ID," I said trying not to let my voice crack and show the daughter that I was surprised. The daughter was staring directly at me with an anxious look on her face to see if I'd fall all over myself for them. Mrs. General handed me her Dependent's ID Card that had the big O-10 in the rank space. It was the first one that I'd ever seen.

"Ladies, have a seat for a minute. I'll be right back."

They smiled pleasantly and sat down. I left the bunker with my sergeants still standing agape. I had the general's wife's ID in my hand. I didn't want to panic in front of the women but as soon as I was out the bunker door I hit a double time trying to find the battalion commander. He wasn't in his office, nor was the XO, S-3 or any captain. They were just like cops, when you needed one, you couldn't find one.

I went back to the bunker and found Mrs. General with an anxious look on her face.

"Ma'am," I said, "I'm afraid that I can't let you go up to the guard post." I handed her back her ID.

"I don't believe you understand," she said. "I want to go to the guard post. Don't you know who my husband is?" The daughter was smiling again.

"Yes, ma'am, I know who your husband is."

"Well, who's your commander?" she asked, as she got a pen and paper out of her purse. She wrote down my battalion commander's name and mine. I spelled my last name as I pointed to the name tab on my uniform. The women left in a real snit.

I looked at my sergeant and said, "I can't believe that I just ruined my career over a box of damn cookies!" We all laughed but I wasn't really sure I should be laughing.

In two minutes the general's daughter knocked on the bunker door. I opened the door; she stuck her head in and asked, "How do we get back to the bridge?" I reached in my desk drawer and pulled out two bus tickets. I gave them to her and told her how to get to the bus stop. She slammed the door on the way out.

"I'm going to go find the battalion commander," I said as I left. I ran around the whole compound twice before I even found a company commander. I didn't bother to tell him what just happened. In this case, what he didn't know wouldn't hurt him. I decided to check the motor pool. As I was approaching, I saw the XO's driver working on the jeep.

"Hey, Boston, where's the battalion commander?" He got his nickname from his hometown of course. He looked around a second until he spied me on the hill. I was waving my arms to help him locate me.

"He went up to JSA but he should be back by now."

"Okay, thanks!" He evidently didn't recognize me from that distance or there would have been a "Sir" in there somewhere.

I ran back to the Headquarters building but the battalion commander still wasn't there. The XO wasn't either, nor was the S-3. However, the S-1 was there. He was a captain, but talking to a washing machine would be more meaningful.

I'd just run about a mile in 200-meter intervals and only found out where the battalion commander was not. Waiting outside of his office seemed like a better way to find him.

My sergeant came and got me in a few minutes. We needed to beat down some alligators that were growing on my desk in the bunker. Before I left my post at the door to the battalion commander's office, I asked the S-1 to give me a call in the bunker if the commander got back. There was a fifty-fifty chance that our S-1 would comply with my request.

Thirty minutes later my sergeant and I had just about taken care of all the paper work by putting the preponderance of it in the round file. The phone rang and my sergeant answered. "Sir, it's the S-1."

I took off like a greyhound. I was just about to knock when the S-1 said, "You can't go in now. He's on the phone with General Williams."

"But I've got the answers," I said and walked straight in. The battalion commander gave me one hell of a look and then chuckled into the phone in response to the general's small talk. I grabbed a pen and paper off his desk and wrote the words: I KNOW ABOUT HIS WIFE, and handed it to him. He looked at me a little puzzled because the general hadn't mentioned her yet. The puzzled look left his face as he listened intently. I grabbed the paper and wrote: I WOULDN'T LET HER GO TO THE GUARD POST, SHE RETURNED S. OF RIVER 30 MINS AGO.

The battalion commander said, "No, Sir, as a matter of fact she's already been here and we didn't let her go up there." I waited for the end of my career to come from the other end of the phone. The battalion commander chuckled a few more times and then said, "Keep up the Fire," and hung up.

I stood waiting. "How did you know?" asked the battalion commander.

"Know what?" I asked back.

"Know that the general told his wife not to come up here?"

"I didn't, I just told her that I didn't want her to go up to the guard post."

"Well lieutenant, you managed to save my ass because I probably would have let her go. The general said that he would've had to reevaluate our situation if we were stupid enough to let her do it. Thanks, go back to work." As I was walking out the door, I heard him say, "I owe you a big one." And I was thinking, *Damn, I did something right.*

Even better, about a week later, the cute general's daughter called me from her daddy's office one day to tell me that she thought I had style. Amazing how one's opinion changes so quickly, all of a sudden, I liked her. She told me that she wanted to get together with me during her stay in the ROK. I would have liked that very much but I just didn't have the time. I really didn't have twenty spare minutes to take a leisurely crap, let alone get down to the land of the big PX at Seoul for a social dalliance.

The guys heard about it through the XO and gave me a hard time. I didn't mind, it added to my growing reputation. I was starting to become a legend, well, maybe just in my own mind, but I'd been there as long as anyone, so there was more of an opportunity to find a story that involved me.

"A lot can happen to you in six months," my old XO said, referring to Vietnam. The same was applicable up on the Z, a place like no other in the world. In 1980, it was as close as you could have gotten to combat in the US Armed Forces. My officer evaluation report described the situation like this: "Most forward deployed US battalion located within three kilometers of the Korean DMZ and operates in an environment similar to that found in combat."

Patrols kept coming and going with no incident, which was fine with me. It made my job a whole lot easier. I had nothing to complain about except living in a dump, working sixteen hours a day in a hole in the ground, being 10,000 miles from home three days before Christmas, being cold and lonely and having to send tired, but good men out to do a job that people back home could give a shit about, no women, no sex, I'd used up my ration of hot chocolate and my leg hurt badly enough to impair my functioning. There was a lot to bitch about I guess. It was a soldier's right to bitch but there were things to be thankful for also. I felt good about what I was doing, only twenty-seven officers since the Korean conflict ended had ever done the job that I was doing. I grew up too. I was twenty-seven years old (I was born 4 days after the Korean conflict officially ended) and I finally felt mature. I'm not ashamed to admit that it took a little longer for me than most.

One of our brigadier generals made a trip to the guard posts two days before Christmas to see what it was like. He made the boys up there take down their Christmas tree and throw their decorations away. Usually I can tolerate the general officers and all their idiosyncrasies but I couldn't understand taking down the Christmas tree. He said that it would just remind them of home and lower morale. Bullshit! The general, in one fell swoop, did more to lower morale than any other single incident in the entire eleven months that I'd been there.

Now is when I needed General Williams's wife to show up and visit the guard post. She'd run tell her four star husband that a one star was tearing down the Christmas decorations. Bastard. I felt like I was in the story of "The Grinch Who Stole Christmas."

The day before Christmas, the recon platoon leader and I went out to Guard Post Ouellette, the one that's the closest to North Korea. He and I took over some of the duties in the scout tower just to give his men a break on Christmas Eve. It was a really horrible time in my life and I'm sure the other soldiers felt the same way. This was the second year in a row that I'd missed Christmas at home and on top of that my leg was hurting me constantly. It was progressively getting worse.

The recon platoon leader, Pat, and I sat in the tower most of the afternoon watching the enemy move back and forth along their fence lines. One particular North Korean caught our attention. He was very close to the tree line just on the enemy side of the Military Demarcation Line (MDL). He was carrying something that looked like a bag full of bowling balls, and, of course, an AK-47.

He was walking perpendicular to the MDL and then cut directly parallel, all the while searching the ground. He walked for a hundred meters, knelt down, and took three disc type objects from the bowling ball bag. We assumed that the objects were antipersonnel mines. They looked like they were homemade and that each one may have contained about ten pounds of explosives.

This dumbass North Korean just gave away one of his minefield positions. Pat and I quickly plotted his path on a map and checked it with our secret maps of enemy obstacles. The map showed a "suspected" minefield in that area, which we filled in as "confirmed." We called it in to a higher Headquarters and spent twenty minutes on the horn trying to explain to them what went on. I could hear music in the background because higher Headquarters was having a party of some sorts and could care less where we thought a confirmed enemy minefield was located. I got disgusted and hung up on the clerk at the other end of the secure line.

"I'll tell them later," I said to Pat. We walked out of the tower into the freezing evening air. We were only wearing fatigues and flak jackets. The wind stung our arms but couldn't penetrate our armored vests. We stood behind a sandbag wall and watched the North Korean begin to dig a hole to emplace one of the mines. We assumed that he was trying to plug a gap in the defense or he could have just made some mines to stay busy.

"Maybe he'll blow himself up," I said.

We were cold and were just about ready to go back into the wooden tower when explosions roared across the MDL. Pat and I felt a slight air-shock touch our faces as white smoke engulfed the area that the North Korean had occupied. We grabbed our binoculars and searched for the North Korean soldier. There were four puffs of smoke coming from the ground. All of them were around the North Korean's position.

"You know what?" asked Pat.

"What?"

"I think he blew himself up."

"I think you're right," I said. "Look, two meters to the right of the largest crater," I said.

"I think that's his boot," said Pat.

Smoke was rising from the ground like steam. Since the mines were homemade, there must have been a flaw in the fuse mechanism and as the mines began to cool in the freezing temperature, the fuse contracted and exploded the three mines simultaneously. The overpressure and concussion caused three more mines buried in the field to explode in rapid succession.

After we got through smirking at the irony we had just witnessed, we tried to call in the incident. The higher Headquarters' party was still raging and we had a very difficult time explaining what happened.

"Who died?" they kept asking.

"A North Korean soldier," we continued to scream into the transmitter.

After another twenty minutes, we said, "Hell with it, we'll transmit later."

I couldn't believe that the brigade commander would allow a party in the operations center. It must have been occurring without his knowledge. After I hung up the transmitter, I turned to Pat and said, "A man vaporizes right in front of our eyes and it doesn't even make a wart on a frog's ass." We smirked again and began preparing the tower for night operations.

As the sun was setting in the North Korean hills, our men began filing out of their sleeping quarters and into the trenches on their way to the bunkers. We made radio checks to all the bunkers and loaded our weapons. We weren't supposed to load our weapons but one of our adversaries destroyed himself right before our eyes. After his comrades collect the remains, which amounted to a partial leg and foot, they might get blood thirsty and go on the warpath.

We expected heavy propaganda from the large speakers and they didn't disappoint us. Thirty minutes after darkness, the speakers cranked up. We got our resident KATUSA to translate for us.

The speeches by the propagandist that night varied from the usual. Instead of the standard persuasive speeches, it was reduced to name calling because of the incident that resulted in the disintegration of the North Korean. They accused us of killing him with pinpoint mortar fire and said that they would "cut off our balls and stick them in our mouths." At least that's what the KATUSA translated. The KATUSAs tended to translate very loosely and interject some of their own imagination but it's all we had to go on because my Korean vocabulary was up to twenty-eight words and none of them were useful in this situation.

At midnight, the beginning of Christmas, the speakers fell silent. Pat and I continued a very diligent watch into the blackness. At 0430 our relief came in and we got a little sleep in the living quarters bunker. I do mean a "little" sleep. We got up at 0600 for breakfast and to watch the early morning mine sweeps, perimeter checks and the shit barrel burning at the outhouse. Some poor soldier for Christmas morning, instead of opening presents, drinking cocoa and eating candy canes, had to burn our shit. Merry Christmas.

At 1300 (1 PM) I found myself on the back of an open air supply truck, freezing my ass off, trying to get back to the compound in time to go out with the afternoon recon patrol. I had my rifle, my helmet, a flak jacket, and dozens of shiny brass bullets. Of course Pat, my recon platoon leader was with me. He was going to be the patrol leader for my recon patrol.

He and I were sitting with our backs against the cab of the truck. Usually we would have ridden inside because we were lieutenants but we gave the two enlisted men a break and let them ride in the heated cab. We jumped off at the main gate and the truck continued on to the combat support gate. When my numb feet hit the pavement, my knees buckled and I nearly went down. Pat grabbed my parka, jerked me up, and kept me from falling over. "Your knee?" he asked.

"Don't know," I said. "I can barely feel anything below my neck."

We hustled into my bunker to get ready for our patrol. A little face paint, a couple more rounds of ammo, a half a dozen flares, and we were ready. We were the perfect one-two punch. I had the patrol briefing down to a science and Pat had the patrol order worked up and memorized from two days before. He had it written down on a folded 5 X 8 card to make sure he didn't forget anything, although I never once heard him forget a single thing.

We briefed the patrol and marched up to the Headquarters area to be inspected. We rehearsed a few things on the way up, just to reinforce our memories. We had rehearsed for four hours three days prior. The S-3 inspected us and we loaded back into another truck. This truck was one of the covered patrol vehicles designed so the indigenous personnel couldn't see that a patrol was going out. Pat and I sat next to each other in the dim light.

"These damn sandbags are frozen solid," I said to no one in particular. "They hurt my butt cheeks." I shifted my weight. Sandbags in the truck helped prevent mine shrapnel from slicing through a soldiers' private parts so I would rather have them than not.

"Get out your DMZ passes and get ready to lock a magazine," Pat said.

Even though I out ranked him, he was the patrol leader and I was the assistant. Such is the way of the world. When you're a staff puke, you never get to lead anything. Of course, these guys were his men, why shouldn't he lead them?

Pat reached in his pocket and pulled out a waterproof bag. He kept everything in waterproof bags. This bag was filled with hard butterscotch candy. He gave one to every patrol member and said, "Merry Christmas."

I'd forgotten that it was Christmas Day. The soldiers unwrapped their "presents" and sucked on the candy. That was our Christmas 1980. I saved mine. That one little piece of candy would be embedded in my memory as one of the most meaningful presents I'd ever gotten. I saved it for 20 years, until one day, I just couldn't remember where it was anymore.

My melancholy was broken by the brakes of the truck halting at the southern boundary of the DMZ. We were cleared through and loaded our weapons. Christmas was over, it was back to business. One of our men was killed in the DMZ just before Christmas last year. I didn't want to be the one this year. A bad feeling momentarily swept over me. I thought for a fleeting moment *for Christ's sake, why am I on this patrol? I am such a dumbass.* I was on this patrol because I volunteered to replace a good soldier on Christmas Day. *Why do I do these stupid ass things?*

Before I could think about it anymore we were off the truck and into the woods; the point man jacked a round into the chamber. We moved out smartly and became a well-oiled combat unit. There weren't many people I'd trust with automatic weapons on my flank but I trusted Pat and his men.

Six hours later we were re-boarding the vehicle for the ride back to the compound. We would forego the official debriefing since I was the man who did that. Pat and I made the official report for the record and then we cleaned and stored our weapons. We still had to call in some of the information from the Christmas Eve guard post tour, including the disappearing act of the North Korean soldier.

After a hot shower, we got to the battalion operations center at about the same time and began passing our information up to higher Headquarters. They asked us why we didn't inform them sooner about the death on the DMZ. We told them that we had reported it at the time that it occurred. They didn't believe us, which resulted in another twenty-minute argument.

It was 2100 (9 PM) by the time we finished our reports. I was barely awake. We'd only had an hour and a half sleep and we'd conducted a lot of mentally stressful and physically fatiguing activities.

"Supper or what?" asked Pat.

I was hungry but too tired to eat it. I just said "Or what?"

"Steak and potatoes tonight," said Pat, "I earned it."

"I'm going to hit the bunk," I said.

"Right," said Pat as if he were skeptical.

We had to walk passed the Officer's club to get to our hooches. As we came even with the club door, both of us, without saying a word, made a left face and entered. I should have known better. The S-3 and the assistant S-3 cornered the chaplain and me and forced us to play a game of spades. The chaplain and I had lost two games by 2230 (10:30 pm). We quit and I called the operations center to see if all was quiet on the northern front. It was quiet and I went and collapsed on my bunk, while visions of sugarplums ... and Christmas Day ended.

CHAPTER 18

River Blindness

When the 26th rolled around, my leg was noticeably sorer than the previous day and drastically sorer than the previous week. I thought it might have been due to the heavy combat load I carried around on patrol.

On the way to the dining facility for breakfast, I slipped on an ice patch and caught myself in an awkward position. My knee burned like fire. I sat down for a moment, until the immediate pain subsided into a throb. I went on and ate a large breakfast of biscuits, gravy, bacon, hashed brown potatoes, three eggs, and two glasses of whole milk, a glass of orange juice and a bowl of Frosted Flakes. In 1980, cholesterol and triglycerides were not part of an American's vocabulary. I felt silly but I stuck two biscuits in my pocket for later. I ate both biscuits right after the morning briefing at 0730 but I was still hungry. I went to my bunker and ransacked my desk looking for the remains of a care package my mother had sent to me for the holidays. It was beef jerky, Big Red soda, water, and some candy. Unfortunately, I'd shared most of it with the mice that inhabited the bunker. I found four Peanut M&M's rolling around in the bottom of my junk drawer and I ate them.

I sat behind my desk, rubbing my knee, which still throbbed slightly. It hurt differently than it ever had before. I pulled my fatigue trousers down around my ankles and stared at both my knees. I touched them and the injured one felt warmer than the good one. My first thought was blood poisoning. I looked for tracks down my calves and shin but saw nothing.

I pulled my pants up and started shuffling patrol schedules and preparing the briefing for the day's patrols. We had a bunch of new guys and for their sake, I tried to make the briefing as dramatic as possible, trying to pump them up and make them realize how important their job was for America. However, it didn't matter to anyone back home. The home folks didn't even know that we were here, let alone know what we were doing. Dwelling on this subject made me cynical so I changed my thoughts.

Before I knew it, the 28th of December popped up on the calendar. That was my father's birthday. I tried to place a call to my father through the overseas operator in Yongsan but the holiday season calls clogged the lines. I gave up on the phone call and wrote a letter that would take seven days to get there. The US Postal Service in Korea was always a good excuse for being late.

Patrols kept coming and going. There were no incidents that deserved mentioning, a couple of frostbite cases, a three inch cut on a guy's butt where he accidentally sat down on his bayonet and another guy got a burn on his thigh from having an overly hot hand warmer in his pocket. He put it in his fatigue pockets, then put field pants on over that. It was virtually impossible to get it out after he put it in so it stayed there throughout the patrol and caused a 2 X 3 inch blister.

On the night of the twenty-ninth, an unusually cold wind began to blow, bringing a snowstorm that was blinding. We had a command and staff pow-wow to figure out if we really wanted to send out patrols in such poor weather. The soldiers were familiar with patrol operations in limited visibility but the vehicle drivers couldn't see well enough to stay on the roads.

We decided that we would call higher Headquarters and try to get out of the patrols and see if they'd let us stay home. It was a real wimp thing to do but we cared a lot about our soldiers and didn't want them to get hurt needlessly. We figured that no infiltrator would try to make it across on a night like this anyway. Higher Headquarters said, "Wimp!" And we sent patrols out, not in vehicles, but we marched them out over the three-foot high drifts of snow. Walking out made it worse for the soldiers. They'd work up a sweat getting to the site and freeze after the ambush was emplaced.

We were concerned about the patrols, but there were many others out in this weather, like the guys walking on that frozen bridge over the Imjin River. The wind cuts through you on the bridge. Nothing but frozen steel girders to protect you. The air flows under and over the bridge, super cooling it, causing a permanent sheet of ice across the railroad ties. The South Barrier Fence guards were a concern also, but they had a warming tent in which to thaw out. You really couldn't get warm in the tent, but it was just enough to keep you from looking miserable when VIPs drove past. The sixty men on the guard posts were a special concern. Of course they had bunkers. It kept the wind off of them but it was still twenty degrees inside.

Nobody in their right mind would try to infiltrate on a night like this. Then I remembered the frogmen who swam twenty miles down the river hiding among the icebergs. Maybe they were fool enough to try; maybe this was the perfect night. I slowly began to convince myself that something was going to happen.

My intuition told me that the problem would be at the bridge. I'm not sure why, but mostly because on average we had a shooting spree at the bridge every thirty days and it had been a month and a half since someone pulled the trigger. I borrowed the staff duty jeep and headed to the bridge. The open jeep was cold and the snow was piling up quite high. The jeep got up over heartbreak hill and more or less slid down to the bridge. I wasn't sure if we could get back up.

The bridge was frozen, the wind was twenty knots at least, and visibility was fifteen meters at best. I didn't envy those poor bastards down there. I was the only person from battalion to visit them during the holidays. The bridge was a terrible beginning for a new soldier in Korea.

I spoke to everyone on duty..."God," I nearly cried. I must have been getting soft because my legs felt so frozen that I couldn't stand very well. I felt like I was about to collapse, a little faint too. I made it back to the guard shack and massaged my knee in front of the big silver bullet gasoline stove.

"I'm going back to my Quonset hut," I lied to the men. I was actually going to the Officer's Club to eat if I could get there before the kitchen closed. "Call me if you need anything or if something happens. I have a gut feeling about tonight."

"The trick knee telling you something, Sir?" asked the E-5 guard.

"It's telling me that I'm old and beat up," I said sarcastically.

"Don't worry, Sir," said the sergeant. "We'll take care of anything that happens."

"I don't doubt that a bit," I said.

I got in the jeep and just as I suspected, we couldn't get up the hill. I left the driver at the heated guard shack and began hiking. The last time I hiked in the snow I ended up pulling a six-inch stake out from underneath my kneecap. It brought back terrible memories of my first patrol.

I began slipping in the ankle deep snow because the wind in my parka kept me off balance. I had to go down on all fours twice to keep from falling. My leg really began to hurt so badly that I considered stopping at the ROK compound halfway up the hill and calling for help. The ROKs would probably string me up. I'm surprised that their guard hadn't shot me already. I assumed that I was saved only by the fact that the snow was falling so hard that the guard couldn't see me even if he was looking directly at me. I skidded around for another fifteen minutes trying to get to the top of the hill.

About a dozen grunts and leaps more and I made it to the crest. Going down was about as funny as climbing up was miserable. As I was sliding on my butt past the ammo dump I heard one of the walking guards yell, "What are you doing?"

"I'm trying to get to the Headquarters. What's it look like?" I yelled back.

"It looks like your trying to wipe your ass on the pavement!" He said with all sincerity. I'm pretty sure that he did not recognize me as an officer because I sure didn't look like one. I stood up, continuing to slide by the guard shack...backwards. Three feet later, I fell down, ten meters later I fell down again. My knee was getting banged up badly.

I finally made it to the secondary gate. The Korean guard nonchalantly peered through the Plexiglas of his hut to see who it was, then he looked back down. I could have been a Russian soldier and it would have triggered the exact same response. Ain't no way that dude was getting out of his warm hut for nothing.

I walked past the guard shack towards the hot dog stand. I heard the old Korean cook ask me, "You want hot doggie?" I just glared at him from underneath my pile cap. There was a frosty border around my glasses so I could barely see him. I continued across the parade field being the first one to walk over the snow. After I made it to the other side, I had to stop and look back at my creation. The only thing more satisfying might have been to pee in the snow while I was crossing the field.

When I was climbing up the stairs to the Headquarters parking lot, I laughed out loud. I was thinking back to moments ago when the old Korean cook asked me if I wanted a hot dog. Hell no, I didn't want a hot dog. I wanted a heater but I realized what he was doing. The hot dog stand was open unusually late and the Korean cook, by standard operating procedures, was not allowed to have the stove on unless he was cooking hot dogs. I remembered seeing, through my crystalline glasses, a stack of cooked hot dogs a foot high. There must have been thirty-five of them. He'd been cooking hot dogs all night long to stay warm and knew he had so many he'd never get rid of them all. Maybe he should just start cooking them again. I'm sure double cooking hot dogs wasn't contradictory to the standard operating procedure that allowed him to keep the stove lit.

I walked into the Headquarters' foyer and knocked the snow off my boots. I stamped my feet but couldn't feel either foot. My slick, black Army boots had given all they could give a half hour ago. I went in the S-1 office to visit the staff duty officer. He was in a real whirlwind.

"There's been a shooting," he said.

My stomach turned. "Where?" I asked.

"At the bridge."

"Shit, I just got back from there! It must have happened in the last ten minutes," I said.

"It did. Take my jeep," the staff duty officer suggested.

"I did," I said. " Does the old man know about the shooting?" I asked.

"Not yet."

"Tell him now. I'll get him a full report as soon as I can. Oh, and get the wrecker driver rousted out. Your jeep is stuck at the bridge. It can't get up the hill."

"Damn," I heard the staff duty officer say as I walked out. *What's he bitching about,* I thought. *I'm the one who has to walk back to the bridge.*

I started double-timing. When I passed the hot dog stand, the stack of hot dogs had grown another six inches. "Hot doggie?" I heard him ask as I jogged by. In the midst of all the shit going on I still laughed to myself.

I got about halfway to the bridge when I realized that I didn't have a weapon and I had no idea what I was walking into. I was afraid to walk by the ROK compound again. If they heard the shooting, the ROK commander would have them fully alerted. I walked down the middle of the road, hoping if a sentry saw me, he wouldn't suspect me of trying to infiltrate since I was walking down the center of the road.

Luckily, the ROKs were asleep. At the turn that led down the hill to the riverbed, I stood and surveyed the situation. I could see six men on the near end of the bridge, all on their bellies with their rifles at the ready, aimed toward the north bank on the down river side (if the river was flowing but it was frozen solid).

"I'm coming down," I yelled.

"Okay," someone yelled back.

I apprehensively started walking down to the riverbed. I felt tired, cold, and scared. Something was going on here that I didn't fully understand and I didn't like it at all. I took another couple of steps, stood, and listened. I was truly afraid. I would have felt safer with a weapon, but all I had was a one and a half inch blade gentlemen's knife and combination finger nail file. *Sleep well, my fellow soldiers.*

I ventured closer to the bridge entering that fifty-meter stretch between the guard shack and the steel girders. I inched forward, looking in the direction that the guards pointed their weapons. I couldn't see or hear anything.

On my next step the sergeant in charge yelled, "FIRE!" and every soldier on the bridge started poppin' caps.

I buried my face in the snow. "Oh, God," I said out loud without meaning to. The shots came so quickly that they sounded like one long burst.

When the echo subsided, I got up and ran toward the bridge. I slid into position alongside the soldiers. Blue smoke and the smell of cordite momentarily engulfed our small band of men and then drifted away on the wind. The bridge was filled with bullet holes from the real war and the smell of combat for it was a familiar sensation, but this was scaring the living hell out of me.

"What's going on?" I screamed.

"There's someone over in the bushes about 150 meters down the river bank," the sergeant said.

"How are you doing on ammunition?" I asked.

"Count off! How many rounds do you have left?" ordered the sergeant.

"None."

"Two rounds."

"Don't know."

No one had more than two bullets left.

I took charge. I told one of the men who was out of ammo to double time to the north end and get the can of emergency ammo and bring it back. I sent a messenger into the bridge platoon billets to roust them all out and I sent another soldier to call in a report to Headquarters. Within minutes, the ammo can was at our location and everyone had a fresh eighteen round magazine in their weapon and another magazine in their pocket. The reserves from the platoon scrambled out and I stationed them tactically on the bridge the best I could. I then began to interrogate the sergeant in charge.

"What did you see? What did you do? What happened then?" I questioned him until I was satisfied that I could justify everything to the battalion commander.

In ten minutes, the battalion commander's jeep rumbled on to the railroad ties of the bridge. I explained everything that happened. He was a little perplexed but the men had followed the rules of engagement, as long as they actually saw an unidentified person to begin with. All I saw was snow. All the battalion commander saw was snow. And none of the soldiers could tell me exactly what they saw but we'd already made our bed and now we'd have to lie in it.

The battalion commander told me, "Stay on top of this. Spend the night on the bridge and monitor. Remain alert. At dawn plus one hour, run a patrol out to see if you can find any concrete signs of infiltration activities. Be careful," was his last instruction. Then he said, "I'm going back to the compound."

"I don't think your jeep will make it up the hill," I said. "Mine didn't."

"Nonsense," said the commander. "Mine's a commander's jeep. Yours is a staff jeep." He smiled. I smiled too when his jeep slipped over into the ditch halfway up the hill. He got out and walked. I don't know if I actually heard it or not, but I think there was a blue streak of curses in a word bubble following him up the hill.

I was kneeling behind a girder and a very bundled up bridge guard was in a prone position beside me. He was wearing so many layers of clothing that he looked like an animal of some kind. I was jealous. I was numb, especially from my wounded knee down. I figured that the circulation was impaired somehow and that my foot would probably freeze solid to the bridge when I stood up in the morning.

Sometime during the night, the soldier next to me looked up and said, "Is this shit for real, Sir?" I didn't have a response because I wasn't sure myself.

By the dawn's early light we readied plans for our security sweep of the area. We hadn't heard or seen anything all night and I doubted that we would on the sweep but I had to go through the motions and I had to do it right. We gathered together a six-man patrol and stationed an over-watch on the bridge itself. The morning vehicle traffic was halted until I gave the okay. We made a radio check and started out as the sun was breaking over South Korea. I was beginning to warm up from the movement and from the red sun.

"Alright men, move out." I'd been waiting to say that ever since I saw my first episode of "Combat" on TV eighteen years earlier. The point man slid down the bank towards the river. The primary radio operator went next and I followed. By this time I had an M-16 with eighteen rounds of ammunition. The armorer brought it to me fifteen minutes prior to going on the patrol. I think I would have somehow been warmer if I'd had it the night before but better late than never.

The chaplain was just sitting down to hot biscuits and gravy when our point man reached the wooded area. The battalion maintenance officer and the assistant S-3 joined the chaplain. They began to inquire about me because they had wanted to play cards the night before but I was nowhere to be found.

"Where's the S-2?" was raised several times at breakfast.

Even people who were here, sometimes really weren't "here." They didn't know what was going on. How could they, sleeping in their own bunks, worrying about playing cards, eating hot biscuits and gravy for breakfast? While they slept, I squatted on a railroad tie suspended above a frozen river, leaning against a bullet riddled steel girder, watching the blackness close in around me. I used to hate the people back home for not knowing or caring about our purpose. Half of them didn't even know what side of the world Korea was on. I somehow resented everyone. However, I forgave them because if my own fellow officers, only a mile away, didn't know what was happening, how could the people in the States have a clue. All that crossed my mind between the time the point man hit the woods and the time I did. I put all of those thoughts out of my head and got down to the work at hand.

The trees were thick but all the leaves had frozen off, making visibility fairly good. About eighty meters into the woods, we circled the wagons for a conference.

"What I saw was about fifteen meters further ahead," said our point man, who was the main shooter last night. You always take the guy with you on patrol who has first hand knowledge.

"Well," I said. "Let's continue on. We're still in sight of our over-watch so we're alright. Go ahead and chamber a round. Lead the way." We moved out slowly. I gave a wave to our over-watch and one guy waved back. I just wanted to make sure that someone on the bridge was paying enough attention to back us up.

We hadn't walked ten steps when the point man screamed out, "Oh Shit!" Somewhere between the "Oh" and the "Shit" he fired a round. The blast was deafening. Snow dust flew off the tree branches around us. Everyone but the point man was crouching in the snow. I raised up in what must have been three seconds and asked the point man, "Are you alright?" He stood there, staring out in front of him. I moved forward until I stood beside him. I waved to the other men to stay down.

The point man looked at me as serious as a heart attack and said, "He caught the river blindness, didn't he?" The point man was referring to a common affliction contracted by people in the area, you go down to the river and get your eyes shot out.

"Yeah, he did," I said and meant it.

There was a dead Korean man slumped backward over a bush. He was an enemy soldier. He had an AK-47 with short stock next to him. He'd been shot in the back of his head. The bullet exited right between his eyes. Both eyeballs had been blown out of their sockets. One hung next to his ear suspended by some kind of retinal tissue. The other had burst and was stuck flat on his cheek like a fried egg. The whole mess was frozen stiff. He'd died last night. There was a small puncture in his leg where the point man fired as a matter of reflex.

We made a search of the area meanwhile calling in our situation on the radio. In thirty minutes the colonels came, in an hour the generals came by helicopter and in four hours there was a press conference. The lowest ranking man at the press conference was a major, except for me, a first lieutenant. I got a token seat in the back.

The general explained to the press exactly what happened. Everything he said was true but it didn't feel that way while it was happening. He neglected to mention how tired we were, how cold it got and how hungry our bellies were after staying up all night and missing breakfast. He didn't say how a scared private shot the dead man again out of fright, or how we'd fired over a hundred rounds to hit him once in the back of the head. The man who first saw him was referred to as a "guard." I wasn't referred to at all, even though I was the officer in charge and was on the patrol.

Our medics didn't even get to bag up the body. United Nations Command people came and got the body. Our battalion commander got a job well done in writing from some big muckaty-muck. He passed it down to us but somehow we just didn't care.

That day was hard to get through. No sleep and my leg never returned to normal after the long, cold night in a crouch. In the midafternoon I went to the latrine to sit on the commode. While there, I was rubbing my knee. It felt hot again. Feverish. Worse than before.

I got dressed quickly and went to the doc's. I was surprised when I got there because this doc was a different guy than before. The newly assigned doc poked around my leg a bit, the same type of poking that other docs had done before. He pulled the cigar from his mouth and set it in a bedpan near his desk. He went to a cabinet and pulled out a syringe with a needle on it that looked like a water pipe.

"I'm going to draw some fluid off it," he said.

I started to jump up and say, "Like hell," smack him over the head with a jar of tongue depressors and make my escape, but I didn't. My heart just sank with my spirit as he pushed the needle up underneath my kneecap.

He sucked with the syringe and sucked some more but nothing came out. The reason he thought no fluid came out was that the needle was in the wrong place. He stuck it in again from the side but still nothing. He made me lie on my stomach and stuck the damn needle in through the back.

I was getting pissed off by this time and told him, that if he didn't know what was wrong, fine, just tell me, it's no sin. However, he continued to gouge and pull and bend, and then, as I was sitting up on the edge of the examining table with my eyes shut, trying to concentrate through the pain, he hit me with that damned ol' rubber hammer! That was it! No more!

"You send me to someone who knows what the hell they're doing!" It could have been an order and should have been. A first lieutenant outranks a warrant officer every damn day of the week especially when he's hitting you in the sore knee with rubber hammer.

He wasn't concerned with my rank, however, I was four inches taller, and twenty-five pounds heavier and he suspected that I was about ready to knock the starch out of him. This was the third doc assigned to the battalion this year and he was a tiny little shit.

"Well, I'll see what I can do about getting you in to Camp Edwards for an X-ray."

"Call me at my office in the next fifteen minutes and let me know when I go to my appointment."

As I was pulling my fatigue trousers back up he told me that he thought I had a stress fracture.

"That one has been used before, doc. Twice!"

I started walking up the hill to my bunker. The ground still had some snow and ice on it and I had to walk in a funny manner to keep from slipping down. I couldn't tell if it was the inch by inch way I was walking or the make believe stress fracture that made my knee hurt worse than it had before. But more than likely, it was the five freaking fresh needle punctures.

I got to my bunker, propped my leg up, and kicked back. I only got up if someone who outranked me wanted something or a patrol needed a briefing or debriefing. My friend, Pat, the recon platoon leader, walked in wearing his .357 magnum.

"I thought they told you to carry a regulation side arm," I said.

"Yeah, they did, but we're back at 'war' now," he said using hand quotations. "What did you find out about the KIA down at the bridge?"

"I haven't heard very much, because of course you know that..." I paused, "We don't make a wart on a frog's ass," we said in unison. It was a universal saying in the battalion.

"You'd think they'd tell us something, after all, our soldiers shot him and he was on our turf, so to speak. They can't say that we don't have a need to know."

"You're right, Pat, why don't you call the general and ask him to release some more information," I said slyly because Pat and the general did not get along at all.

"Sure, I'll give Barbwire Bob a call. What's his number, one eight hundred

I've got two stars and you don't, bitch."

"What are you bothering me for anyway?" I asked

"I don't know. I'm caught up on everything so I'm just kind of hanging out."

"Me too," I said. "So, sit and hang out here." I pointed to a beat up grey military chair.

Pat sat down. "How the hell are ya?" he bellowed.

"I'm tired..."

"Yeah, I'm doing fine too."

This guy was a true friend. He and I had totally different styles but there was camaraderie that was unequaled. Anybody who would stick my dirty feet into their armpits to stave off frostbite after a long bitterly cold winter patrol was alright by me and Pat had done it a few weeks earlier.

We talked for hours, about explosions in the night, rifles, death, about serving together in Alaska and his Malamute dog named King. King couldn't come to Korea, which made Pat sad.

We changed the subject because Pat never got sad, furious with his troops for screwing up, furious at the high command for being blind and mad at himself for not being better, but he was never sad, except when he thought about his dog. Sadness was catching, I felt it the minute he felt it. His poor puppy got left with a relative stranger 10,000 miles away from his master.

"Hey," I said changing the subject. "That damn shrimp of a doc was supposed to give me a call two hours ago."

"I don't like that little prick," said Pat. "What do you need a doc for?"

"I'm getting an appointment to get my leg X-rayed. You weren't here when I went on my first patrol. I'm glad too, you would have never let me live it down."

"I knew that you got hurt."

"The pain is getting worse. It's been eleven months and I'm not sure how much longer I can do my job."

"Tell the doc to fix it."

"I went to the doc four times with three different docs. The last time was that little piss ant"

Pat grabbed the phone and called the aid station. I snatched it out of his hand and hung up before they answered on the other end. "You bastard," I said.

There was a knock on the door that separated my side of the bunker from the operations center half of the bunker. I looked through the small peep door.

"Sir, patrol's comin' in," said a voice through the hole.

"Thanks," I said. "Pat, why don't you debrief the patrol with me, after all, they are your guys."

"Okay, but if they screwed it up, I'll beat them to death."

"Maybe you should let me do the talking."

Pat grabbed his field jacket and headgear and went to the briefing room. I stayed behind and made a check of the office. I was the only one there because I'd given my sergeants a half a day off so they could play cards in their hooch. After all, they worked Christmas Eve, Christmas Day, and the last six weekends in a row. A half a day off during the holiday season wasn't unreasonable, was it? I really didn't know anymore.

As I shut the iron door to the bunker my leg went numb and I fell to the side of the dirt embankment of the entrance. I just leaned against the sandbags for a while and then I slumped completely as a wave of pain ran the length of my leg. Tears came to my eyes as I held my knee close to my chest. I couldn't think clearly. I used to believe that the pain was imaginary but this wasn't, it made my mind go blank. The only thought I had in my head was that of Pat's dog. I don't know why. I sat for a minute before I stood up. It was a long minute too.

I got to the ready room and debriefed the patrol. It was rather uneventful considering the recent killing. Everyone was excited and wanted to get a piece of the action. They were impressed that I was rumored to have two kills under my belt. After the patrol at the river, my reputation surfaced again.

I was involved with an earlier tragic shooting and now I was the officer in charge of the guards that were responsible for the second killing. At the second one I didn't even pull a trigger. However, I was credited with both of them. I didn't want the recognition, but the troops kept the rumors alive. Everybody seemed to be talking about it. The command looked down on it but you can't stop rumors. The more I told people that I didn't have anything to do with the killing the more they believed that I did. They started referring to me by a nickname: The Oscar Deuce, O-2. That was my rank, first lieutenant O-2 and that was also the initial of my last name and the number of kills. It was not a nickname that I encouraged. However, I heard Oscar Deuce mentioned more often than not.

It was getting late in the afternoon. I went back to the aid station to pick up my X-ray slip. The desk sergeant didn't know what I was talking about. I saw instant red.

"I've had it with this shit," I said. "Where's the doc?"

"He's in treatment room number two," said the sergeant.

I headed down the hall and stepped right into the treatment room without knocking. It startled the doc who happened to have a small wire rod sticking up a soldier's penis. The doc jumped and I guaran-damn-tee you that the soldier jumped too. If I wasn't so mad I would have laughed my ass off.

"Where's my X-ray slip?" I asked, staring at the doc with a penis between his gloved fingers. The soldier just stood, quietly embarrassed, with his fatigues around his knees.

"Not now," said the doc.

I walked to the doc's desk and leaned over on it bracing myself with my hands, "Right this instant," I said, "or I'll kick your medical ass all the way down to Bongilchon." I felt sorry for the Unknown Soldier standing there with his genitals hanging out.

"Alright," said the doc in defeat and he yanked the rod our of the man's penis. The young soldier winced and I did too. One of the foremost things on my mind was the fact that every soldier gets "rodded" before he goes home. It's for a test to make sure that Uncle Sam's soldiers don't take home some strange strain of oriental VD that they may spread to their loved ones or perfect strangers for that matter. The doc would have to rod me sometime in the near future. I may regret pissing him off because one of these days he would most certainly have the chance to get me back.

The doc wiped the specimen into a lab dish and labeled it. Then he methodically wrote me a script for an X-ray at Camp Edwards. The date on it was for 31 Dec. 80.

I wasn't busy on the 31st but I'd scheduled myself for another patrol on 01 Jan 81. I always liked to give some deserving soldier a break on holidays.

We rehearsed for the New Year's Day patrol and again I was going to be the assistant patrol leader. I was also going to carry a claymore mine. I wasn't exactly an expert on setting up the claymore, so I'm glad we rehearsed. The sergeant made me go over it three times with a dummy claymore just in case we had to really use it. It was the mark of a professional, no cutting corners.

We finished up the rehearsal and I went back to the office. I debriefed the recon patrol when it came in and made a quick trip to the guard post to check an incident that was reported. It took about three hours to make a routine check because it was a major chore for me to borrow a vehicle from someone, since I didn't have one myself.

The incident in question was a stalled truck on the road leading up to one of the enemy observation posts. The scouts eventually realized that it was unimportant but had no way of contacting me while I was in route.

I was stuck on the guard post until I could find a ride back. It's probably the fact that I didn't live on the guard post but I enjoyed spending time with the men up there, searching the enemy terrain with binoculars. It was fun to watch the enemy work during the day, knowing that at night they would try to kill you. I got to thinking about killing and how many people had been killed, and I got excited about pulling out all the files and compiling the information.

It was well into the night when I got back to my bunker and after midnight when I finished my KIA calculations. I penciled it neatly into chart form so I could brief the battalion commander. When I was finished I sat back and looked at it, letting it all soak in.

The most staggering figures were thirty-three dead enemy during my tour with a shooting incident occurring every ten days and I still had one month to go.

The ambush patrol came in and I debriefed them. They were cold and tired and I could tell that the new guys were disillusioned. They asked, "Is that all there is to it?"

I just said, "Wait ten days." They didn't understand what I was talking about so I gave a mini briefing to them with my newly compiled statistics. I concluded by saying, "It's inevitable that sometime during your Korean tour on the DMZ, something will blow up near you, someone will shoot at you or you'll shoot at them, someone will drown in the river or someone will drown in their own vomit after a heavy drunk, someone will die or," I paused not really needing a dramatic effect for this one, "someone will shoot their own balls off, just ask Spalding." I walked off leaving them to put that in their pipes and smoke it.

CHAPTER 19

Bad News

I woke up at 0500, just in time to make an appearance at the briefing for the Listening Post/Observation Post (LP/OP) patrol. Then I sat in the operations center listening to the radio traffic of the day. There was a rhythm to it that was soothing. Everything had its place, the mine sweeping of the road to the guard posts, the manning of the bunkers, the arrival of the chow truck, the patrols coming and going and the spot reports of North Korean activity. The LP/OP patrol was a short one and came back in at 1100. I debriefed them and briefed the afternoon recon patrol right after that. My X-ray appointment was at 1400 (2 PM). I'd have time to get back from the X-ray before the recon debriefing.

I ate lunch, a very miserable, over cooked hamburger and tried to confiscate a vehicle to take me to Camp Edwards where the medical facility was located. I couldn't find a jeep for all the fish in the Imjin River. I pulled some Myungjin bus tickets out of my wallet and went to the bus stop. The bus from the south came by as I was standing there. Mike, my friend from Camp Casey stepped off.

"Howdy, Oscar Deuce," he said.

"I can't believe you just called me that."

"You're famous, what can I say?"

"What the hell are you doing up here?" I asked.

"I'm making a liaison run to the ROK right flank..."

"Bullshit," I said.

"Yeah, I know, I'm dicking off for the day and thought I'd come up to the Z."

"Mike, you are the strangest human being," I said. "You're the only guy I know who would take a day off and come up to the Z. Most normal people try to get away from here."

"Ain't that somethin'," he said smiling.

"Well, I'm heading to Camp Edwards to get my leg X-rayed."

"What's wrong?" Mike asked.

"You remember a year ago when I got hurt on patrol?"

"Yeah."

"Well, it never got better, I'm going to have it checked out for the umpteenth time."

"Let's go."

The bus came and Mike and I left the forward area and headed for REMF (rear echelon motherfucker) land at Camp Edwards and the village of Yongtori. We walked around the village for ten minutes before we entered the compound. It was a small supply and medical facility where some American Army women were stationed which gave convincing evidence that the camp was well in the rear. It was still very much a man's Army on New Year's Eve 1980, but times were changing.

Today the medical staff was X-raying dependents for Tuberculosis. I could feel TB infiltrate my lungs the instant I walked in. The doctor was present this time. Last time, eleven months ago, I was X-rayed by a novice technician and he said, "What the hell. It ain't broken." I went back to work and the pain persisted, forever, it seemed like.

The desk person ushered me back to the radiology section of the Quonset hut hospital where a black female X-ray tech sat reading a Cosmopolitan magazine.

"Drop your pants," she said in a matter of fact tone as she dog-eared a page of her magazine. I dropped my trousers down to my boot tops and stood there waiting for further instructions. "Sit on the table with your legs up," she said. I sat on the table with my legs up but I was facing the wrong way. "Sir, you need to turn around and put your legs in this position." She pushed me around, spinning me on my butt until I was in the proper position. All the while my pants were tangling around my boots making me look like Captain Ryan fighting his pants.

"Now, don't move," she said as if she were talking to a three year old.

"Okay," I said.

She went behind the lead shield and snapped one shot. She came back and very gently pushed me around into another position knotting my pants around my ankles even more. When I was through it took me a full minute to figure out how to unravel my britches enough to pull them up.

When I got out to the waiting room, Mike was flirting with the Korean woman behind the front desk. She was maybe five foot tall and sitting down. Mike was 6'4" and standing up. The physical statures were so disparate that it looked like courtship through intimidation. I chuckled because I was in the best of spirits. I hadn't felt so at ease since ... I couldn't remember.

In a moment the X-ray tech came out and told me to go back and see the doctor.

"I'll be back in a minute," I said to Mike.

The doctor was very young, about my age, twenty-seven.

"Sit down," he said. "Have you ever been X-rayed here before?"

"Eleven months ago. I think the first week in February." I said not too sure about the date. The doctor scurried out of the office and left me sitting by his desk. You can bet a dime to a donut that this doctor was the most junior one around and they stuffed his ass over in the Western Corridor at Camp Edwards and made him work on New Year's Eve. But at least he was a doctor.

He came back with both X-rays. He was very excited, worried actually. He looked at me and laid it out straight, something that I've always appreciated. He said, "Look, lieutenant, I'm too new and not good enough to tell you what's wrong with your leg but there's a definite problem and it may be serious. I hate to use this word but it appears to be something like ... cancer. I'm going to send you down to the 121 EVAC Hospital for testing. You'll be there a couple of days."

"When?" I asked.

"Right now," he said.

"I can't. I have patrols out in the DMZ and I need to debrief them. I, personally, go on patrol tomorrow."

"No, lieutenant, you won't. As of this minute, you're out of the war."

"Out... of..."

The doctor said something about making arrangements for an ambulance to transfer me to Seoul. I wasn't listening. I was trying to let what he said soak in.

"Can I at least go back and pick up some things?" I asked.

The doctor appeared to be deep in thought for a moment. Then he said, "Yes, but I want you in the hospital tonight." It never fails, I've been trying to get medical attention all year long and now, when I've got other things to do that are very important, I get so much medical attention that it prevents me from doing them. I went back out to the front desk. Mike was scoring big points with the Korean woman.

"Mike, why don't you go back to Camp Casey? I'm not going to have time to visit today. I've got to go to the hospital," I said trying to be calm.

"What for?" he asked.

"I don't really know," I said.

"What did the doc tell you?"

After a very long pause, "Uh, cancer," I said.

"You got to be shitting me?"

Mike and I sat in silence. The Korean woman kept flirting but Mike paid no attention. After a half an hour of just sitting and contemplating, Mike said that he had to get back to work. We shook hands, with the long, firm grip of friends and Mike was gone.

I hopped on a bus trying to figure out what was happening to me, the war over for me. I couldn't even fathom the idea. The bus ride back took an unbelievably long time. Once back at my Quonset hut, I threw a few personal articles in an AWOL bag, grabbed a couple of hangers full of uniforms, shirts, and jeans and went to the battalion commander's office. I was browsing through the briefing maps when the he entered through his private door.

"What's up, Two?" he said. "I hope that bag doesn't mean you're leaving us for a long time?" he pointed to my AWOL bag.

"As a matter of fact it does, Sir." The commander did a double take. "I just got back from the doctor's at Camp Edwards. He thinks I may have cancer."

I could tell the commander was a little taken back but he didn't waiver one bit. Cancer mortality rates were 50% higher in 1980 than they are now; so just saying the word was frightening.

"What do we need to do to get you taken care of?"

"I don't think anything. An ambulance will take me down to the 121 EVAC Hospital from Camp Edwards. I'll be there a while for tests, maybe a couple of days. I don't really know." I shrugged my shoulders feeling a little disoriented. When I regained my composer, I said, "I've got a patrol out. Pat can take care of that. The schedules and routes are made up for the next week so you won't hit a crunch until then."

"I'm sure Pat can handle it. If not, I'll get the S-3 to do an honest day's work and double up doing your job too."

"Okay, Sir, I'm going to take off. I'll call from the hospital if anything drastic happens. We shook hands and saluted, "Keep up the Fire!"

I stood under the bus stop shed. It was cold and beginning to rain. The bus rumbled over the hill and I boarded heading south. I was the only English speaking person on the bus and once again I was alone and scared. During the year, I'd prepared for and confronted some ugly things but I was not prepared for this.

My knee ached more than normal which I knew was psychological but I couldn't help it and, on top of that, I felt a little sick. I'd never gotten motion sickness on a bus before but I was close. I started thinking about how long I had been in pain. That was plenty of time for cancer to metastasize to every part of my body.

Camp Edwards was deserted when I got there. Most of the offices had closed for New Year's Eve. The medical facility was manned by the same desk person I saw earlier and I explained what was going on. She prepared a slip for transport to the 121 EVAC Hospital. The ambulance was leaving at 1800 (6 PM). I sat and waited, feeling much smaller than I did yesterday. The "feeling useless" syndrome had already set in.

I must have dozed off because 1800 (6 PM) came too quickly. An ambulance driver strolled through from the back and was looking around for people to transport.

"Sir, are you the only person here?" he asked.

"There's some people here but I think I'm the only patient." I hated stupid questions. There were two of us in the room, the desk person, and myself. I hate it equally as much when someone calls the office on the phone wanting someone of rank and asked my sergeant, "Is anyone there?" Who the hell did they think answered the phone?

The ambulance driver was a specialist/4 and he tried to make me lie down in the back of the vehicle. I finally made it clear to him that I wasn't going to do it and we started the drive to Seoul. An hour and a half later I was dumped at the emergency entrance to the 121 EVAC Hospital. The driver and I each handed a stack of records to the emergency room orderly. After reviewing the records, the orderly asked, "Could you come back day after tomorrow? We're kind of closed for the holidays."

The ambulance driver scurried off to safety. I nearly detonated. I held it back but I was really getting fed up with the apathy in the rear areas, it was even at the hospital.

"Listen, don't bother yourself. I'll find a room to stay in." I grabbed my gear and wandered down the hall. The orderly was calling someone on the phone as I turned the corner. More than likely a flock of Korean security guards or MPs were now headed my direction.

I found a desk that was labeled, "Admissions." I plopped down in a chair beside it and decided to camp there until someone showed up, even if it was three days later. Three minutes was more like it. A female lieutenant made the scene and explained that they didn't usually admit non-emergency patients on holidays.

"That's okay," I said. "I'll just stay with you at your hooch until the holidays are over."

It only took seven minutes for her to fill out the paperwork and assign me to room number 207, a four-bed hospital room. All three of the other beds were filled. The one nearest the door on my side had a young artillery soldier in it. His leg was in traction. He told me his plight; "Got drunk on Christmas, fell down and fractured my leg in four places." The bed next to him had an older NCO in it. He fell in the bathtub and slipped a disc. All I could think was, *they have bathtubs in Yongson Garrison?*

The bed next to me had a young engineer private in it. He was 6'2" and weighed 235 pounds without an ounce of fat, nineteen-inch arms, and the like. He hurt himself lifting the back end of a jeep out of a mud hole.

Then my story..."I was on patrol in the DMZ ... eleven months later, cancer." By far the most impressive story of the lot. The four of us cripples spent New Year's Eve, 1980, together in the hospital.

The engineer woke up once complaining of spasms in his back. A nurse, who had obviously been asleep, administered three medications to the engineer. One pill was to relax his muscles, one was a stool softener, and the other was a laxative.

When the first sun of 1981 woke us, the young engineer asked us, "What does a stool softener do?"

The older NCO said, "Son, I think you need to worry more about the laxative."

"Why?" the engineer sounded confused.

"What do you think, lieutenant?" asked the NCO. "Do you think he'll figure it out in about ten minutes?" The engineer started to get up and move toward the latrine. His stomach was gurgling.

"I'd say about thirty seconds," I said and the NCO nodded back.

The engineer closed the latrine door behind him. Loud explosive spurts and groans bellowed forth. Fifteen minutes later, they were still sounding. It was humorous but you couldn't help feel sorry for the guy. It was a hell of a way to start the New Year.

When he finally came out, we all told him, "That's what stool softeners and laxatives do."

Midmorning rolled around and a doctor came through. He made a cursory glance at everyone's chart. He said that he'd start my test after the holidays, since I wasn't an emergency. I was kind of getting sick of being labeled a non-emergency.

I read the rules of the hospital and found out that I could leave, as long as I was back by 2100 (9 PM). I got out of my hospital uniform (striped pajamas) and into a pair of fatigues. I went to a post movie. I made it back, just under the wire, 2055 (8:55 PM) and had my striped pajama uniform on when the nurse came through for bed check. I felt a little bit guilty because I could leave the hospital but the other guys couldn't.

A normal working day for the hospital started at 0800. The doctor made it in at 0900. He made me go to an examining room that smelled like formaldehyde. I dropped my pants and he pulled around on my leg like everyone else had done. He sent me for X-rays, urinalysis, a blood draw, and a couple of other things that I didn't know what were. I was sent back to my room to wait. I watched TV, the only English station. I'd never watched it during the day before. What trash, worse than American soap operas.

At 1500 (3 PM) I was back in the examining room. I sat on the edge of the table waiting for the doc. He came in carrying a small stack of lab slips and X-rays. He stuck the X-rays on a lighted viewer. Then, he took off his glasses and while he was cleaning them, he nonchalantly said, "There's a chance we'll have to cut your leg off."

For just a fleeting instant, I thought he was kidding. He wasn't. Then I got mad about his lack of bedside manner and for another fleeting instant I thought I might kick his ass so hard that he would have to stand up to sit down. Then I remembered that I was the guy who liked it straight up.

He pointed to my X-rays. "I won't go into all the medical jargon but that large discolored area," he made a circle around it, "we think, might be a giant cell bone tumor. It's a mutation caused by trauma, a severe blow." He pulled out another X-ray and stuck it on the viewer. "This one was taken eleven months ago. See the mutated area is only a pinpoint, caused by the direct impact of whatever hit you. In eleven months, it's grown to enormous proportions." He pointed to the later X-ray and encircled the tumor area again. "If it's benign we can cut it out. If it's malignant the leg will have to come off."

We both sat, motionless and speechless for quite some time. I was a little short of breath. Finally I asked, "What's next?"

"Well, the facilities here are not equipped to handle this kind of operation and you've already completed your tour so we're going to send you home."

"When?"

"On the next Medevac flight out."

"When's that?"

"On the seventh." That was five days away.

"Can I go back to my unit?" I asked.

"No. If you break your leg at the tumor, all the king's horses and all the king's men couldn't get you back together again. The bone is nearly eaten through with the tumor. It's like a honeycomb. I want you to take it easy.

Don't do anything that will put a lot of pressure on the knee, no running, no jumping, no climbing stairs."

I went to the hospital library and found a couple of books on leprosy. I flipped through them looking at all the pictures. Those folks were really screwed up. Then I imagined myself, a one-legged man. No comparison, I was lucky. I was thoroughly convinced that I could have had a lot of things more terrible than a tumor in my leg. I could have gotten the river blindness. All I had was a little tumor, the size of a golf ball. No biggie—as they say up on the Z.

I made my own arrangements for the Medevac flight and got someone to take care of my things at Camp Greaves. I made a side trip to the big PX and bought Miss Yi and Miss Kim, our dedicated waitresses, small presents. I sent them back to the unit with the first sergeant, who came to visit. He was the only person who visited me in the hospital. Of course, everyone was busy with the mission.

On 06 Jan 81, a day before my Medevac flight, I was given the bad news that I'd been bumped from the flight. I never understood how a patient could be bumped from a medical flight and I didn't want to know.

The next tentative date for a flight was 09 Jan 81, just two days later than the original date. I wasn't pleased but I could live with it. That morning I was called to the hospital administration office to pay my bill! I owed twenty-seven dollars. I thought medical care was one of the benefits you got for serving your country? It is, as long as you pay three dollars a day for it. Actually, it's the basic allowance for subsistence that the government takes back. In other words, I had to pay for my meals.

On the evening of the eighth, I got a wild hair and took a taxi to the Walker Hill Complex, the huge resort area for foreigners. I'd always wanted to go there. I found the casino, sat down at a table, and began to play Blackjack. Four hours later I had amassed a pile of chips worth 650,000 Won, a little over $1000. I'd started with a twenty-dollar bill.

At 2000 (8 PM) I had to make a split decision: quit gambling and make it back to the hospital just before bed-check or continue gambling and make it back to Yongsan compound before the curfew at midnight or stay at Walker Hill Hotel and make it to the hospital in time to catch the ambulance that was supposed to take patients to the Medevac plane. I thought I'd better get back for bed check. Something might happen and they could pull my name from the flight manifest. I'd already been bumped once.

I took 250,000 Won and laid it on the table. "Last hand," I said. The Filipino woman gambling beside me was impressed. This was my final assault on getting rich quickly. I was trying to be cool but seeing 250,000 Won stacked up on front of me made me get a little nervous. It didn't last long; I was dealt a king and seven. The dealer had a ten and a nine. I didn't have time to worry about it. I had to cash in and grab a taxi. The cashier gave me four checks worth 100,000 Won a piece. I asked her what the hell I was supposed to do with them. "Same as money," she said.

"I want real money," I said. She was disgusted at my arrogance but she counted out eighty bills, each worth 5000 Won. I went around to the hotel desk and asked the clerk to give me American dollars for the Won. He acted like I was crazy and said that I had to go to the bank. Great! It's 2030 (8:30 PM) and my plane leaves at 0900 the next morning for the States. What am I going to do with 400,000 Won?

I paid the taxi driver a little extra to get me to the compound on time. Taxi rides in downtown Seoul scared me more than any patrol I'd ever been in the DMZ. When the nurse came by for bed check I was standing in the middle of the room in my underwear with one leg in my hospital pajamas.

I didn't sleep at all. I got up at 0600, got my things together and headed for the Central Finance Office, which opened at 0700. I told the clerk that I wanted to exchange some Won for dollars.

"How much do you want to exchange?" she asked.

I pulled the wad of eighty bills out of my pocket and plopped it down on the counter. "Four hundred thousand."

"I can't," said the clerk a little too aloofly. "We're only allowed to exchange a hundred dollars worth."

I didn't waste any time. "I want to see your boss." The clerk went and got a 2nd lieutenant who immediately stated that it was against regulations to cash in more than a hundred bucks worth. I disregarded his statement and explained my situation ... DMZ, patrol, cancer, gambling. The 2nd lieutenant kept blankly staring at me. I told the story again and he continued to stare. Obviously, he was not listening to a damn thing I was saying.

Finally I blurted out in a loud command voice, "What the fuck are you looking at?" Everyone in the finance office froze.

He flinched, cleared his throat and then meekly asked in a low voice, "Are you the Oscar Deuce?"

"I've beaten people to death for saying that out loud," I said in a low menacing tone.

The 2nd lieutenant counted out six hundred and forty-four US dollars. He was smiling uncontrollably. I don't know what he thought he knew, but he was certainly happier than a pig in shit.

The ambulance was pulling out from the emergency area of the hospital when I showed up. The driver gave me a ration of static but he wasn't about to suffer the wrath of the administration for leaving me behind.

It took a long time to load the C-9 Nightingale Airplane. There were lots of patients going home. The stretchers were carried up a ramp that led to a large door in the fuselage of the airplane. The stretchers were then placed on racks inside. The walking wounded (that's me) were allowed to board only after the last stretcher was strapped down.

There were at least twenty of us walking wounded. Everyone, except me, looked hurt with cast, stitches, bandages, crutches and one guy had his legs hobbled together and his hands shackled, a third strap connected his wrist to his legs. He was led on to the plane by a leash joined to the third strap. He was obviously a severe psychiatric patient.

The seats on a C-9 Nightingale Medevac Airplane face to the rear. I didn't like the feeling of taking off backwards. The engines roared and the man who was tied up became restless. The plane taxied into position for takeoff and the bound man was sedated with about a pint of medication. The medics buckled their seat belts and the plane shot down the runway. Wheels came up, the plane banked and I got a last glimpse of Korea out of the porthole window. It was over.

Epilogue

The flight home was a rough one, especially for the guys who were really hurt. We stopped in Japan to pick up more wounded and then on to the Philippines to spend the night. Some of the not-so-wounded asked me if I wanted to go down to the village and get laid. I told them "No," I was through with that. I was going to leave it all behind me.

From the Philippines we flew to Guam, then to Hawaii, then to San Francisco. The nurse who greeted us at Travis Air Force Base was Korean. The first American woman I saw stateside had to be of Korean descent.

The next day I flew from San Francisco to San Diego, then to my final destination, San Antonio, Texas. The first three cities I was in all started with the "San," I don't know why that stuck in my mind.

There were two of us who got off at the Air Force base in San Antonio. The ambulance took us to the massive Army Medical Center at Ft. Sam Houston. The other patient was a lieutenant also. I think he was an transportation officer. I couldn't understand him when he talked. He was paralyzed from the neck down, along with part of his face. He had been stung by a bee and had a severe reaction. Four weeks later he could speak clearly, walk twenty paces and could carry light objects like a toothbrush. That was the last time I saw him but prognosis was good for a full recovery.

I checked in and was assigned a bed on the orthopedic ward. All beds were set up like a barracks. The building was a dump. There was a bed within three feet on each side of me, forty-three all together, packed full of crippled bodies. Motorcycle wrecks were the worst. The two men on either side of me were also knee patients. One guy was in the Navy and had problems with his football knee for years. The guy on the other side of me also had a football knee but he was a dependent.

I spent the entire first month having tests conducted: X-rays, Cat Scans, and a bunch of other modern nuclear medicine tests. I even had to stand up in front of a caucus of twenty doctors who used me as a training aid. It's hard to talk to a crowd of colonels, majors, and captains when you're standing on a desktop with a pair of boxer shorts on with all of their eyes at crotch level. I started my story, "I was on patrol in the DMZ..." I wish I could have worn pants.

A week before my operation date, the guys on either side of me had their operations. They got back from surgery late in the evening. Before lights out at 2200 (10 PM), both managed to throw up and one urinated all over his bed because he was given a spinal and couldn't control his functions.

The thought of burping up and pissing all over myself didn't contribute anything positive to my confidence about my operation. My worst fear was that I might wake up without my leg. The doctor promised me that if my leg needed to come off, they would wait and amputate later. They also told me that if the tumor was too far into the knee joint, they'd fuse my leg together, making it a stiff leg. I had to prepare for waking up like that also. They were going to try to excise the tumor and save an eggshell layer of bone in the knee joint and then take bone matter out my hip to remake the leg. Sounded awfully complicated, good luck with that.

I really wanted a rest my mind after the duty on the DMZ. But the loneliness and pain that guys felt on the DMZ wasn't anything like what I saw in the hospital ward. One young 2nd lieutenant ranger parachuted into a power line. Burns were all over him, his leg was burned completely off, and when he finally fell out of the power lines, he cracked his back. He alternated between the orthopedic ward and the burn ward. He walked on his wooden leg with just a little limp and his serious burns were grafted over. He was tough. He would be the role model for my recovery. He never felt bitter and he didn't slow down a bit. He swept a young gorgeous pharmacy intern off her feet and married her. Six months after they were married, I saw him again, getting his new modern prosthetic leg. His wife was with him and she was still just as goo-goo eyed as before and noticeably pregnant. I really admired him and had a great respect for her.

I guess I identified with him because he was hurt while doing his duty, just like me. I didn't have a whole lot of sympathy for the motorcycle wrecks or the guys who were fighting and crushed their hands on someone's face and the other guy with a crushed face in another ward somewhere.

The men on either side of me were moved out when they became better. Then it was my turn to go under the knife. I was supposed to go the first thing in the morning but it was postponed until 1000. Meanwhile I couldn't eat or drink. I was given a shot of Demerol and a Valium pill. I tried to make a conscious effort to experience how the drugs affected me but I went to sleep too fast.

The Army anesthetist knew my father, who was a Certified Registered Nurse

Anesthetist. My father was a staff guy at one time in a teaching hospital so a lot of his students remembered him. After finding out who my father was, the doctors treated me like royalty.

I was given a spinal to begin the operation. It was good for grinding the tumor out of my leg but I woke up just as the doctor smacked a chisel with a hammer that cracked off the top of my hipbone. I raised my head up a little and I must have looked panic stricken. I never felt any pain but I felt the blows from the hammer and chisel as it jerked my body down the table. The doctor's eyes met mine and he said, "Put this guy out now."

I heard the anesthetist say "Goodnight," and that was it. They gave me a general anesthetic to finish breaking my hipbones to do the iliac graft to reshape my leg. I just shut my eyes and don't remember anything after that.

I woke up at 1700 (5 PM), in my bed on the ward. There were some flowers on the table. They were black carnations. For an instant, I thought I'd died, but they were from my high school sweetheart. I wore a white tux and a black carnation at the prom with her. I hadn't seen her in years but she'd heard through my small town grapevine that I was going under the blade at that particular time.

My parents were there along with my good friend, Jim Locke. I woke up just long enough to see that they were there. Before I acknowledged them I looked down to see my toes sticking out of the end of a full-length leg cast. I relaxed a little but all it meant was that the doctor hadn't cut my leg off yet.

I went back to sleep for another hour or so but woke up again when a volunteer came around with milk and juice. I had a very dry mouth and I wanted something to drink, but the pain was too great. I was on the verge of dry heaving. The anesthetic was completely gone now and the pain was immense but strangely, my knee didn't hurt as much as my hip. I had a tube running out of my hip into a bottle that was filling with blood. The reason for the drain was to let the large incision on my hip close from the inside out without the swelling effect from the blood and other fluid.

The surgeons had gone in and knocked off the top my pelvic bone and spooned out the soft bone. This material is what they used to reshape my leg. The reason for my knee, hurting less than my hip was explained it to me like this: "Your knee was bad and we fixed it but there was absolutely nothing wrong with your hip and we went in and wrecked it." For some reason my butt hurt so much that I couldn't lift it off the bed. I didn't ask why.

A respiratory therapist came around and gave me a little pump device to blow into. She said, "A lot of people don't take that one deep breath they need after an operation," so I blew into the pump on a regular basis.

When the lights went out that first night after the operation, I was wide-awake. I don't think I was in great pain, maybe I was, I'd been in pain for so long I couldn't distinguish between regular pain and great pain. The nurse came around several times during the night to see if I wanted a shot. Shit no, I didn't want a shot. I was a Manchu Warrior. My dignity was reduced enough already with tubes hanging out of me, bloody bottles attached to the tubes, a cast from crotch to ankle and a pitcher to try to piss in. I couldn't even piss yet because I hadn't had anything to drink plus I was still numb in that area from the spinal. I tried, but I just couldn't get it together enough to take a leak. They told me if I didn't start peeing in the next few hours they were going to insert a catheter. Every five minutes during night I tried to squirt a few drops of urine into the pitcher. I did not want another tube sticking out me, especially out of my penis.

When morning came, breakfast was served. A private, dressed in hospital whites, cranked my bed up and pushed a tray of food in front of me.

"Roll me back down. I think I'm going to throw up again." Earlier I'd belched up just enough in my little kidney shaped bowl to make a scene.

"You have got to eat something," he said.

"I don't want anything to eat," I said. "Roll me back down."

"Do you hurt so bad that you can't eat?" he asked.

I didn't say anything because I was just about ready to pass out from the pain. He rolled me back down, I winced, and he took the tray away.

"Have you had a shot this morning?" he asked.

"I haven't had one yet," I said.

"Goddamnit, lieutenant, you're getting a shot right now!" Thank the Lord for take-charge privates. The nurse came and gave me a shot of an unknown narcotic. Within ten minutes I felt great. I ate my breakfast and went to sleep. I didn't mean to go to sleep but with the lack of sleep from the night before and the drug-induced relaxation, I couldn't help it. I woke up hours later with the doctor pinching my toes.

"Checking to see if your cast is too tight," he said.

I became a little more alert. "How am I?" I asked the doctor.

"You'll be alright. We removed the tumor with no problem. It wasn't into the joint so you should have at least sixty percent flexibility. I'll talk to you about it during morning rounds. Right now I want you to start your physical therapy. The doctor went to the next bed.

"Hi, I'm your physical therapist." It was a very attractive and healthy looking female captain.

"Howdy."

"Come with me to the therapy room."

I struggled to get up. She adjusted crutches for me and taught me how to walk with a straight leg cast while carrying my outflow blood bottle in one hand and the IV pole and inflowing blood bottle in the other. It took several minutes for me to reach the therapy room even though it was only thirty feet away.

Once there, I lay down on a mat and suffered, and I do mean suffered, through twenty-five leg lifts. My cast weighed ten pounds at least. With a crushed hip and new knee bone, the pain was intense, but I wanted to run and play like all the other kids so I kept at it. Plus the physical therapist was so attractive it was intimidating, and I just couldn't wimp out in front of her. I remember MAJ Thiel, commander of the Butch Brigade, laughing at me during my last physical therapy session.

And so went the road to recovery:

1981

09 FEB: Operation

10 FEB: Fitted for crutches—1st physical therapy session, twice daily from then on.

12 FEB: Old straight leg cast had blood soaking through—new straight leg cast put on.

14 FEB: IV (antibiotic) in hand removed. Happy Valentines Day.

15 FEB: Blood drainage tube from hip removed (hurt like hell).

17 FEB: Promoted to captain while lying flat on my back trying to figure out the proper position for a prone attention. Presented a Meritorious Service Medal and given a debriefing stating that I couldn't discuss anything

that happened in Korea for 25 years. "Okay, I won't."

19 FEB: 30-day convalescent leave at home.

28 FEB: Used a pair of pliers to take the wire (not stitches) out of hip incision (not smart)

19 MAR: Reported back to the hospital

29 MAR: After six weeks in the second straight leg cast, they removed it and yanked out the ingrown wire from my knee incision. I surely liked stitches better. They took X-rays as I continuously scratched my leg for two hours. New full-length flexible cast was put on. It was cut at the knee and had heavy plastic hinges.

05 APR: Moved to Minimal Care Ward one-and-one-half miles from the main hospital. It was a hassle going to physical therapy twice daily.

01 MAY: Removed the full-length flexible cast. Took X-rays and I continuously scratched my leg while waiting for the results. New half size cast put on, covered foot and ankle. For the first time I could apply touch pressure to the bottom of my foot.

02 JUN: Scheduled to get cast removed forever, but doctor was on leave and resident refused to take it off. Strong dislike and lack of respect for my doctor developed.

05 JUN: Removed final cast, X-rays okay, still on crutches.

12 JUL: Moved to Bachelor Officers' Quarters, still assigned to Medical Holding Company as an outpatient.

29 JUL: Issued a cane. Drove out of town, smashed my wooden crutches to pieces on a guard rail on a country road and ceremoniously set them on fire.

30 JUL: Paid Finance Office fifteen dollars for unreturned crutches. (I wish I knew this yesterday).

31 JUL: Happy Birthday to me. I was 28 years old.

02 AUG: Physical Evaluation Board convened. I stood in front of them like a piece of meat. All the colonels just shook their heads. I was thinking, *this is not good.*

08 AUG: Placed on TDRL (Temporary Disabled Retired List).

Discharged from the hospital after 220 days. I paid $660 for "medical treatment" just like in Korea. Three bucks a day for the food.

09 AUG: Stepped off the post a temporary retiree with a cane and a limp.

1983

28 FEB: The Physical Evaluation Board reconvened. I stood in front of them again, feeling like an aged piece of meat this time. Although in decent physical condition, I was declared unfit for further military service. I threatened to get a JAG Officer and force them, through legal means to reinstate me. The board chairman said "Son, it's a medical decision not a legal one. A lawyer will do you no good." I was awarded a ten percent disability and an Honorable Discharge. From captain's pay to fifty-three bucks a month. All benefits were discontinued. I was a civilian.

They used me up—and threw me away.

The End

Made in the USA
San Bernardino, CA
23 October 2015